A
BRILLIANT
MADNESS

A BRILLIANT MADNESS

Living with Manic-Depressive Illness

PATTY DUKE

AND

GLORIA HOCHMAN

BANTAM BOOKS

NEW YORK • TORONTO • LONDON • SYDNEY • AUCKLAND

A BRILLIANT MADNESS
A Bantam Book / July 1992

The text was designed and the project was supervised by M 'N O
Production Services, Inc.

Library of Congress Cataloging-in-Publication Data

Duke, Patty, 1946–
    A brilliant madness : living with manic-depressive illness / Patty
Duke and Gloria Hochman.
      p.   cm.
    Includes bibliographical references and index.
    ISBN 0-553-07256-0
    1. Manic-depressive psychoses—Popular works.   2. Duke,
Patty, 1946-   —Mental health.   I. Hochman, Gloria.   II. Title.
RC516.D85   1992
616.89'5'0092—dc20   92-5878
[B]   CIP

Published simultaneously in the United States and Canada

Bantam Books are published by Bantam Books, a division of Bantam
Doubleday Dell Publishing Group, Inc. Its trademark, consisting of
the words "Bantam Books" and the portrayal of a rooster, is
Registered in U.S. Patent and Trademark Office and in other
countries. Marca Registrada. Bantam Books, 666 Fifth Avenue, New
York, New York 10103.

PRINTED IN THE UNITED STATES OF AMERICA

BVG   0 9 8 7 6 5 4

For my steadfast soldier of Grace, Michael Pearce
—Patty Duke

For Sarah and Abe
for Anndee
and especially for Stan
—Gloria Hochman

CONTENTS

MY FRIEND ANNA

by Mary Lou Pinckert

Those of you who have read *Call Me Anna* or saw the television dramatization based on that book know that Patty Duke's life was, to say the least, a turbulent one. While all of us marveled at her dazzling performances—as we applauded her Oscar-winning portrayal of Helen Keller in *The Miracle Worker*, or as we hummed the catchy "cousins" song from her television series *The Patty Duke Show*—we didn't have a clue about Anna, the troubled and tormented little girl who lived inside the mind and body of Patty Duke.

I think that few of us could have imagined the "stranger than fiction" existence of this awkward child who grew up to become a brilliant actress and one of the most sensitive, tortured, and electrifying people I have ever met.

Anna and I met, literally, out on the street when we were neighbors in Westwood, California. Our kids were young and they would play together, so Anna (as Patty prefers to be called) and I eased into a relationship. At first we'd be out and wave hello to each other. Then we got into conversations and found that we spoke easily, and that we enjoyed running into each other's houses.

In the early days of our friendship, I was not familiar with the ups and downs of her life. But as time went by and we became closer, she told me about her upbringing—her mother; her father; her sister, Carol; her brother, Raymond; the Rosses.

Many of the things she said—some of which I read later in *Call Me Anna*—were unbelievable, shocking for me to hear.

Her father was an alcoholic who couldn't hold a job or keep his life in order. When she was six, he moved away from the family, and Anna rarely saw him. He died at fifty in a furnished room. To this day, she has never quite come to terms with that tremendous loss.

Her mother had her own problems. A number of times—the first when Anna was little more than a toddler—her mother was taken to the hospital for depression. When she was home, she had loud and explosive temper tantrums, made suicide threats, and experienced what seemed to Anna to be endless periods of melancholia, punctuated by unpredictable times of rage and unbridled emotion. Sometimes, when she couldn't sleep, she would take Anna for midnight rides on the Lexington Avenue bus. They would just ride up and down, from one end of the line to the other, until, thoroughly exhausted, they would end up back at their four-story walkup on New York's East Thirty-first Street. Once Anna's mom turned on the gas jets, vowing to kill herself and all of her children. It was a feeble attempt, Anna told me, because she left the windows open.

But it was not her mother who transformed Anna into Patty and forever altered the course of her life. John and Ethel Ross, who managed child actors, met Anna through her brother, whom the Rosses had been placing in television shows and commercials. Later, when Raymond was eighteen, he and the Rosses had a parting of the ways, and he joined the Army. Although Anna had never demonstrated an interest in dramatics—in fact, she really imagined she would be a nun—and the Rosses had reservations about her talent, not to mention her straight hair, her skinny legs, and her general demeanor, they saw in her an untapped potential they were willing to take a chance on.

From that moment on, Anna never again lived in the world of children. She studied every day after school to lose her New York way of speaking. She learned a clipped English accent, a Southern drawl, a Tennessee twang.

When she was eight, the Rosses abruptly changed her name, from Anna Marie to a "perkier" Patty. They told her, "Anna Marie is dead. You're Patty now." Anna and I burned a lot of midnight oil raking over the damage that comes when someone's identity is snatched from them.

The Rosses were rigid and demanding taskmasters. They taught Anna how to be interviewed, how to measure her words, how always to have the "right" answers. They taught her how to lie, how not to have opinions of her own, and to do what they kept telling her was "for her own good." She said she grew up feeling like a "perfect Stepford child."

As it became more evident that Anna had a unique talent and was destined for stardom, the Rosses made certain that she felt totally dependent on them. Anna remembers that they said, "If it wasn't for us, you'd be a hooker or you'd work in the five-and-dime."

Meanwhile, contact with her family, by edict of the Rosses, dwindled down to nearly zero. At first she didn't spend all her time with Ethel and John Ross—just every day after school to study and be coached. Soon it was overnight at their posh Upper West Side apartment when there was a job the next day. Then weekends. Then longer weekends. Finally they told her she would have to live with them because her work was going to demand their constant attention. At twelve, once she had become a Broadway star, she never again lived with her family.

Anna's contacts with her mother were orchestrated and monitored by the Rosses. Mrs. Duke was allowed to come to a set, by invitation only, mainly when Anna needed baby-sitting. She was explicitly told to keep out of the way and say nothing. One of her jobs was to answer Anna's fan mail; another was to come to the Rosses' home every week to do the laundry. There were days when, for reasons she couldn't explain, Anna remembers, her mother would show up on the Rosses' doorstep crying. Often she would come into the house, then spend all day and into the night sobbing. Anna never knew why.

Meanwhile, Anna ran the gamut of emotions about her

mother. She was angry because her mother had turned her over to these two strangers whom she feared and was fascinated by and in whose presence she told me she felt powerless. She was afraid because she didn't know what would happen to her if she showed any signs of defiance. And she understood that her mother desperately needed the money she was earning. Anna told me she felt as though she were in a prison to which someone had tossed away the key.

On the other hand, there were the tantalizing perks. Dinners every night at fancy restaurants. Attention from other performers. The rigorous training she received from John Ross, which she acknowledges played a major role in her success. The growing recognition that she was good at what she did.

That recognition peaked opening night of *The Miracle Worker*, when she was twelve. In her earlier book, Anna wrote: "I'd never experienced the exhilaration of real live human beings I didn't know screaming, 'Bravo! Bravo!' for all those curtain calls. It was the best moment of my life and I started to feel tears that came from I don't know where."

Jobs came easily to Anna after that, but her life was not one anyone could have envied. She had no friends, no hobbies, and lived in the insulated world of show business, with Uncle John and Aunt Ethel as her "playmates." They chose her clothes and decided how she would style her hair. But as her popularity increased, their insecurities intensified. Without her, where would they be?

Both were heavy drinkers, and Anna says that Ethel could easily down a fifth of vodka in a weekend. Unfortunately, they exposed Anna to alcohol, too, and when she was in her early teens, she already knew the buzz that booze gives. Eventually they fed her what she calls "happy pills"—later determined to be Thorazine or another antipsychotic drug or Percodan—just to make sure she would sleep well or to calm her down if she seemed a little hyper. There began to be subtle sexual advances by John, usually after he had been drinking.

Even her happiest moments—such as the one when she won

the Academy Award for best supporting actress in the film of *The Miracle Worker*—were laced with sorrow. The Rosses would not allow her mother to attend the ceremonies. They considered her a nuisance and an embarrassment. So Anna missed what all children long for—for their parents to be with them, to support them, to approve of them, to be proud of them, and to cheer them the loudest when they have achieved something wonderful.

So here was my friend Anna, at sixteen, the actress who had grown accustomed to standing ovations . . . the captive of deeply troubled people whom she loved, hated, and feared . . . the little girl who yearned for her family . . . the child star who felt anger, guilt, and confusion and wondered if she would ever know what it meant to be happy. It breaks my heart whenever I think about it.

When Anna and I first met, I think that she and her then husband, John Astin, *were* very happy. She would, as she put it, have her moods. I noticed them, but it never occurred to me that they were symptomatic of a problem as serious as it turned out to be.

I did see that she would snap very quickly at something, sometimes at her kids. She seemed to reach a breaking point too soon, often at some little thing that didn't seem to call for such an extreme reaction. And I would worry, from time to time, that I would do or say something that would trigger off something that would get her going. But that never happened.

The first time I saw serious depression in Anna was one New Year's Eve early in our relationship. She and John were giving a big party, and all of a sudden she got very depressed, so depressed she couldn't come out of her bedroom. She stayed there for the whole party. Later, I began to see more of that. She would retreat into her room, sometimes for weeks.

During those times, I'd call and John would say, "Anna's sick," or "Anna's sleeping," or "Anna's not feeling well." Later I learned that she was too depressed to talk even to me during those times. Then one day I'd see her up and around again. And I'd ask her, "Where have you been? Were you working?" And she'd admit that she hadn't been feeling well.

After that, Anna confided to me that she had dramatic mood swings, that there were times when she would get violent and throw things and have wild outbursts.

But the first time I actually witnessed any of those episodes was the New Year's Eve she and John had another great party. Everything went smoothly and everyone seemed to have a good time. Afterward we were cleaning up, and John's son David said something that triggered a reaction in Anna.

She got that look on her face which meant trouble. I could see it coming, and suddenly dishes were clanging and champagne bottles were breaking. She was throwing wine bottles all over the backyard, which was tented in. She was calling John every name you could think of. She just went nuts, talking drivel I couldn't understand. And you could see that she couldn't stop. She was fighting for herself in a way that made me think it was her New York street childhood coming out.

In the weeks that followed, I began noticing other things: a hole in the wall, a broken antique, knife cuttings in the kitchen cabinets, doors hanging off the hinges. Anna told me she did it.

Some nights, after she'd taken too many sleeping pills or had too much to drink—I'm not sure which—I'd see John walking her up and down the street for hours until she came out of it.

That's when Anna began to feel safe enough with me to admit how serious her highs and lows really were. We'd spend some nights, until three in the morning, lying across her bed talking. She cried a lot those nights and she would say, "Please, Mary Lou, don't ever leave me. Promise that we'll stay friends no matter what happens."

In fact, Anna has been a wonderful friend to me. I always feel I can count on her one hundred percent. When my son, Eric, was hit by a car and in a body cast for an entire summer, that woman never left my side. And if I called her tonight and told her I needed her, she would be there for me. But the way she remembers it, I gave her everything and she gave me nothing.

Anna is a unique person who has enriched my life. She has the capacity to feel intensely, and I admire that so much. I often think

it must be wonderful to feel joy and happiness so exquisitely. But on the other hand, she feels hurt and pain deeply also, and it seems to last longer than it does with most of us. I know that Anna still tortures herself about not having been a good mother. She carries incredible guilt. But you only have to look at her sons now to see what a terrific mother she was.

I was thrilled when Anna told me she was writing this book. Because of her unique compassion and incredible honesty, every person who reads it has the chance to get close to a brilliant and caring woman and to come away with a new appreciation, as I have, of the agony of mental illness. Through what she has written, I believe that my friend Anna will make a difference in the way sufferers of mood disorders and their loved ones face the future.

A DISEASE? THANK GOD!

"Anna, I have wrestled with this and wondered about it, and suspected for some time now that you may have a condition that I want to discuss with you. I didn't make this diagnosis before because it's a very difficult one to make. It is a diagnosis that comes with a painful stigma, and I didn't want to hang you with that and be wrong. Don't be frightened, but I think you are manic-depressive."

Even now, it's weird to tell you what my reaction was. In my entire life, I had heard the words "manic-depressive" only three or four times—in some completely unrelated way, certainly nothing to do with me. But the words just made sense. As my psychiatrist, Dr. Harold Arlen, said them, I remember nodding my head as if I had known this all along. They were the best two words I ever heard. They described how it felt to be me.

Through most of my adult life, when I was either manic—doing so many bizarre, off-the-wall things—or depressed, taking to my bed for weeks refusing to see anyone, I kept thinking, "There *must* be *something*, something I could take that would make this all go away, that would make me stop behaving this way." Wouldn't you know that I would find that something at a time when I least expected to?

It was June of 1982 and I was going through one of the few times in my life when things were, more or less, on an even keel. My motor wasn't running, and I didn't feel racy or panicky. John

Astin, to whom I had been married for ten years, and I were separated. I was the in-house parent—Sean was then eleven and Mack was nine. I was working with the actor Richard Crenna on a television series called *It Takes Two*. It was a comedy about a powerful chief of surgery who was married to a just-as-powerful lawyer. And I liked the feeling of it. The characters were actually intelligent and they loved each other, and I enjoyed coming to work each day. I loved every minute of it. The show was running on ABC, and I had a wonderful relationship with Lou Ehrlict, their top programming executive. In fact, I had a great relationship with everyone in the show. And what's more, the show was doing well—or at least it seemed to be. Our ratings were up there. I could have been content doing that show for years.

After twenty-two episodes were aired, for some mysterious reason I never fully understood, the series was yanked. It was especially odd considering that I had been given a People's Choice Award for being the most popular television actress based on my work in that show. So who really knows?

But this was before any of that happened, and I was feeling fine. It had been quite a while since I had had any symptoms of depression. Working, of course, had a lot to do with it. I usually didn't get depressed when I was working. And, as I recall, there had not been outrageous behavior for some time either. Mistakenly, as it turned out, I believed that John's and my separating and deciding to divorce was the reason I wasn't having mood swings. It turned out I was wrong.

We were in rehearsal for an episode of *It Takes Two*, and I began to get very sick. At first I thought it was a cold. Then I developed flu-like symptoms, my throat began to hurt, and it progressed to laryngitis. This happened over the course of five days—maybe there was a weekend in there—but by the time it came to what we call tape day (we rehearsed in the morning and taped the show before an audience twice), I could barely talk. So calls went out to find the best ear, nose, and throat person, someone who could make a miracle happen.

I was also seeing Dr. Arlen, even though I was not in depression, which was the only condition that had sent me to a psychiatrist in the past. But I was trying to be an adult. And since I was going through a trauma—the divorce, which was imminent—I was going to approach it in a healthy fashion. But Dr. Arlen was not aware of this throat problem because I wasn't seeing him every day.

We found a highly respected throat doctor who diagnosed me as having nodes on my vocal cords. I kept saying, "But, Doctor, you don't understand. I have to do a show tonight. I have to be able to talk." So he gave me a shot of cortisone to shrink the nodes. The man had no knowledge whatsoever of my prior medical or behavioral history except what he got from me, and that was precious little. I went back to the studio. We had about four hours until show time. The cortisone did work. I rested and did the show. But I still didn't feel so hot. I went home and had insomnia for the first time in a long time. I even had a couple of panic attacks during the night. Now, I know that a lot of people have panic attacks, and most of those people are not manic-depressive. But my panic attacks, my ups, my downs, and the unusual way I grew up are all part of my history, and it is impossible for me to pry one apart from the other and to know how much overlap there was.

In fact, that night I felt terrified—as terrified as I've ever been in my life. What was going on in my mind was constant rumination about the inevitability of death. But it had nothing to do with any immediate danger from my throat. By the morning I was very agitated and very frightened because I didn't understand why I was so agitated. There was no stimulus for it.

Also, I was beginning to have worsening physical symptoms—diarrhea and vomiting. Yet I continued to go to the studio for almost a week. I was becoming more and more agitated. Not outwardly. This was something different from the kind of tantrums I was famous for. I wasn't barking at people or being ornery or difficult. It was just a frenzied feeling inside—I could feel the motor revving up—along with the continuing physical symptoms. I was constantly running to the bathroom, and finally, one day at work, I just passed out, and someone took me home.

By then it was clear that my problems were more than just the physical ones associated with the flu. I spent another sleepless night. I was panicky. My motor was racing. I felt paranoid. I did a lot of pacing, pacing, pacing. The next morning, my whole body shaking, I went to Dr. Arlen's office.

That was when he broached the topic of manic depression. He told me he had suspected for a long time that I might have this condition, and he believed that it was the shot of cortisone that had triggered this episode.

Dr. Arlen was worried about my reaction to the "stigma" of manic depression, but I had the benefit of ignorance on my side, so I wasn't frightened by it. I was only relieved that after all these years of feeling whatever the hell this was, it had a name. And before he told me that it had a name, he told me that it had a treatment. So for me, all my anxiety, all my stress, all my pain came *prior* to hearing those words.

A lot of people might have asked a whole bunch of questions. I did not. I just wanted to know: Do I take the pill now or five minutes from now or what?

Dr. Arlen explained that I would be hospitalized for baseline tests. That worried me a little because it meant I couldn't work, and there's always a bit of panic that goes with a performer's not showing up. So I felt it was important to speak candidly to the producers of *It Takes Two*, to take them into our confidence. But I didn't want this to be blurted out publicly because there *was* a stigma at that time to mental illness, and not just for someone in my profession. Mental illness scares people. They don't understand it, and they tend to feel uncomfortable with anyone who has it.

So it was all handled very privately. I went home. I told the boys, and I explained that I was going to have to go to the hospital. That didn't frighten them very much because they understood that it was for tests, and that maybe we were looking at a solution, the possibility of a more normal way of life. I honestly do not remember worrying that it wouldn't work. From the moment that man told me I could be helped until now, I knew I was going to be okay.

I went into Cedars-Sinai Hospital for five days for tests to make sure all of my organs were functioning correctly. There was a lot of blood work and CAT scans. I guess the blood work was somewhat sophisticated because of my diagnosis, but it felt to me as though I were just there for a head-to-toe physical. It was not a psychiatric setting. There is always that little bit of fear about psychiatric hospitals, so it was nice to be like a regular patient in a hospital bed in a regular room.

The last evening of my stay, Dr. Arlen came into my room. He was carrying Josh Logan's book *Movie Stars, Real People and Me*, which he had told me about earlier. It was about Josh's manic depression and how he dealt with it. He placed the book in my left hand and my first lithium pill in the right. I'm sure there was a moment right after taking the pill when I expected to jump up and scream, "I'm healed," but it didn't work quite that quickly.

I went home the next day, taking my pill in the morning and at night. Dr. Arlen had told me that somewhere in about three weeks I would begin to notice a change. But I think it was sooner than that. In about ten days I started to feel easier. It wasn't anything dramatic, the way a tranquilizer might make you feel. Things were just easier. It was easier to get up. It was easier to carry on a chitchat with somebody. It was easier to be. For the first time in my life I felt "normal."

When I wrote *Call Me Anna* in 1987, it was not to address manic-depressive illness but to fulfill a promise I had made to my mother twenty years earlier. I promised her I would write something to "set straight" the record of my life, something that would give the public a more accurate picture of me than what had been published for years in the newspapers and fan magazines. I knew that the story of my life, bizarre as it was, was full of drama and human interest, and I hoped it would enlighten some people who read it. But, at the time, I had no idea of the kind of response I would get. And I certainly didn't realize that the response would come from people who identified with me because I had been diagnosed as having manic-depressive illness.

The letters started arriving, bundles at a time, and I don't know that I'll ever be able to describe the impact those letters had on me. Total strangers telling me how much I had helped them, how they finally got their mother or their brother or their best friend to a doctor. Some of them came addressed, honest to God, to "Patty Duke, America." It was beyond anything I could have imagined. I began to travel to psychiatric hospitals to speak to patients and their families, and I testified at congressional hearings about the need for more funding for mental illness. Without ever intending it, I became a mental health advocate.

In 1989, Bantam Books, the publisher of *Call Me Anna*, approached me about writing a book specifically about manic-depressive illness. Both they and I wanted a book that would focus on more than just my story. While we believed that people would benefit from hearing about my experiences with this strange disease, we felt it was essential to share the wealth of information and research about manic-depressive illness. We wanted to show that the illness has many faces, and that there are many different ways that other people experience the condition. They suggested I work with Gloria Hochman, a medical writer, who could help bring this broader perspective to the book.

Gloria and I met; we clicked right away and knew that we could become lifelong buddies. After talking with each other for a long time, we were sure we wanted to work together. Much of Gloria's writing, in the past fifteen years, has focused on mental health, and she and I had the same goals. We spent a lot of time together. Through long and often trying days, we shared words and tears, experiences and information. In the end, we decided to write the book in alternating chapters—my personal story, then the critical information that people with the illness and their families and friends need to know.

My story has a happy ending. I am married to a wonderful man, Michael Pearce. We have a three-year-old son, Kevin, whom we adopted when he was a baby; two daughters, Raelene and Charlene, both busy and happy students; two sons, Sean and Mackenzie, both busy and happy in the entertainment industry; and three more sons, David, Allen, and Tom, busy and happy leading healthy adult lives. I feel blessed, and wish for all of you the peace and love that feel even sweeter to me because they were so long in coming.

—Patty Duke

◆

ILLNESS OR ECCENTRICITY?

All of us experience unexpected, inexplicable changes of mood— days when we feel energized and peppy, and days when we want to hug the covers, stay in bed, and shut the world out. For most of us, these moods come and go and don't interfere significantly with our daily lives. But for approximately twenty million Americans, mood shifts dramatically alter the way they live. They suffer from the psychiatric condition that tormented Patty Duke— an *affective*, or *mood, disorder*.

The most common is *unipolar depression*, which its victims commonly describe as "a black cloud that won't lift."

Manic-depressive illness, another mood disorder, plagues at least two to three million Americans. It is often called *bipolar* illness because, unlike unipolar depression, its victims experience not only the depressive states, but mood swings that cycle between two poles, bouncing them from reckless ecstasy to morbid despair. Because the condition is so often misdiagnosed, mental health experts insist that the numbers who suffer from it are far higher than statistics indicate. Dr. Janice Egeland, the director of a major study on manic-depressive illness, calls the disorder the "bipolar iceberg."

The National Institute of Mental Health defines manic-depressive illness as involving episodes of serious mania and depression. The person's mood usually swings from overly "high" and irritable to sad and hopeless and then back again, with periods of normal mood in between.

Someone in the depressed cycle may have any or all of the following symptoms:

- persistent sad, anxious, or empty mood
- feelings of hopelessness or pessimism
- feelings of guilt, worthlessness, or helplessness
- loss of interest or pleasure in ordinary activities, including sex
- decreased energy, a feeling of fatigue or of being "slowed down"
- difficulty concentrating, remembering, making decisions
- restlessness or irritability
- sleep disturbances
- loss of appetite and weight, or weight gain
- chronic pain or other persistent bodily symptoms that are not caused by physical disease
- thoughts of death or suicide; suicide attempts

A person in mania may have some or all of the following symptoms:

- excessive "high" or euphoric feelings
- a sustained period of behavior that is different from usual
- increased energy, activity, restlessness, racing thoughts, and rapid talking
- decreased need for sleep

- unrealistic beliefs in one's abilities and powers
- extreme irritability and distractibility
- uncharacteristically poor judgment
- increased sexual drive
- abuse of drugs, particularly cocaine, alcohol, and sleeping medications
- obnoxious, provocative, or intrusive behavior
- denial that anything is wrong

Not everyone with manic-depressive illness experiences all of the symptoms. Not everyone who is in a manic state gambles away the house, nor does every person in the depression phase of the cycle try to commit suicide.

The illness has many faces and covers a spectrum of behaviors, which are described fully in Chapter 2. Chapters 4 and 6 explore the causes and treatment of the illness; in Chapter 8, you will learn about mood disorders and their association with creativity.

Manic-depressive illness was identified at the turn of the century by Emil Kraepelin, an Edinburgh psychiatrist, who described several hundred cases in his care and made it clear that this was not a rare disorder. Since that time, the condition has captured the imagination of layperson and professional alike, partly because of its intriguing link to artistic creativity and superior leadership.

While mental health experts acknowledge that there are psychological components to manic-depressive illness, they see it primarily as a medical condition, one that results from abnormal brain chemistry—a condition for which there is enormous hope because usually it can be treated successfully. Unfortunately, a 1991 survey by the National Mental Health Association revealed that 43 percent of Americans believe that depression is not a disease but a personal or emotional weakness. And most people with the disorder continue to blunder through the medical system, as Patty Duke did, for years without learning what is wrong with them. Drs. Frederick K. Goodwin and Kay Redfield Jamison, in their book *Manic-Depressive Illness*, estimate that only 27 percent of those with the illness get treated—the lowest percentage of all major psychiatric disorders. So Patty Duke, you might say, is fortunate.

But until she was diagnosed and treated in 1982, she had little control over the dictates of her abnormal body chemistry or any mastery over her life.

Since that time, she has worked diligently to help others with mental illness. In *A Brilliant Madness*, she reveals the details of her diagnosis, her treatment, her family's reactions, and her thoughts about the connection between her illness and her extraordinary talent. As I worked with her, I was struck by her sensitivity and her compassion for people, her willingness to forgive, her hope that she would be forgiven, and her sincere efforts not to hurt anyone. I could understand why her husband, Michael Pearce, described her to me as "just sweet, someone with a good heart."

Patty and I hope that as you read her story and the alternating chapters about the many forms of manic-depressive illness, its causes, its treatment, and its association with dazzling creativity, you will gain a new understanding of this bizarre disorder, which Dr. Kay Redfield Jamison calls "the only mental illness that has a good side."

Both of us want to express our appreciation to the many mental health experts—those who work with patients and their families and those on the cutting edge of new, exciting research—for their time and their expertise. Without their contributions, this book would not have been possible. A list of those interviewed appears on pages 274–277. We thank the mental health organizations for all they do to act as advocates for and to offer support to patients and their families, and for their support of our work.

Our special appreciation goes to Dr. Hagop Akiskal, senior science adviser of affective and related disorders, National Institute of Mental Health, and Dr. Jay Amsterdam, director of the depression research unit, University of Pennsylvania School of

Medicine, for taking our midnight telephone calls and holding our hands every step of the way.

Many thanks to Steve Rubin for having conceptualized this book; to Linda Grey; to attorney Mitchell J. Dawson; to agent Cynthia Robbins for her support and encouragement; to Stuart Applebaum for his creative thinking; to Lauren Field for her attention to detail; to Amanda Mecke; to research assistant Joan Spivack; to librarian June Strickland; to associate editor Linda Gross; and to Toni Burbank, our editor, for her skills and her vision.

And our sincere gratitude to the patients and their families—whose names and identifying characteristics have been changed to protect their privacy—for sharing their stories with us to let other people with mental illness know they are not alone.

—Gloria Hochman

A
BRILLIANT
MADNESS

CHAPTER ONE

LOOKING BACKWARD

I knew from a very young age that there was something very wrong with me, but I thought it was just that I was not a good person, that I didn't try hard enough. As with many people, the overt symptoms of my manic-depressive illness didn't show themselves until my late teens. And that was with a manic episode. From that time on, until I was diagnosed at the age of thirty-five, I rode a wild roller coaster, from agitated, out-of-control highs to disabling, often suicidal lows.

As the cycles increased in frequency, they also increased in intensity—this is what the experts call the "maturing" of the illness—and as the years went on, the span of level time became shorter and shorter. I would have a manic, then a depressive, episode every three to four months, with the depressions lasting much, much longer than the manias.

But when I make myself think about it now, when I look all the way back to my childhood, long before my first big, public manic episode in 1970, I know there were other signs, other portents that I was very, very ill.

I do not recall any manias before I was nineteen. Oh, I can look back at certain things and speculate that maybe there were some manias going on, recollections of exciting times, opening on Broadway and things like that, which were exhilarating. But I don't think they really hold up to a test of mania.

But the panic attacks—they happened as far back as I can

1

remember. I can remember them prior to having language to go with them. I'm not sure what they have to do with—feelings of loss, maybe abandonment—but they became very clear to me around the age of eight. I still have them, but very rarely now. When I do, the same exact feelings I experience now I experienced then. They always have to do with death, *my* death. The very few times that I've been able to intellectualize about these feelings, I felt guilty that I wasn't ever worried about anyone else's death, only mine. About *my* nonexistence. It's only recently that I've been able to talk about this at all.

For instance, I can remember as though it were happening this minute a scene that took place outside the apartment house in Queens where my mother lived. I was about twelve—I was already living with the Rosses—and I had gone to visit my mother. I was getting ready to go inside the building, and it was a beautiful day. There was a little patch of grass in front of the building, and I thought to myself how very green it was. The light was bright, and across the street were a Catholic church and a Catholic school with a cross on top. There were milk bottles outside the apartment building, and I bent down to pick them up, then stood up. I could feel the air and see the light as it was hitting the building and that little grassed area. And then it happened. There was something about the beauty of that day, the smell, something that suddenly threw me into absolute terror that someday I would never see this again. I screamed and ran into the house with the milk bottles and dropped them on my way up the stairs. I just kept running in this frenzied, frenzied way. Then I ran into my mother and I was embarrassed. I couldn't tell her what it was that had happened to me. So I did what I always did in those cases when there was another person around. I made up something: A mouse ran across the hallway and I got scared.

When I visited my mother, the bus I took back to Manhattan passed two cemeteries. As soon as we passed Calvary Cemetery, I would be hit with a panic attack. I did a lot of throat-clearing and wheezing, trying to pretend I was having an asthma attack.

Sometimes it would be so late when I left that my mother would give me taxi money for the trip to the city. That was even worse. The statues at the cemetery's entrance were lit up at night. You could see the cross and the Virgin Mary. It was worse because I didn't even have anything else to look at to distract me. Plus I was drawn to that sight, fascinated by it. Once, when I was about ten, I jumped out of the cab just at the entrance to the Fifty-ninth Street bridge. I just screamed, "I gotta get out. I gotta get out." And I got out. The cab driver was scared. I was a little kid. I ran across the bridge, ran and ran and ran and ran. That was the only thing that would make it go away—physical exhaustion—which makes me wonder now what physiological thing is happening in those panic attacks. At the time I only knew that the best solution was running, the next was screaming, and the next was clearing my throat. Finally I got smart and took the subway so I didn't have to pass the cemetery anymore.

But it wasn't just passing a cemetery that brought it on. I can't, even to this day, track a pattern of what triggers it. That gorgeous day at my mother's house did it. And once it happened right here in my house. I woke up. It was a beautiful morning. I was listening to the birds, and all of a sudden it hit.

The panic attacks usually occurred in that sleepy zone in the morning, just after awakening, or at night, just before going to sleep. My symptoms would be deep, heavy breathing, hyperventilating, and screaming and running. I would jump out of bed. I couldn't stop myself. I'd just run around and scream, and the attack wouldn't stop until I was physically spent from either screaming or breathing funny for long enough to just about pass out. Sometimes I was able to contain my running around to the bedroom so I didn't disturb the children. But my screaming was so ungodly I'm sure the children heard it. The easiest thing to tell anyone was that I had been dreaming.

When I lived with the Rosses, the panic happened just about every night when I was going to sleep. Early on, I would scream, and I'm telling you it was a bloodcurdling, horrific scream, so it scared everybody who was around. I always lied and said it was a dream, a bad dream. I lucked out because the Rosses never asked me what the dream was about.

The panic happened during fully awake moments, too, when I was watching television or doing my homework. And there would be other people in the room. So I didn't scream, but cleared my throat so loud and vigorously that it was very disruptive. First I would be told to stop doing that. But I couldn't. I remember one time Ethel saying, "Why are you doing that? What's the matter with you?" And I blurted out what was bothering me. I told her I was afraid of dying. I didn't know exactly how to say it, but I tried to explain to her that I didn't mean I was afraid I was going to die this minute, but that someday I was going to die. The Rosses' response was logical and unenlightened. They said, "Oh, you don't have to worry about that for a long time. Look at us. We're not worried about it, and we're a lot closer to it than you are." I was embarrassed and I felt belittled. I don't think they meant to belittle me. That's just what you say to somebody who's saying things that are alien to your ears. So I went back to lying. And that's how it went for my whole life with them. I guess they never thought it was unusual that I had so many nightmares. And the coughing and the throat-clearing became a real habit, a crutch so that I wouldn't scream.

This is the kind of thing people don't talk about much. But one night when I was playing in *Meetin's on the Porch*, in Los Angeles, I did a very dangerous, too-revealing thing. A group of women had come to see the show, and they stayed afterward for a question-and-answer session. The play is about the friendship of three women from the time they are seventeen until they are eighty-five. All of the scenes take place on the porch of Haley's house—Haley's the character played by Susan Clark. In the first scene we're in our mid-forties, in the next we're eighteen, then we're all the way up to eighty-five, and in the final scene we're in our thirties. Well, we were talking about the first scene where Haley tells us that she killed her husband; but it is never mentioned or referred to again. One woman in the audience asked about that, and I jumped in without even thinking. I said, "Perhaps it speaks to the extraordinary ability we have to deny. I guess we have to be good at denial or we'd be running around twenty-four hours a day screaming, 'I'm going to die. I'm going to die.'" And as soon as it was out of my mouth I couldn't believe I had exposed myself that way. But what interested me was all the nodding of heads out there. Yes, it told me, we all do think about it. You're not the only one. It is a question that fascinates us all and terrifies us. It really is *the* question that we all have in common. But it's true. We have developed this unbelievable ability to deny. We have to. If we didn't, we'd go crazy.

Now, I know that a lot of people who have panic attacks do not have manic-depressive illness, that panic attacks are not a symptom of manic depression. But people who go to doctors complaining about anxiety often describe symptoms such as sweaty palms, fast-beating heart, jumpiness, dizziness, faintness, upset stomach, and trembling—symptoms that they call "anxiety." Sometimes that's just what it is—anxiety manifested in panic attacks. But sometimes it is depression. Many of the symptoms are similar. In my case, I believe that my panic attacks and my manic-depressive illness are probably independent of each other.

Oddly enough, I've not been incapacitated by panic attacks. When I was younger, I used to think they would eventually go away. I'd say to myself, "When I'm nine, I won't feel this way." Twelve. Fifteen. Well, when I get to be twenty. Thirty. Well, here we are forty-five, and from time to time up jumps the devil.

It's as annoying as hell that I've gone through all of this—the highs and lows and the treatment—and I still have this other stuff to deal with. But deal with it I will!

Aside from the panic attacks, I don't think I was a sad child. Maybe a bit melancholy. I was a serious little girl, but I also had the capacity to have fun and to laugh and to look forward to things. I think my real depressions started when I was about sixteen. I was living with the Rosses and *The Patty Duke Show* was on the air. I worked a five-day week from seven in the morning to seven or eight at night. I'd come home and do my schoolwork, rarely watched TV, and had no social life, no friends—none, zero. I would go to bed at about ten o'clock on a Friday night and I would not get up again until six-thirty Monday morning.

Today the Rosses would probably be described as dysfunctional—Ethel was drunk a good deal of the time—and as long as I was out of the way I wasn't bothering anybody. I didn't have to be entertained. If we all knew then what we know now, two weekends of that would say to you that there was something very wrong. But there was a strange relationship going on there as well. The Rosses mixed pills and alcohol and did some pretty irresponsible things, including making me their bartender and giving me first drinks, then drugs like Thorazine or phenobarbital or Percodan—things they knew nothing about but acquired through a friend.

There was a time when they took me every week to a weird doctor in New Jersey who put me on an examining table that had metal coils on the top. He would turn the lights out and flip a switch, and the coils would undulate beneath me. I hadn't a clue as to the purpose of this. The Rosses kept telling me that what the doctor was doing would make me feel better. They paid no attention when I told them I didn't feel sick in the first place.

So I keep going back and forth on the fence of how much of what I was doing was my genetic illness and what was in response to my environment.

When I was eighteen, I was still doing *The Patty Duke Show*, but I had fallen in love at a distance with Harry Falk, the man who eventually became my first husband. That was sort of a shot of adrenaline in my life, and though I still had no social life, I was a little more reluctant to disappear, even into sleep for a weekend.

And I was arguing more with the Rosses, especially about Harry. Finally they decided to keep me away from him by transferring the series to Los Angeles. That made me crazy. I balked and Ethel went on a rampage, carrying on about how she and John had given up so much for me and I was nothing but an unappreciative little slut. It was the last straw. I snapped out, told them I hated them and was leaving. There was much hullabaloo and trauma, but I did leave and spent most of that summer at Harry's place in Manhattan or out on Fire Island. But in the fall, I had to go back to L.A. to do the series. For the first time in my life I lived alone . . . in a luxury apartment on Sunset Strip. For a few days I loved the idea, but then I got lonely and restless. I didn't like staying alone, and I didn't know the first thing about how to manage on my own. My motor started to run. I couldn't sleep, and I would drive around at night or end up on the beach. Sometimes I stayed on the beach all night just because I couldn't stand going home to an empty apartment.

That's when I began running around with what was left of the Rat Pack. I was the youngest and littlest member, but I loved it—hanging around with Peter Lawford and Sammy Davis, Jr., drinking too much Jack Daniel's—so much that I was showing up on the set looking hung-over. I don't want to use it as an excuse, but I'll bet there aren't too many manic-depressives around who haven't, at one time or another, abused alcohol or drugs. I think it is an attempt to self-medicate, to suppress the high end to calm down a little, and on the low end to go the rest of the way into oblivion.

I was also learning to smoke and to swear. I guess my behavior on the set wasn't so great because I got nicknamed the "little shit." After all these years of taking orders, I liked the idea of giving them. I know now that my behavior was a classic attention-getting device. But did it also have something to do with an illness I didn't yet know I had? In retrospect, I certainly think so.

But the first manic episode I can remember came in 1965, when I was eighteen. Little did I know that it marked the beginning of a fifteen-year-long nightmare. I was at work on the set of *The Patty Duke Show*, and I got sudden, severe pain in my stomach, my side, and my shoulder. I was rushed to the hospital, and I needed emergency surgery for a ruptured appendix and a cyst on

7

my right ovary. Who knew then that certain drugs, such as those contained in anesthesia, could be bad for me? But after I came home from the hospital, I literally went crazy. I was hallucinating and raving and ranting and not sleeping and not eating and spending a lot of money. Luckily, Bob Sweeney, producer of *The Patty Duke Show*, visited me a few times and could see that something was drastically wrong. He insisted that I recuperate at his house with him and his wife and daughter. I spent six weeks there and I remember that I felt safe and loved in their home. In that environment I recovered from this manic episode, which I'm convinced was brought on by the anesthesia I had during the surgery.

Harry flew to California to see me, and two months later we got married. I was euphorically happy. Now, I don't mean that in the same sense as maniacally happy. I just felt wonderful. But it didn't last. Two or three months into the marriage, the depressions started again. I felt inadequate, I didn't know anything about making dinners for guests, the series had been canceled, so I was not earning money and therefore I was useless. I didn't know anything about sex. I didn't know anything about anything.

But instead of my going to sleep for days at a time the way I did in my teenage years, this depression showed itself in other ways. I was afraid—I didn't know of what. I cried all the time and I was completely unable to function. I'd stand in my closet for hours on end. I'd go in there to get dressed to go to the supermarket, and Harry would come back hours later and find me still standing there.

I also went on a diet at that time, a really swell diet of cigarettes, coffee, and Diet Rite cola. I went from 108 pounds to 73. This was twenty-five years ago, before we knew about anorexia, but I would guess that behavior pretty much falls into the anorexic category. Today we're all becoming more and more aware of the mind-body connection and that one thing triggers another. In retrospect, I have no doubt that the anorexia and the depression were feeding each other.

I had other physical symptoms, too. Everything gynecological went wrong. I cried—day in and day out I cried. It's hard to believe anyone has that many tears in her body. I was frightened, frightened of everything. If Harry suggested going to a movie, I would go into spasms.

This would go on until I got a job. Though petrified, I would pull it together enough to go and perform. I don't know how or why this worked for me because this is not the case with many people.

Perhaps it was something about the training I had as a child at that very vulnerable sponge-like age. Discipline and the fear of not fulfilling my obligations were so thoroughly branded into my soul that I was able to have some kind of manic, total craziness for forty-eight hours—right up to two hours before performance time—and then go to work. Once I was out in public, no one ever knew. Unfortunately, my ability to function probably delayed my diagnosis for years.

There were only a few times when the illness interfered with my work in an obvious way. And then it was the manias that caused the problem, because that's when I was brazen enough to say, "I don't care who you are, I don't care what studio you own, get off my back." In the depressions, I was interested only in pleasing, but even that didn't make me feel satisfied. For instance, let's say I would cry all Friday night, Saturday night, Sunday—then Monday, get up and go to work, do a good job, but on the way home Monday night I'd be crying again, more fearful, more fretful.

There *were* times when all of this leveled off, but I never knew what made it stop, what made the crying stop, what made me not be afraid that day. I also didn't question it. Once things seemed to be okay, I didn't mess with it. This was also a way to deal with the shame attached to that kind of behavior. It's everyone's shame, the family's as well. It's as if we said, "Oh, okay, it's stopped now, let's not talk about it anymore." Number one, talking might bring it back, and number two, it's just too embarrassing to look at.

9

But the depressions always came back. They defined my life. Sometimes I would manage to get up and get out of the house. But I always felt tense and anxious and I always wondered if everyone out there knew what was happening inside me. Are they staring at me? Do they know that I'm a loony?

During this time I became very clever about how to obtain and stockpile pills—tranquilizers, usually Valium. At home, I picked fights with Harry; then I would fly into the bathroom and swallow half a bottle of whatever pills I had—Valium or librium or Librax or whatever I had been able to get my hands on. These weren't real suicide attempts because I never did them unless someone, usually Harry, was there to make me throw up. I think they were a classic cry for help. It was as though there were demons inside me making me do all these crazy things. And the only way I could get away from them was a long sleep.

The real attempts to end my life didn't come until later.

Harry and I thought a vacation where we could relax and just be together might help. What a disaster that turned out to be! We went East to Fire Island, and I was impossible. I couldn't sit still. I couldn't read. I couldn't hold a normal conversation. I paced and screamed and threw things. And again I swallowed a handful of pills. Of course, Harry heard me in the bathroom and made me throw up before any real damage was done.

But the next day he insisted that I see a psychiatrist in Manhattan. That was a shrink I will never forget. The words she said that day haunted me for the next fifteen years. She told Harry right in front of me, "This is a very sick girl. And she probably will never get well." She talked about me like I wasn't there. And it sounded as though my life were a fait accompli. Finished. Final.

Now my suicide attempts became real. I can't even remember how many times I tried to kill myself. Not all of them got as far as actually taking the pills or digesting the pills. And it was almost always pills, although I did make a show sometimes of trying to use razors. But I always chickened out. A couple of times I tried to jump out of a moving car. But I didn't seem willing to inflict physical pain on myself. Some of the attempts continued to be attention-getting devices. Others came out of so much pain. I just wanted it to stop. I wish I had a more colorful, more profound way to describe it, but the only thoughts that went through my head were "Please make this stop. Please make me brave enough to die so that this anguish will stop." If someone could have handed me some other solution, as Dr. Arlen eventually did, I would have opted for that just as much as the pills in the bathroom. And, as perverse as it sounds, after all the suicide attempts I made, it is still very hard for me to imagine someone really killing herself.

Most of the time I didn't know why I was depressed. But in 1967 it was different. I became pregnant, but the pregnancy turned out to be ectopic, or tubular. That *was* grounds for another depression, but I would characterize that one differently because there was a reason for it. Losing my pregnancy *was* depressing, I could understand that reaction, whereas a lot of the other depressions seemed to come from nowhere.

By 1968, my marriage was faltering. I got a job in New York and Harry decided to stay in Los Angeles. And that created some volatility in me, that he was not coming with me. It was his choice to stay in Los Angeles, to rent out the house and get things in order. But I was determined to approach this as an adventure. I was a grown-up, I was going to New York to do a movie, *Me, Natalie,* and find an apartment and really function as an adult. But this was one of the times when I knew that the motor was starting to speed. I didn't know, of course, that I had an illness, but I was aware that something not quite normal was happening inside me.

The mania started with insomnia and not eating and being driven, driven to find an apartment, driven to "do" New York, driven to see everybody, driven to never shut up. The first weekend I was there, Bobby Kennedy was assassinated. I had been speaking publicly on his behalf—my first foray backing a political candidate—and I had an overwhelmingly out-of-proportion reaction to his assassination. I know those were insane times and we all had enormous reactions to those

11

assassinations, but for me it was as if he had been *my* brother or *my* father. This is not an exaggeration—at least two weeks went by without sleep. Now, I don't know how that's physically possible unless you're manic. The only other people who have ever done this that I know about are people who are chanting and fasting. Otherwise, it has to be a manic episode.

Harry came to New York for Kennedy's funeral, went back to L.A. for a week, then came back to New York. And we had major blowups. I remember myself in rage and acting very wicked. I had an incredible command of the language at these times, and I was doing alliteration stuff—"horrible, hateful, hideous Harry"—just spewing it out of me. I had insights I would never have had at any other time, and in the rage I was feeling I didn't edit any of them. Some of them were really vicious.

The day when all of this stuff spewed out of me was basically the end of my first marriage. And I did try to commit suicide within twenty-four hours. This time I was serious.

I did it with pills, after a day's work in the studio. This was different from my earlier attempts or from the pattern that developed later, after my marriage to John Astin. Those times it was all done privately and quietly at home and could easily be covered up. Here I ran the risk of being found out . . . or being dead. I had the pills with me. I had gotten them through someone who worked on the set. I never had a prescription of my own for any of these pills. And none of them were from drug pushers. It was astounding how easy it was to get them—people think they're helping. "Oh, yeah, I can get my prescription renewed. Is your back bothering you?" That kind of thing. And I might save the pills for months and months at a time, one here, three there.

That day I had Seconal, the red ones, and I sat on the floor in the dressing room and took them all, along with I don't know how much wine, a couple of glasses at least. I apparently called Harry and he decided it was better for him to stay away. I'm not quite sure what happened because this was one of the few times where I lost consciousness. From what I gather, Harry did come and took me to the hospital, had my stomach pumped, and then called Fred Coe, the director of the movie. He basically turned me over to him. He said, "I'm not helping here, I'm only making things worse."

I felt so responsible for creating such trouble for Fred and the other people connected with the movie that I woke myself up the next morning and went to work. Ironically, I did some of the best day's work I've ever done. I'm not so sure I was in control of my senses because I still had the residue of the effect of the pills. But I did it.

And then I was fine for a while, for a couple of weeks maybe, but I was now in a whole new environment. I was staying with Fred and his family at their New York apartment. I was being watched and cared for and probably catered to. All of a sudden I decided I was going to have the youth that I never had. In the movie I rode this little motor scooter, so after work I began taking the motor scooter home and staying out till all hours and cavorting with God knows who I found in Greenwich Village. I mean, right to splashing around in the Plaza fountain.

I was also trouble on the set. We were always losing half a day here and half a day there because I would show up late. Or I'd have a tantrum on the set—behavior I had never exhibited before. Once I told Fred to take his movie and shove it up his ass.

Finally, with much pain and everyone trying to figure out what the hell was going on, the picture was over and I had to come back to Los Angeles, and start a new life. And as soon as I moved into my new apartment I entered a depression.

This was one of the sleeping ones: stay up all night and sleep all day. I took the phone off the hook, disconnected it any way I could. I wanted no contact with the world. I felt like I was suspended in time, and I was tired, physically tired, yet I hadn't done anything to expend any energy. I really *would* sleep, and I'd wake up after four or five hours, go to the bathroom, and go right back to bed until ten o'clock at night. Then I was up. It was all-night television. And food deliveries—I never went to the supermarket. I lived on deli food. I couldn't have gotten it together to go out and shop. I didn't make any decisions. I made sure that I eliminated any possibility of having to make a decision. If your agent can't reach you on the phone, you can't be called upon to answer if you'll take this next job or not. But even the silliest things—what to eat—you just can't decide, and it's not like those days where you just don't know what you want. You *really can't* decide.

I wasn't drinking during this time. I never drank when I was by myself. There *were* times when I drank socially that I drank a lot. Usually white wine. When things were going well, champagne. What fascinates me is that I never became involved with other kinds of drugs, grass or cocaine. I never dropped acid, and that was going around big in the late sixties and early seventies. I remember being afraid that I would go off on some mental journey and never come back. I thought I would lose my mind. And I was ignorant enough of the effects of alcohol to think that that was okay.

I felt hopeless. Hopeless is really the word. I felt this was the way it was always going to be. There was nothing I could do to change it. I didn't think the phrase "I must be crazy," I really didn't think that. But I always thought there was something wrong with my character. I never talked to anyone about it. But I remember feeling so bad that I could never think the way other people did. I would hear people talking about plans, whether it was plans for two weeks from now or plans for their lives or plans for a house. I never was able to think in those terms. I almost didn't understand how you go about thinking that way. I always thought the solution was outside of me. I would have thoughts like, "If only I could meet a man like so-and-so or if only I had a home like so-and-so or if only I had children . . . " It was always those if-onlies that were going to save me.

When I moved out of the bleakness of a depression as deep as this one it wasn't as if I woke up one day and, boom, everything was fine. The manias and the depressions seemed to have a life of their own. I've been guilty of describing my mood swings in a way that makes them sound like a pendulum—an action and a reaction—and that's not all that accurate. It's far more accurate to talk about the ending of manias and maybe some down time, but not always. Sometimes I think that even in the smaller manias I exhausted myself so—just physically and emotionally exhausted myself—that I *had* to go to bed, and that began the depression.

When the mania starts to ebb and you return to the planet, you begin to recognize that you have done some very strange things. And sometimes the crisis was so practical and so real that I didn't have time or energy to worry about the wacko kind of things I did. I had to worry about what I had done with all the money or how I was going to get more, how was I going to cover those checks.

After I had been in this depression a month or so, I began to make an effort. I would take a shower and curl my hair and put on some clothes. That might take half a day, and then I had to figure out where I was going, because by now I had shut everyone else out of my life. I would try to go out. Sometimes I would just go to the supermarket and buy a quart of milk, but I had accomplished something, I was proud of myself. Then, little by little, I would put the phone back on the hook or see somebody in the elevator that I knew and I would be invited someplace, and that's how I got back into a bit of a social life. I'd be fine at whatever the event was, whether it was a dinner at someone's home or dinner out, but as soon as anyone would ask about seeing me again, I would retreat. I stayed in that kind of push me pull you place for a couple of months. Finally I got back into the social whirl—dating, dancing, and drinking.

Inevitably, I found myself smack in the middle of another mania. This one was particularly scary.

I was on the freeway, on my way from a tennis lesson, when I began to hallucinate. This is something I've not talked about before because I was afraid of being judged as someone who was truly crazy. Voices talked to me through my car radio. Bizarre headlines spoke to me personally in the form of a news report.

The voice told me someone was taking over the White House, and that I could be of assistance in this matter. I had to get to Washington! I was on a mission. I *did* call people before I left and say, "Have you been listening to the radio? There's been an invasion of the White House . . . " And of course what could anyone say to that except, "Gee, I think you'd better calm down."

I took off to Washington. And for the whole trip I was *on* a trip. When I got there, the house of cards began to fall and I began to feel paranoid. It was one of the few times that I really felt as if I were being watched. I was frightened because I knew this secret no one else knew. I checked into a swanky hotel in Washington and made all kinds of phone calls to different government offices. And then, almost like somebody flipped a switch, I realized I was behaving crazily, and I left the hotel. It was easy to move around because I had brought nothing with me.

I remember going out to the airport. It was snowing and the airport was closed because of the weather, only I now decided that it was closed because of this great invasion and that I was going to be captured. They had closed the airport to capture me. I paced through that airport until daylight, when it finally reopened. As I wandered, I just kept going in and out of reality. Sometimes I was completely in touch and saying to myself, "Oh, my God, what am I doing here?" But it was going through the unreal states that allowed me to survive that night. If I had stayed in reality very long in that airport, I would have freaked out.

Some of these things are convoluted in the telling because they *are* so nutty, almost like dreams. By the time I got back to Los Angeles I had not completed the manic phase, but I was clear enough of the hallucination to be very embarrassed about it. I couldn't remember whom I had talked to on the phone, so I spent several days worrying every time the phone rang that it was one of those people I had told my story to.

This ability to disappear for a while, then return—if I heard some of those stories about someone else I would say, "How did they do that? You can't just fall off the face of the earth.

Somebody must know where you are, especially if you're a celebrity." But I was able to do that in my early twenties—be totally involved with whatever the social scene was and then disappear, get into a whole other lifestyle and create a whole new reality. And within that reality I was normal. It was as if none of the other stuff ever existed.

This was also the period when I got absolutely maniacal about safety-deposit boxes. I kept putting stuff in safety-deposit boxes all over town. I'm talking about a Kleenex in one, an earring in another. But, boy, they thought I was very busy at those banks.

And my sex life . . . well, this was the sixties, I was a single person, and I got into what I guess we called free love. I certainly didn't know it then, but, looking back, I see this as another part of the mania. Sexual promiscuity is not exclusive to this illness, but it is a symptom of it. And there did come a point when I was, for *my* taste, *very* promiscuous. It really didn't matter who the person was, I went home with him. Or brought him home. I was awfully lucky that I didn't get some hideous disease. Now that I know about the prevalence of promiscuity among manics, I find the knowledge helpful because what I did then does not fit in with my personality. Yes, I like to have a healthy sex life with my mate, but really I am a monogamous person. So all of that running around and winding up with strangers and having to be drunk, not knowing who that person was in my bed, was unbelievably painful, not pleasurable. Mania does not excuse this behavior, but it does help explain why someone who, under other circumstances, wouldn't dream of going to bed with somebody she didn't know did it so often. It wasn't part of my reality and yet there I was, doing it. When you're manic, there are no consequences.

Once again I got into a pattern of running around all night and staying in bed all day. But I also had insomnia. And I still couldn't accept the split with Harry. So one night I took a whole bottle of pills. I did it after I drove to Harry's house and found a woman there. I don't remember much after that, but somehow I drove back to my friend Sandy Smith's house. I stayed there a

17

lot because I couldn't bear to be alone at night. Sandy was asleep. And I tried to kill myself—with an overdose of pills.

She called my manager and he got someone to admit me quietly into Cedars-Sinai Hospital. It was accomplished without fanfare and without publicity.

This is a good example of how being a celebrity complicates a disease like manic depression. Sometimes celebrity works for you; other times it hurts you. I feel especially lucky that despite my outrageous behavior, there were enough people in my life who cared what happened to me—for business or personal reasons—that I was frequently rescued from near death, and in a way that didn't destroy my career.

On the other hand, I was able to get away with a lot that someone else might not have, such as spending money I did not have. I know that there are lots of manic-depressives out there who do that, but I'll bet more often than not—if it's someone who is an accountant or a butcher or a baker—somebody says, somewhere along the line, "May I see your identification, please," or "May I call your bank?" It is astounding, it is shameful, but back then, if you were a celebrity, people just assumed you had the money. They didn't want to offend you by checking. That has changed somewhat over the years. These days, when I use my credit cards, they run them through just as they would anyone else's. But the places I frequented then catered to celebrities who were used to being recognized the moment they walked through the door— it's a rarefied atmosphere. Now, in most cases those people could probably afford to pay for what they were buying. I couldn't. But it was easy for me to check into hotels with nothing. I had nothing. I certainly never had any cash. There were also times when I didn't have credit cards or checkbooks or anything. Still, the door opened. The piper had to paid later on, but it was certainly a manic's dream.

After my suicide attempt, I was on the critical list at Cedars-Sinai for almost a week and it took me several months to recover after my release. Because of my Catholic background—good little Catholic girls don't do all that carousing and all that free sex—of course, I had to do pennance. So I went into a depression. And I became celibate. I took the pledge, and did everything else that went with straightening out my act—except getting real help.

I was saved when Bob Banner, the producer of *My Sweet Charlie*, a play that was being turned into a TV movie, offered me the female lead. I was overweight and didn't look too great, and I had a rocky start with my co-star, Al Freeman, Jr. But the four-week shoot turned out to be a big success.

When it was over, in late 1969, it was back to the same old pattern, back to the apartment, back to the bed, back to the effort to get up and get out again.

A few months later, John Astin came into my life. I was first drawn to this older, brilliant man because he shared my fixation on death. We were both at a wrap party for the film of a mutual friend and we got to talking about John Kennedy and about his dying so young. I saw something in John's face—a certain look, a fear—that made me know that he, too, was afraid of death. We talked nonstop for a long time and ended up spending the night together. John told me he was separated from his wife, so we saw each other a couple more times and I thought I was in love with him. That's when I found out that I was pregnant. I don't think those things happen by accident. It kicked off the next and most obvious, most manic episode in my life. It is hard even for me to believe that I did so many off-the-wall things in the space of just a few months.

My behavior on a detective show called *Matt Lincoln*, where I was doing a guest shot, was atrocious. I threw tantrums on the set, which cost time, and I made a very ugly display in the office of Sid Sheinberg, head of MCA. I had been called into his office probably to be lectured about wasting time on the set, and I felt I had a very legitimate case. The crew was being mistreated, blah, blah, blah, and I was now going to be their great champion. It turns out the crew all said they were fine, they didn't have any problems. Anyway, while I was in there with Sheinberg, I threw his Mickey Mouse clock at him and called him all kinds of names and just ranted and raved and tossed myself about his office. I thought I was the great Queen of England—I was suspended from my contract.

When I was nominated for an Emmy for *My Sweet Charlie* in the spring of 1970, so much was going on in my life. I was pregnant and unmarried. And I had just gone through a terrible trauma over the death of John Ross.

Although I hadn't seen John or Ethel for more than five years, I had a visceral connection with them. I had, in fact, written to them saying that I'd like to see them, but was advised by my manager not to mail it. Two weeks later, John died. I never had my chance to say good-bye, and it made me very sad. As though that wasn't enough, Ethel didn't want me at the funeral. I was so devastated that I asked a friend to intervene. He did, and Ethel finally relented. But she was so hostile to me at the funeral that it triggered another of those periods where I couldn't eat and couldn't sleep.

It happened that the Emmys were being presented on my mother's birthday. She had never been included in anything like that, so I wanted her there and sent her a plane ticket to Los Angeles. My mom's visit went poorly. She didn't like any of the clothes she and I had bought for her to wear to the award ceremonies. She cried a lot for no reason I could figure out. And the night of the awards, she was impossible. She sat in my bedroom and just wouldn't talk. I ended up dressing her in the dress I had planned to wear, and became so distraught myself that I went bananas. I threw together the most bizarre-looking outfit for myself, just odds and ends from my closet that didn't go together. But by that time I didn't care. I just took my mother, and off we went to the Emmys.

What had happened was that all of these pressures—all of these very real triggers—were going off at the same time. I apparently made a very strange acceptance speech at the Emmys, very disjointed, very erratic. I just stood there and mumbled, "The best words I've ever learned were 'hello' . . . and 'enthusiasm.'" Then I left the stage to go to the press area, and by the time I got there something had really snapped in my head. When they asked me the usual questions—how do you feel about your Emmy and so on—I answered, "I don't want it, take it back, I don't need this shit. I'm going to be a doctor." Suddenly I was leaving show business to go into medicine. I told them I had enrolled at UCLA. And I was going to become—what else?—a psychiatrist. I think there was a part of me that thought this was very funny and that I was being outrageous and screw 'em anyway.

Before I left for Chicago to rehearse for a play, a bedroom farce called *The Paisley Convertible*, I sublet my apartment in Los Angeles. I have no idea why. At the time I didn't need the money, though I would very shortly. I rented it to a young man that I saw standing in the lobby of my building inquiring about an apartment. I didn't know him from a hole in the wall.

By the time I got to Chicago, I was in even less touch with reality. I was staying in a Holiday Inn down the street from the Drury Lane Theater. There was a beautiful apartment suite with a dressing room connected to the theater, but they didn't allow me to use it because I had flown my dogs in with me, my white German shepherd, my Great Dane, and my miniature dachshund. Before I was in the Holiday Inn forty-eight hours, I had opened up the living room portion of the suite like a hospitality room—for total strangers. It was one loud party going on in there, people I never saw before in my life, never saw since. I don't know if they knew who the hell I was or if they cared. And the dogs were running around all over the place.

I had insomnia again, as I often did when I was manic, so I was physically exhausted, not to mention having morning sickness from the pregnancy. Plus I was wandering around the hospitals of Chicago looking for a baby to adopt. And I couldn't learn my lines for the play. I was throwing up all the time and the dogs were all over the Holiday Inn. So for the first time in my life, I got fired.

I closed the door to my hotel suite, left my dogs at a kennel nearby, and flew back to California. By now I was losing the manic energy and I was getting really tired and really sick. I went back to my apartment and told the poor guy who had sublet it that he had to get out. I was really sorry, but things had changed and I was back and he had to move. He was still there when I got on the telephone and started calling people about my pregnancy. I had been dating Desi Arnaz, Jr., before I went to Chicago and there had been a lot of sleazy stories that I was pregnant with his baby. I didn't protest because I was just too sick to do anything rational. So I called Desi and he said, "You know my situation. I can't get involved. You have to get help." Desi was seventeen, and you can imagine that his parents weren't too thrilled about any of this. I got off the phone with him and I was hysterical, ranting and raving about being pregnant and not married. This guy—my tenant (his name was Michael)— said to me, "Do you want to get married? I'll marry you." I said okay. It was if he had said, "Would you like a ham sandwich?"

At the time I would have liked to think of myself as free-wheeling and not caring what anybody thought, but the fact of the matter was that there was the core of the good little Catholic girl who does things by the rules. I was almost embarrassingly concerned about having a child without being married. Now, I don't think that's a good enough reason to go and marry somebody you don't even know. But there *was* an element of that in it as well as the maniacal element.

Within an hour we were on our way to Las Vegas and we were married that night. For the next thirteen days, I picked up my new husband's markers, which were hefty, all over Las Vegas. Then I decided I wanted to go someplace else. Michael wanted to visit his family in New Jersey and I thought, "Why not?" And on the way we'd pick up my dogs that I had left in Chicago. I didn't want to travel on a regular airliner, so we rented a Lear jet. We went to Chicago, then to New Jersey, then to New York where I wound up on *The Dick Cavett Show*. My manager had no idea how manic I was, so he was still booking me. Meanwhile, the Lear jet I had rented sat in an airport in New Jersey with the meter running. I forgot it was there because I was off doing twelve other crazy things.

On the show, I told Dick Cavett and I don't know how many millions of other people that I was pregnant and that I was going to build an ark in the desert between Barstow and Bakersfield. Again I humiliated myself in front of a national audience. After that show, I began to regain just a little bit of touch with reality because at least I felt embarrassed by what I had just done on national television.

But the mania wasn't over yet. I picked a fight with this "husband" in our hotel room on the nineteenth floor of the Americana, and I began throwing things. Just like at the Holiday Inn in Chicago, it was set up like a hospitality suite, bottles everywhere, glasses—and dozens and dozens of our "closest" friends. I began throwing everything in sight. Chairs, tables went out the nineteenth-floor window, and then I called Annie Bancroft.

I had been very close to her when we worked together in *The Miracle Worker*. I would tell her my troubles and she would really listen. She treated me like a young adult instead of a child, and I have always appreciated the relationship we had. But I hadn't talked to her in years. I don't even know how I got her number. I called her agent maybe, and in return she called me. I obviously didn't sound so swell on the telephone, and she came right away. She got in touch with my lawyer, who was the only person I felt I knew in Los Angeles anymore, and he arranged for me to fly back. Annie put me on the plane that afternoon, and, to the best of my knowledge, I never saw Michael again. The marriage was annulled. I don't know how the lawyers proved it, but the annulment was based on the marriage's not having been consummated. In fact, it never was. When would there have been time? Thirteen days with this person and I don't think I could ever, by the slightest stretch of the imagination, describe it as a marriage. I still have no idea about his side of the story.

Cleaning up the debris of that episode didn't stop the mania.

I decided to rent a house in Palm Springs for a couple of months and calm down, but I wound up flying to Las Vegas again, for what reason I do not know, on another rented plane with the meter running. And I met a woman who was a stewardess on this little plane and she told me a sad story about how she didn't have anyplace to live with her little baby. So she and the baby moved in with me. Before long, another girl, an artist whom we met in a restaurant, came to live with us. Now I was running a commune—and getting more and more pregnant, of course. There was no money, but that didn't stop me from writing checks or running up charges as if it were going out of style. I know that spending money with abandon is one of the telltale symptoms of mania, and I certainly did more than my share.

There was that cockamamy dune buggy I bought in Palm Springs, for instance. I don't know why I bought it. Like Mount Everest, it was there. That's the childlike part of the mania. It's whatever you see you want, that's it, it's yours, with no thought, not the slightest anxiety about what it takes to get it or how you're going to pay for it. It really is like believing that the money's all growing on trees. When I walked in the door of that store, I knew I didn't have money for the dune buggy, but between door and dune buggy—which I couldn't even drive because it had a stick shift—any kind of logical concept like that was gone. The dune buggy was for my new playmates of the moment, whoever they were—somebody I met in a bar or at a hairdresser or at an ice cream store. A week after I bought it, I went back to Sears—I was trying to mend my ways and shop in a less expensive store—saying, "You have to take it back. Don't you understand? I don't have any money, you have to take it back."

My judgment about finances of any kind just didn't exist. The worst blunder I made involved two guys who, on a whim, I had made my business managers. It was another one of those things like the guy who said, "Do you want to get married?" And me saying, "Sure."

I had met these guys literally in the parking lot of The Bistro restaurant. And frankly, I thought one of them was hitting on me. I had no idea *how* he was hitting on me. I freely gave out my phone number. I didn't know these two guys from a hole in the wall. They called immediately and said could we have lunch, that they were business managers. And I didn't question why I should go have lunch with two people I didn't know. So I had lunch with them, and the next thing I knew, they were my managers. Well, they managed my money right into their account and did a very good job of disposing of it. When I brought a criminal investigation against them in 1974 no money could be found. Plus they had charged things to my charge cards, and I never looked. I didn't pay my own bills. They went directly to them. I used to say, "Oh, pooh, pooh, pooh, I don't do that. I'm an actress, I don't do that." There was always a willing helper.

As my pregnancy progressed, manic as I was, I knew that I needed to take care of myself physically. So I left my house in Palm Springs and went back to L.A. to be nearer my obstetrician. The artist left, too, and while I was gone, the woman with the baby cleaned my house out. She took all the furniture and vanished, but she left our dogs. Before I found out about it, they had been locked up in the house for nearly ten days and eaten everything in sight, including walls and floors, and made a mess. Needless to say, the whole thing cost me a fortune.

Then the mania ended. This was one of the times when the gloom descended quickly. I was six weeks away from delivering Sean, and I spent those six weeks in bed around the clock, barely eating, seeing no one, and doing nothing. Still, this depression wasn't as intense as some others, and I think that was because I was calling on every bit of discipline I had for the pregnancy.

But once Sean was born, the big mood swings stopped. There *was* some depression—there were just the two of us—and a lot of sleepless nights, but at least there was this little toy to play with, and I took very good care of him. The depression lasted about a month, until I got a job, which gave me enough money to get another house to live in. Then for the next eight months I was alone with this child—I really became a recluse—very responsible and very at peace. It was lonely, except that I had this little buddy who wet his pants, who needed to be changed. It wasn't a time I was jumping for joy, but it was lacking in hysteria, so, by comparison, it was almost heaven. And this was really it for the manias for a very long time.

CHAPTER TWO

THE MANY FACES OF MANIC-DEPRESSIVE ILLNESS

It seems incredible that Patty Duke, an intelligent and articulate woman, a famous actress with access to the best and most sophisticated medical and psychiatric care, had to endure fifteen tormented years before she was given a reason for her bizarre behavior. It appears even more astonishing because Patty's sharp mood swings were the symptoms of classic manic-depressive illness, the form one would think would be easy to recognize. Why then did she—a woman in obvious agony, crying out for help— ricochet from doctor to doctor, move in and out of psychiatric facilities, and make countless suicide attempts before hearing the diagnosis that changed her life?

Unfortunately, there is no definitive laboratory test, no X ray, that can confirm manic-depressive illness. It is like diagnosing a heart attack without the benefit of an electrocardiagram, or a brain tumor without viewing the results of an MRI. The diagnosis is largely one of exclusion, and rests in the hands of a probing and knowledgeable physician.

Dr. Hagop S. Akiskal is an Armenian-born psychiatrist who has devoted his professional life to the study of personality and mood disorders. He became well known for his innovative, sometimes provocative, views about manic-depressive illness when he was professor of psychiatry and director of the affective disorders program at the University of Tennessee. Today he is senior science adviser of affective and related disorders at the National Institute of Mental Health. He speaks passionately and eloquently about manic-depressive illness and why it takes the skills of a medical detective to tease out a diagnosis.

"Unfortunately, manic-depressive illness is not as clear-cut as it might seem," Dr. Akiskal explains. There was a time, he says, that manic depression, also called bipolar illness, was thought to be a disease *only* of psychotic highs and suicidal lows—a condition that could make its victims feel as though they could conquer the world or convince them that life is not worth living. Today it is known that the disorder has many forms and that it does not always follow a predictable course. Sometimes the highs are muted, hardly recognizable even to the person experiencing them. Some people have many manias and few depressions; more have just the opposite. It is not uncommon for a person to have only one or two manic episodes that punctuate a life marked by long periods of gloom. Others go through something called "mixed states" or "dysphoric mania"—hyperactivity, and "flight of ideas" laced with irritability and apathy. Even depression that keeps recurring may be another form of manic-depressive illness. In between the depressions are periods that may not qualify as "highs," but contrast enough with the lows to count as "cycles." In Europe, a large proportion of recurrent depression is acknowledged to be a form of manic-depressive illness. Such authorities in this country as Dr. Akiskal and Dr. Frederick K. Goodwin, director of the U.S. Alcohol, Drug Abuse, and Mental Health Administration, among others, have conducted research to support that concept. This doesn't mean that all recurrent depressions are manic-depressive illness; the best way to distinguish is by noting a more or less cyclical or recurrent pattern in someone who has a manic-depressive first-degree relative—that is, a mother, father, sister, brother, or child.

BIPOLAR I: CLASSIC HIGHS AND LOWS

Patty Duke suffered from the classic form of manic depression, the one we tend to hear most about, though it is not the most common. Doctors call it "bipolar I."

During manic episodes, people with this form of the illness do outrageous, outlandish things. They may book passage for India on a whim (no matter that their bank account is registering empty), buy three new cars even though they don't drive, marry someone they met at last night's party. They feel invincible, see no consequences for their behavior, and, in fact, believe they can conquer the world. Sometimes they are certain they are God and have been entrusted with a special mission.

People in mania often feel spectacular. They may talk about elation, euphoria, ecstasy. They have boundless energy and need little sleep.

Fifty-four-year-old Marjorie says she would have a hundred ideas and feel that she could implement every one of them—write a movie script, paint an entire apartment in a day. She'd call friends at six o'clock in the morning and talk nonstop, just because she was up and feeling vigorous. "I would do a lot of physical things—like moving all the furniture, cooking for an army, polishing all the silver. My thoughts raced, and my ideas seemed brilliant."

Steven, who was not diagnosed until he was forty, insisted he was charged with saving civilization from famine. For years he hoarded cans of food in his basement from floor to ceiling, until there wasn't an inch of space left.

In the grip of extreme mania, people's energy becomes misdirected and their judgment vanishes. They spend money extravagantly, drive recklessly, become sexually promiscuous, conceive grandiose schemes, make outrageous business investments, gamble away the house. They may also become irritable, quickly outraged, and intolerant of the needs of others.

In full-blown psychotic manias, a person loses all touch with reality. He has delusions and hallucinations, is extremely impulsive, becomes hypersexual, and has a total lack of insight and judgment. Words and sentences roll off his tongue, with ideas and concepts, usually disjointed, tripping over one another. Unlike trying to understand schizophrenics, whose words often make no sense, someone listening closely can follow the leaps and jumps of the manic-depressive's flight of ideas, but it is stunning—and wearing. Energy is boundless and the manic-depressive can get along on amazingly little sleep. In this state, people often become belligerent and move around in such a frenzy they could literally die of exhaustion. They may reach a level of destruction so severe—to themselves or to others—that they need to be hospitalized.

When the gloom descends, it is debilitating. Its mournful symptoms often feel the same whether someone is in the depressive cycle of bipolar illness or is going through a major depression.

Some people, like Patty Duke, take to their beds and smother themselves under the covers for weeks at a time, emerging only to go to the bathroom or, perhaps, to attempt suicide. Others manage to get out of bed, if not in the morning, then some time during the day, but complain that they feel flat and slowed down. People in this condition enjoy nothing. They lose interest in sex, have no self-esteem, can't make decisions, and find it difficult to concentrate. Feelings of hopelessness—that "life will never be brighter for me"—are common. There are physical complaints, too: loss of appetite, heart palpitations, queasy stomachs. "All of you is in pain," one woman says. "You can't stand your eyeballs. Even your hair hurts."

These depressions are dramatically different from the "down days" or "blue moods" that all of us experience from time to time. While "the blues" come and go, clinical depression is like a black cloud that won't lift. Those experiencing it feel that they have been condemned to a devastating fate from which there is no escape.

But not everyone with this form of the illness rocks back and forth between mania and depression the way Patty Duke did. Some people experience a lifetime of recurrent depressions, punctuated by one or two episodes of mania.

Dawn: Only One Mania

Dawn, forty-five, says it was her only manic episode that saved her.

"Since I was in my twenties, I had been seeing doctors for depressions that came and went about every six months," Dawn says. "They were worse during the winter months, around Christmastime and during the long, dark days of January and February." During those periods, Dawn felt totally slowed down. She couldn't make decisions, she didn't want to see anyone, and she felt hopeless. "I never tried to commit suicide, but I did think about it," Dawn says. "Whatever it was I had felt terminal."

Like Patty Duke, Dawn was tormented with unexplainable physical symptoms: spastic colon, bad gums, endometriosis. Her husband would become irritated and tell her to "snap out of it," to shake herself. "That was like telling Mickey Rooney to grow six inches," Dawn says. "It was ridiculous."

Then Dawn had her excursion into mania. She was in a new, high-pressure job as a research pharmacologist, working long hours, drinking lots of coffee, and taking work home every night. One night at work, she got the feeling that she had to "save" all of the patients in the hospital, that it was her mission. When she went to her boss's office to discuss her new calling, she began hallucinating. "I was seeing fluorescent creepy-crawlers, like bright silverfish, creeping all over the floor. I kept scratching my skin. I thought I had fleas. I was talking nonstop, with words that made no sense tumbling out of my mouth. Then I left and somehow ended up in a fetal position outside the elevator. I don't know to this day how I got there."

31

Dawn was taken to a mental hospital and given drugs to sedate her. The next day she plunged into a depression; a staff psychiatrist diagnosed her as having manic-depressive illness. It was the beginning of her journey into health.

◆

THE LESS-THAN-HIGH "HIGHS"

Dr. Akiskal has pioneered the study of what he has called the "soft bioplar spectrum," manic-depressive illness characterized by less-than-high highs. People with these milder forms of the illness—which have different names and mean different things—are often erroneously labeled neurotic or personality-disordered.

BIPOLAR II

People with bipolar II play out a different scenario than Patty Duke, with her sharply defined highs and lows. They have recurrent depressions, but without the psychotic manic episodes. Instead, they experience brief "hypomanic" (less than manic) periods, during which they feel mildly euphoric and have lots of self-confidence and energy. These hypomanic episodes may last from two to ten days, and they don't require hospitalization. It has been speculated that many successful salespeople may operate in a hypomanic state, a sort of toned-down mania.

Beverly: A Bipolar II

Thirty-five-year-old Beverly, an artist, never knew what to call her illness, but says there was never any doubt in her mind that something was very wrong with her. She was plagued with low-level depression that every once in a while escalated and became incapacitating. In between the depressions, she had mild to moderate—but never psychotic—manias.

32

Her first depression came when she was sixteen, when, for no reason she could understand, she cried all day and most of every night. She couldn't eat, broke into heavy sweats, and had heart palpitations. She remembers a painting she created —the background was flames, the flames of hell, and there was a woman who had no head. She was carrying her head on a stick. Beverly says that painting mirrored how she felt—detached, as though she didn't know where her head was.

From that time on, her depressions came and went, and varied in severity. In between were the blessed periods of elation. When she felt good, she didn't want to waste time sleeping. "It was like—hurry up and do everything because you never know when you're going to feel bad again, and then you won't be able to do anything," Beverly says. "I had this creative burst in my brain and there would be so much going on. During those high times, I'd be more daring, take more risks with color and design. I was more sure of myself, and I was very productive. I didn't know where the energy came from. If only I could have kept it up, life would have been spectacular."

Like Beverly, people with bipolar II are frequently thought to be highly productive. "Their minds work faster, they may be sharper, even sharper-tongued," says Dr. Akiskal. "They can accomplish a lot, and even though they take risks and sometimes act impulsively, they are charming and intense. They generate a sense of excitement, people catch their highs and tend to like them."

The hypomanic periods often come at the end of a long depression during which the person has vegetated and accumulated a long list of obligations. The period of heightened energy allows him or her suddenly to discharge these responsibilities quickly, effectively, and efficiently, so that people are enormously impressed. If this productivity is averaged over a year and measured against that of other workers, it may not be so dramatic. But, at the time, it is striking. Dr. Akiskal says that during periods of hypomania a salesman might sell twenty-five cars when others are selling only two or three. This unevenness characterizes them.

Bipolar II's are often wonderful at parties, fun to be with, and can be great on vacations, but they are very difficult to live with. Their relentless exuberance can be wearing and their shifts into gloom jolting. When they feel good, they reject any kind of help. Why would they want it? It is only when the depression hits that they may be willing to see a doctor.

Dorothy, a Chicago woman who suffers from bipolar II, says she wishes she could bottle her mania. When she is "up," she feels fantastic, beautiful, and supercompetent. She can get along on almost no sleep and feels as though there is nothing she can't do. But, inevitably, along come the lows, and then it is as though the highs never happened.

How can hypomania be distinguished from just plain happiness? How does a doctor know it is a condition that needs treatment? Dr. Akiskal says that "hypomania is a *recurrent* condition; happiness is not." And it is especially significant if the high-spirited time has been preceded or followed by depression, particularly if the depression comes in autumn and winter.

THE CYCLOTHYMES: MILD UPS AND DOWNS

To further complicate diagnosis, there is a group of individuals called cyclothymes, the most uneven of manic-depressives, whose high-and-low cycles last only a few days or weeks. When Dr. Akiskal first studied cyclothymes in the late 1970s, he was stunned by their sudden switches from apathy to sharp and creative thinking.

He describes them as "perpetual dilettantes." They start something with great enthusiasm but don't complete it. They move from place to place. They attach themselves to various movements, then become disillusioned. They may get great poetic inspirations, then dry up for weeks. They have an uneven work record, but during their productive times they can achieve remarkable things.

Thirty-eight-year-old Lisa, for instance, moved nine times in three years. Each time she rented an apartment and furnished it, with passion and joy, she found a reason to move on. The view was less than she expected. The neighbors were noisy. She was tired of peach and gray. She preferred a loft. She changed jobs and her enthusiasm for them just as frequently. After a year as a computer programmer, she decided to become an entrepreneur, opening a chic shop for party supplies. After several months, that was "too frivolous" an occupation, and she returned to school to study photography. The camera her parents gave her as a graduation gift is gathering dust in her closet. Lisa is now applying to law school. Through all of these life changes, she lost most of a sizable inheritance and almost all her friends, not to mention the support of her family, who wrote her off as a "drifter."

Lisa has never gone through a serious depression, but her history is one of high-energy periods, marked by ambition and a thirst for new adventure, followed by times of listlessness and inertia during which she could not pursue her dreams.

These cyclothymes represent a vast group of people whose deviations in temperament are often thought, mistakenly, Dr. Akiskal observes, to be personality or character disorders. Their fluctuations are different from the normal shifts in mood that most people have, in that they are more intense and more frequent. "Most people don't go that deep or that high from day to day or week to week," he says. "And they don't lose their judgment."

The most extreme cyclothymes are called "rapid cyclers," with mood changes colliding with each other, from month to month, from day to day, or sometimes even within the same day. These men and women zigzag between highs and lows so rapidly they often feel as though they are about to die. They might bounce from euphoria to despair and back again within hours. They are in exquisite pain, out of control, like a race car gone berserk, and sometimes say that they are afraid of being alone with their episodes because they don't know what they will be doing next.

Rapid cyclers can't make plans because they can't predict their mood even a day ahead. They are like yo-yos and feel as though they are being helplessly manipulated by some force outside themselves. Most rapid cyclers have manias or depressions that last about two weeks; they have them from twelve to twenty-four times a year (sometimes with minicycles in between), in contrast to other manic-depressives, who cycle perhaps four times in twelve months. Approximately 10 to 15 percent of manic-depressives are rapid cyclers. And 85 percent of them are women. In fact, the more rapidly the cycles come, the more likely it is that the sufferer will be female.

This condition is the most difficult to treat; unlike cyclo-thymes, who almost never need hospitalization for their condition, rapid cyclers are usually in and out of the hospital, have a trial-and-error acquaintance with a medley of medications and often need electroconvulsive therapy.

While many people are rapid cyclers from the start, others, over time, "mature" into that form of the illness. They usually begin with depressions that are mild and brief. Later they will experience a "high." Then the depressions come more frequently and last longer. So do the manias. The amount of time between episodes collapses, and the person becomes identified as a rapid cycler.

Nancy: The Agony of a Rapid Cycler

Nancy was thirty and had just had her third child. One morning she was jolted out of sleep and she felt as though something in her head had snapped. She doesn't remember much about that day anymore, but her husband says she was "out of touch" with the world. She accused the neurologist who saw her as an emergency patient of stealing her purse, and she was hysterical in his office. He sent her to the hospital immediately.

During her three weeks there, her behavior became more bizarre. She remembers walking around the hospital parking lot naked and barefoot, but has no idea how she got there. She remembers that she was so agitated she couldn't sit still and would run down the hospital corridors. Sometimes she skipped down the halls without her clothes on.

No one told her what was wrong with her, but doctors recommended electroconvulsive treatments to improve her condition. After three months of those treatments, she was no better. And from that time on, her moods "went up and down like an elevator." One day she would want to kill herself. The next she'd go out on the town, spending money she didn't have on furs and jewelry.

Typical of rapid cyclers, Nancy's mood shifts became more frequent, with manias and depressions almost running together. Like many others with her form of the illness, she has been resistant to medication. One drug after another has been tried, and has failed. There have been—and still are—numerous hospitalizations, mostly when she was psychotically manic.

"During one hospital stay, the doctor found me dancing around the room, pirouetting to the window," Nancy says. "I pointed to the wires that connected the tall lights on the expressway, and told the doctor that I was on my way out of the window to dance on those wires. When I'm manic, I just don't think rationally. Anything I want to do is possible."

When Nancy was interviewed for this book, she was experiencing a fairly level time on a combination of drugs, one of which is lithium. But she needs to be monitored carefully and will probably have to be hospitalized from time to time as her medications need juggling.

THE MIXED STATES

As though the varying types of bipolar disorder are not confusing enough, patients often show a smorgasbord of symptoms that are at odds with each other. They alternate their elation and ecstasy with irritability and anger that may explode into destructive rage. They are hypercritical and complaining, manipulative and often obnoxious. Momentary tearfulness and even suicide threats or attempts are not uncommon. This is the kind of behavior Patty Duke described during the filming of *Me, Natalie*. She was carousing all night in New York, riding a motor scooter, and splashing in the Plaza fountain, but throwing tantrums on the set the next day.

Some mental health experts describe these mixed bipolar episodes as a "despairing anxiety"—a form of depression—coupled with flight of ideas and distractibility—a form of mania. This mixture of behavior reflects both extremes of the illness—the mania and the depression—coming out at one time. So the mood in mania, far from always being pleasant and fun, is often antagonistic and merciless.

Dr. Akiskal's research, supported by the clinical observations of others in the field, shows that the milder forms of manic depression, especially cyclothymia, are probably much more common than the classic bipolar I type experienced by Patty Duke. But those who have them seldom get diagnosed accurately. "This is unfortunate," says Dr. Akiskal, "because such individuals account for 3 to 4 percent of the general population. Full-blown manic-depressive illness has a lifetime risk of one percent; by the time it is diagnosed, it has already caused a great deal of grief and suffering to the patient and his family. That happens because the earlier or cyclothymic phases of the condition go unrecognized."

BIPOLAR III: MEDICATED INTO MANIA

Throw into the cauldron bipolar III, and the waters get even murkier. For people in this group, a manic episode may be precipitated by a drug or by electroconvulsive treatment prescribed for depression. In some cases, as when Patty Duke was tripped into the mania that led to her diagnosis, the drug may be a steroid such as cortisone. Sometimes it is an antidepressant prescribed because the patient was mistakenly believed to have clinical depression. It is not unusual for someone being treated for such a depression to spring into a manic episode; it may mean that he or she is really a misdiagnosed manic-depressive.

MIMICKING OTHER MENTAL ILLNESSES: A DIAGNOSTIC DILEMMA

Sorting through all the forms of manic-depressive illness is arduous enough. But its symptoms overlap with those of other mental disorders—unipolar depression, reactive depression, schizophrenia, schizoaffective disorder—and create a diagnostic dilemma. It takes a relentless sleuth to distinguish them.

Dr. Jay Amsterdam is director of the depression research unit at the University of Pennsylvania School of Medicine. He calls himself a biological psychiatrist—one who focuses on physiology, not psychology as an explanation for mental illness.

Outspoken, blunt, and not averse to challenging traditional thinking, Dr. Amsterdam insists that diagnosing manic depression, or any other mental illness for that matter, is like going on a hunting expedition. "There is no substitute," he says, "for spending a lot of time with patients, observing their behavior carefully, digging persistently into their backgrounds, and prodding them to remember tucked-away details about their own and their family's history. In their histories lie significant clues. Like a skilled detective, we must unearth and piece together pertinent and critical fragments of information."

UNIPOLAR DEPRESSION

People with unipolar depression—more than ten million a year in the United States alone—complain of symptoms similar to the gloom of manic-depressives in their low states. They lose interest in activities they once enjoyed, can't make decisions, have mysterious fears, develop disturbing sleeping and eating patterns, have little energy, and feel hopeless about their futures.

Despite new knowledge about the condition and the National Institute of Mental Health's major national education campaign to inform the public and physicians about symptoms and treatment, only one in four clinically depressed persons gets help.

Unlike bipolar illness, which many physicians believe affects men and women equally, unipolar depression discriminates. More than two thirds of its victims are women. No one is certain why, but there is speculation that women, genetically, may be more predisposed to depression than are men—hormonal factors probably contribute; or that the changing roles of women have produced unprecedented anxiety; or that women may be more likely to seek help than men, so the numbers are skewed; or perhaps that men are better able to distract themselves and focus less on depressed feelings than women do.

A new survey, however, suggests that men may be starting to catch up.

Whatever the cause, unipolar depression, like manic-depressive illness, has been misunderstood and undertreated and has taken a heavy toll on its victims. Fifteen percent of those who have it will eventually commit suicide and, according to research conducted by Dr. George Murphy of Washington University in St. Louis, most of them will have visited a physician within a month before they took their lives.

REACTIVE DEPRESSION

While Dr. Amsterdam is convinced that unipolar and manic depression are physical illnesses, just like diabetes or arthritis, he recognizes that some depressions are "reactive," that is, they are a normal response to a major trauma—the death of a loved one, the loss of a job, the onset of a life-threatening illness. But that's different, he says, from the patients with a biochemical mood disorder. Reactive depression is time-limited. When the stress is relieved, patients can again enjoy sex, food, hobbies, other people.

The way people respond to major loss offers a significant clue about the kind of depression they have. "People with reactive depression grieve for their losses, then restore themselves and go on with their lives," Dr. Amsterdam says. "The people I see with the chemical depressions often can't grieve normally, not even when they suffer one of the most profound insults in life, when someone close to them dies. They can't experience even this extreme pain. That's why they sometimes try to kill themselves. They're locked into this limbo and they can't explain it because there are no words to describe what they feel. They say to me, 'If only I could cry, I'd feel better.' Or, 'I should have feelings, but I don't.' This is different from reactive depression. Someone dies, you cry, you grieve. It's not by accident that every culture in the world has some sort of mourning process. But the patients with the chemical depressions have major league trouble because often they can't do that. Once they can begin to feel again, it's a step in the right direction."

DISTINGUISHING UNIPOLAR FROM BIPOLAR

Because most patients come to him when they are in the black hole of despair (why would they want to be treated for feeling good?), Dr. Amsterdam's first task is to determine whether this is a patient who suffers from unipolar or manic depression. He does a full medical workup, including a thorough physical examination and blood tests to rule out medical conditions that could be causing symptoms, ranging from diabetes to a brain tumor. He will ask about head injuries, which could produce mania, or strokes, which could result in depression. Thyroid function will be studied. When examination results or the nature of a patient's complaints make him suspect an underlying medical problem, he may order additional tests. And for someone who does not respond to treatment, he will probe further, perhaps with brain imaging studies.

Because depression, whatever its cause, is described by patients in the same way—feeling hopeless, having trouble concentrating, losing the ability to enjoy anything—teasing out information that distinguishes unipolar from bipolar illness is challenging and demands Dr. Amsterdam's sharpest sleuthing. He spends hours with patients trying to jog their memories, listens carefully to the answers to his questions, and makes detailed notes that he will scrutinize later, like a lawyer preparing a case for court.

He scours their past for clues, however subtle, about the presence or absence of mania. He probes for evidence of up-and-down cycles. Has there has been a seasonal correlation with mood swings, a pattern common to those with manic-depressive illness?

When did the depressions begin? The age of onset is significant. For those with manic depression, symptoms often become noticeable during the teenage years, and the peak onset is in the mid-twenties. Unipolar depression, on the other hand, usually appears later in life—for women in their late thirties, forties, and fifties; for men, in their fifties and sixties.

The way a person looks is telling, says Dr. Amsterdam. The manic-depressive person, when extremely depressed, looks totally slowed down and burned out. He walks slumped over and barely inches across a room. Even the way he talks is laborious and tedious. People suffering from unipolar depression, although they complain of energy loss, are often agitated, anxious, and keyed up. They may look more tense than tired.

In milder forms of bipolar depression, Dr. Amsterdam looks for what he calls the "great sleep." It is more subtle than sleeping around the clock or refusing to get out of bed, as some people do in major depression. But it is sleeping more than is normally required. Instead of a normal seven or eight hours' sleep, manic-depressives, during their depressive phase, may sleep nine, ten, eleven hours. Or they may sleep eight hours and wake up exhausted. People who are unipolar, on the other hand, often wake up during the night and get up early in the morning.

Dr. Amsterdam rummages through the family baggage, seeking evidence of eccentricities, depression, thyroid abnormalities, or alcoholism. Sometimes he even unveils carefully guarded family secrets.

Diana and Max: Misdiagnosed as Unipolar

Diana had her first episode of depression at eighteen. Now she's forty, and in the past five years she has had four or five distinct bouts of depression where she felt worthless, lost her energy, and thought a lot about ending her life. Diana had been diagnosed as having recurrent unipolar depression. Traditional medication for that disorder seemed to relieve some of the depressive symptoms, but the depressions kept recurring and they were happening more often. It turned out that Diana's condition was really a form of bipolar disease. The "manias" she felt between the depressions were so mild that they weren't noticeable—just times of high energy and significant accomplishments at her job as a nurse administrator.

Dr. Amsterdam had to go on a hunting expedition for other "markers." As a psychopharmacologist, he searched for physical symptoms: changes in energy level, in sleep patterns, in the libido, in the appetite. He wanted to know whether she felt depressed in the fall and winter and energized in the late spring and summer.

To him, taking a family history doesn't mean asking how you feel about your mother or did you hate your sister. That information may be important later as part of a treatment program that includes psychotherapy. But he's convinced it won't help in diagnosing manic-depressive illness. He asked Diana:

- Are there thyroid problems in your family?
- Who had postpartum depression?
- Did anyone in your family try to commit suicide?
- Was anyone in your family an alcoholic?

In Diana's past, he uncovered a history of postpartum depression. Diana and her mother had both suffered from prolonged "down" periods within a year after the birth of their children. This is not the same as normal postpartum "blues," the kind that reflect expected hormonal body changes and psychological let-down after so major an event—and that last only a short time.

And it turned out that Diana's aunt, her mother's sister, and Diana's own sister, Amy, had thyroid problems. For some reason, manic-depressive illness is often associated with thyroid disease on the maternal side of the family.

In fact, some studies indicate that bipolar illness, as well, is often, but not always, inherited from the mother's side of the family, so Dr. Amsterdam scours the mother's family history, in particular. He wants to know about Mom, Mom's sisters, Mom's brothers, Mom's mother, her aunts and uncles.

Once Diana was diagnosed correctly, her symptoms were controlled with lithium. She has been depression-free for the past eighteen months.

Max was a fifty-eight-year-old dentist hospitalized for treatment of severe depression when he came to Dr. Amsterdam's attention. He had become seriously ill six months earlier, did not respond to medication, and had had to turn his thriving dental practice over to a colleague. The first time Dr. Amsterdam saw him, Max was slumped over, without energy, barely able to make his way to the chair in the doctor's office.

Max's referring doctors had diagnosed him as suffering from recurrent unipolar depression unresponsive to treatment. They had traced its roots back thirty-five years, to when Max's father, with whom he had a stormy relationship, committed suicide. Max was twenty-three, a second-year dental student at the time. Six months after his father killed himself, Max had his first major depression, so severe he had to drop out of dental school for a year.

As Dr. Amsterdam talked with Max and read through his medical and family history, bells began to ring. Twenty-three was a typical age for the onset of manic-depressive disease, not unipolar depression. And between depressive episodes, Max apparently functioned well. He had a busy practice, a good marriage, and three children, all of whom were in college or professional school.

Instead of probing about his father's suicide, the seemingly obvious cause of his depression, Dr. Amsterdam asked Max two questions:

"Think hard. Did anyone on your mother's side of the family ever have postpartum depression?" It took a while for the words to come out, but Max mumbled yes, he remembered his mom's saying that six months after his birth, she was depressed, couldn't get out of bed, and Aunt Sophie had to move in to take care of the family.

Dr. Amsterdam's second question was about thyroid disease. Did anyone on his mother's side of the family have thyroid disease. "Yes," Max said, Aunt Sophie, Mom's sister, had had her thyroid removed.

"That was it," said Dr. Amsterdam. "The age of onset, the inertia, the profound motor retardation, his mom's postpartum depression, his aunt's thyroid problem, the periods of apparently normal functioning between depressive episodes—I knew the man had manic-depresssive disorder. His father's suicide was a red herring."

It was not until after Max's depression had subsided that Dr. Amsterdam was able to learn more about him, which reinforced his diagnosis. "Sometimes these people are so apathetic, so slowed down, that you can't get anything much out of them until after they are treated adequately," Dr. Amsterdam says. "While they're depressed, they can't remember back, and they certainly can't remember happy things. Happiness is something they just can't describe."

After ten days on medication, Max was ready to leave the hospital. He was an astonishingly different person—bright-eyed and ready to face the world. He had a dental journal in his hand and said, "Look, I can concentrate again. I want to go back to work. I'm ready to get out of here."

"It was as though he had been moving through his life with a gray haze in front of him, and then it got peeled away," says Dr.

Amsterdam. "Until he was treated, he thought that's what life was—a gray haze. That's what was normal to him."

As it turned out, Max remembered that before each of his major depressions, he had highs—not so bombastic that they spilled over into the psychotic range—but brief periods that were crammed with activity. He would go hunting, take on dozens of new patients, go to shows and concerts, participate in professional meetings—and never felt tired.

So, without meticulous study, his condition appeared to be simply recurrent unipolar depression, attributed to the psychological trauma of his father's suicide. Unfortunately, Max had paid the price of an erroneous diagnosis—years of his life in psychotherapy and eight months on medications that didn't work because they were treating the wrong illness.

SCHIZOPHRENIA

Although schizophrenia and manic-depressive disorder are entirely different illnesses, their full-blown psychotic symptoms are similar. In both conditions, someone may have periodic outbreaks of hallucinations, have delusions, and exhibit outrageously inappropriate behavior such as running down the street naked or claiming to be God. The symptoms are so bizarre that the person having them is not usually able to function.

Like manic-depressive illness, schizophrenia usually begins in late adolescence or early adulthood. The typical age of onset is between fifteen and twenty-five.

The acute episodes can be controlled with antipsychotic drugs, but the course of the illness is often downhill, with briefer normal periods between psychotic ones.

Some people can function for a while as what doctors call "quiet schizophrenics," but most of them eventually burn out, sometimes ending up as street people or back-ward hallucinants. With persistent stimulation, and constant monitoring as early in the course of the illness as possible, they may be able to live "normal" but diminished lives. But their mental organizational skills

46

are poor enough to keep them from being productive and responsible, and their behavior is often grossly inappropriate.

While theories in the past linked schizophrenia to emotional conflicts and patterns of communication within the family, almost all experts now agree that vulnerability to schizophrenia results largely from abnormal brain structure or biochemistry that is partly inherited.

DISTINGUISHING BIPOLAR FROM SCHIZOPHRENIA

A bipolar patient in a psychotic mania can look so much like someone who is in a schizophrenic psychosis—so wildly disorganized, so delusional—that even an astute doctor can find himself in a diagnostic dilemma. But there are differences. While the speech in mania is rapid, each word bursting forth on the heels of another, someone listening carefully can often piece the thoughts together. In schizophrenia, there is a "looseness of associations," so much going on inside the person's head that his speech makes no sense. Someone listening could not make a connection.

And schizophrenics, while they are sometimes agitated, tend to be more apathetic and regressed than the manic-depressive in a psychotically manic episode.

If there is an essence of grandiosity along with increased motor activity and racing speech, in my experience the person is suffering from mania associated with manic-depressive illness," says Dr. Amsterdam. "It may be psychotic, crazy mania, but it's mania. Schizophrenics are more bizarre than just extreme."

Dr. Amsterdam describes George, a thirty-year-old man, who was brought to the emergency room, naked, mute, and with his eyes wide open in a fixed stare. He was paranoid, fearful of everyone around him, terrified to be touched. He found his way to a corner of the room, where he huddled against the wall rocking back and forth, masturbating, and humming. His immediate diagnosis, made by emergency-room doctors, was paranoid schizophrenia, and he was confined to a matted room.

When his family arrived later, Dr. Amsterdam, who had been called in on the case, learned that George's mother had a history of depression and that his mother's brother suffered from mood swings.

"My immediate thought was that George was manic, not schizophrenic," says Dr. Amsterdam. "He was so manic that his humming was actually speaking—it just couldn't be understood."

After George was calmed somewhat with a tranquilizer, he came out of his catatonic-like state. At that point, his humming dissolved into speech so rapid his words could barely be distinguished. He thought Dr. Amsterdam was Sigmund Freud, and he began to race around the room in an agitated frenzy. "You could see, at that point, that he was in psychotic mania," Dr. Amsterdam says. "And since there was a family history of mood disorders, but none of any kind of psychosis, I felt certain that he had manic-depressive illness."

George was treated successfully with lithium.

"Unfortunately, the diagnosis is often made on the way the first episode looks," says Dr. Amsterdam. "When someone is so crazy that he's delusional and he's running around throwing all his money away or thinking he has been chosen by God for special purposes, he usually gets diagnosed as schizophrenic. Often it's not schizophrenia. It's manic depression."

Manuel and Martha: Misdiagnosed as Schizophrenic

Manuel, a New Jersey banker, struggled for twenty-three years with a label of schizophrenia before he learned that he really had manic-depressive illness. In 1944, when he was in his early twenties, just out of Harvard and in the Army, he began to hallucinate. Without fanfare, he was diagnosed as schizophrenic and medically discharged. Two decades later, with no episodes in between, he became seriously depressed. For the next twenty years, he went up and down with deep depressions that felt "like a cloud descending," interrupted by manic highs where "I felt as though I had had ten shots of scotch."

Between 1967 and 1971, Manuel was in and out of psychiatrists' offices and every six months or so had a series of electroconvulsive treatments. It was not until he saw Joshua Logan and his doctor, New York psychiatrist Ronald Fieve, on a television show, that he suspected he might have manic-depressive illness.

The next week, Manuel was in Dr. Fieve's Madison Avenue office. He remembers it as if it were yesterday. "Dr. Fieve looked at me and said, 'I'm going to fix you up. You'll be fine.'" Since swallowing his first lithium pill, almost twenty years ago, Manuel has never had a recurrence of either a manic high or a depressive low.

Martha, a women's clothing buyer for a California department store, was labeled as schizophrenic because her first episode was a psychotically manic one. She awoke one morning believing she was a top fashion designer, instructed by some higher force to change the way women dressed. She wanted to put them all in bustles, bustiers, and crinoline petticoats, in a throwback to the Victorian era.

She arrived at her job, insisting that all of the dresses on the racks were "wrong, wrong, wrong." She began ripping them from their hangers and tossing them into big plastic trash bins behind the service desk. When the saleswomen approached her, she screeched and threatened them with the scissors she was using to cut up the latest arrivals in women's suits. The police were summoned, and Martha was whisked to a hospital, where she was declared to be schizophrenic. She spent fifteen rocky years on medication and electroconvulsive treatments before she was correctly diagnosed as having manic-depressive illness.

If a person's initial symptoms are suggestive of either illness, Dr. Amsterdam will assume, for starters, that the condition is manic depression. The initial treatment, with the goal of calming the patient, is the same. And manic-depressive illness is fixable, so why not begin there?

Although it is reported that the numbers of people with schizophrenia and manic-depressive disorder are about the same, Dr. Amsterdam doesn't believe it. He is convinced that schizophrenia is a rarer disorder, and that many of the people diagnosed with it, especially the ones that are labeled "good-outcome schizophrenics," the ones that improve over the years, really have manic-depressive illness.

SCHIZOAFFECTIVE DISORDER

Acknowledging the difficulty in distinguishing manic-depressive illness from schizophrenia, the revised third edition of the Diagnostical and Statistical Manual of Mental Disorders published by the American Psychiatric Association—DSM-III-R, the psychiatrists' bible—has given official status to another mental illness, schizoaffective disorder. It is a catchall name for a fuzzy set of symptoms that has ingredients of both illnesses but does not meet the strict criteria for either schizophrenia or a mood disorder.

There is a lot of confusion among doctors about what schizoaffective disorder really is, who its victims are likely to be, and even how to treat it. Those labeled as having schizoaffective disorder, says Dr. Amsterdam, are more likely to have manic-depressive illness. Most of the time, the way a person responds to a particular medication determines how he is ultimately classified.

ALCOHOL AND COCAINE: THE DILEMMA OF DRUG ABUSE

There are powerful links between mood disorders and substance abuse, and the symptoms are often intertwined. It is not unlikely that someone who is manic-depressive will abuse alcohol, and a family history of alcoholism is common. Research conducted by the National Institute of Mental Health confirms that there is significantly more alcohol and cocaine abuse in people with affective disorders, especially manic-depressive illness. So doctors must decide which is the primary diagnosis: manic-depressive illness, alcoholism, or drug abuse.

An alarming proportion of manic-depressive patients—60 percent according to the NIMH data—also meet the diagnostic criteria for substance abuse or addiction. That is, they may have a dual diagnosis: manic-depressive illness along with drug or alcohol abuse.

Initially, many manic-depressives use alcohol and drugs as a form of self-treatment. And at first they may help. Snorting cocaine can give someone in depression an intoxicating lift. And a stiff drink can be calming to someone who is agitated. Dr. Edward J. Khantzian, a psychiatrist at Harvard Medical School at the Cambridge Hospital, suggests that the drug a person abuses is no accident. People choose what makes them feel good. Someone who is anxious and agitated typically chooses a sedating kind of drug, such as alcohol.

However, in the long run, alcohol and illicit drugs escalate the problem because they act on brain chemicals that first stimulate, then over-stimulate, then ultimately destroy the brain's fragile relationship to mood. The person then becomes more uneven and experiences even more mood changes.

The symptoms of cocaine abuse and manic-depressive illness are similar. At first the euphoria, hypersexuality, grandiose feelings, loss of judgment, staying up all night, irritability, and hallucinations stimulated by cocaine mirror the symptoms of someone in a manic episode. But the central nervous system in cocaine abusers adjusts downward with repeated use, and inevitably comes the "cocaine crash," bringing with it depression and fatigue—just like the mood swings of the manic-depressive.

When someone is both bipolar and also abuses cocaine, it is not easy to distinguish which came first or whether the symptoms that brought the person in for treatment are those of the drug or the illness.

Peculiar as it may seem, manic-depressives will often use a stimulant such as cocaine or amphetamine not only in an attempt

51

to relieve their depressions, but also when they are feeling high. Part of being high is doing foolish things. And being high feels good. Why not do something that will make you feel even better, allow you to function with less sleep and more energy? Particularly in a society that values push and drive, it makes sense to someone who is already "up" to go a little higher.

Conversely, alcohol, which is a depressant, is often the drug of choice for someone who is already in a depressed mood. Initially, it gives him a lift because it releases inhibitions and blunts psychic pain—and does it quickly because it is so rapidly absorbed into the bloodstream. Eventually, however, alcohol intensifies the depression.

The behavior of alcoholics, like that of cocaine users, often parallels the mood swings of those with manic-depressive illness. The initial high of the alcoholic looks a lot like the euphoric stage of bipolar disorder. The lethargy and inertia that come later match the depressive phase. Fortunately, when the use of alcohol has been mainly to self-medicate depression, successful treatment of the illness often eliminates the need to drink.

With the many forms of manic-depressive illness, its tendency to resemble other psychiatric conditions, and its enmeshment with drugs and alcohol, it becomes easier to understand why diagnosing the condition can become, as Dr. Amsterdam puts it, "a real mishmash." He has identified manic depression in patients who were said by previous physicians to be suffering from unipolar depression, schizophrenia, character disorder, borderline personality, alcoholism, emotional problems, attention deficit disorder, mental retardation, and premenstrual syndrome.

◆

AT THEIR WIT'S END

By the time patients show up at Dr. Amsterdam's office, they have usually been ill for a long time. Often, they have tried to fight the demons of depression on their own . . . and failed. Or,

52

in a hypomanic state, they have made disastrous decisions that are threatening to affect their jobs, their businesses, and their marriages. Most have seen a string of other physicians or may have spent years in psychotherapy, and feel as though they are at the end of their rope.

They are thoroughly confused about why they are depressed. They will say, "I'm well fed, well read, well dressed, nothing terrible has happened to me. Why do I feel this way?"

"They come here scratching their heads," Dr. Amsterdam says.

Even those who try to rationalize their manic or depressive episodes by correlating them with life events are not always reliable reporters. A college student, for instance, may insist that his depression followed a broken romance or failing a course. But discussions with his friends and professors may reveal that his depression came first. That's what ruptured the romance or kept the student from concentrating well enough to pass the exams.

"Once they learn that this is a chemical disease, that attempts to talk their way out of it were destined to fail, they experience a great sense of relief," Dr. Amsterdam says. "They realize they are not crazy. Getting a correct diagnosis is their first big step toward mental health.

"The only way to take that step is to find a doctor experienced in diagnosing and pharmacologically treating mood disorders.

"If that doctor doesn't spend adequate time with you getting a complete chronological history of your mood disturbance, a detailed history of prior treatment, a thorough family history, if he or she doesn't ask the right questions, that should be a major source of concern."

CHAPTER THREE

WHY ME?

My mental illness is a genetic, chemical imbalance of the brain. I know that. But I also had a life that was, to put it mildly, out of the ordinary. I went through a lot of loss, and a lot of things that happened to me would have been enough to make anyone go crazy. So it sometimes gets a bit fuzzy trying to decide which of my manias and depressions came specifically from my illness and which may have had more to do with what was going on in my life.

I know now that my family background makes me a prime candidate. My father was an alcoholic, which is common in family members of people with manic depression. And in 1980 my mother was diagnosed as having unipolar depression, the lows without the highs. Because she had that illness, she made choices and decisions that affected the way I grew up. The results of those choices plus my genetics made me very vulnerable.

On top of that, there was a tremendous amount of loss at an early age. I lost my father when he left our family. I lost my mother when I was given over to the Rosses. I lost my name, which was my identity. I lost my family connections. And I couldn't even deal with my losses the way you do when somebody dies and there's a funeral ceremony, a mourning process. One day my father was there and the next day he wasn't, and there was no discussion of it anymore. The same thing with my mother. My mother didn't die, but I couldn't have her.

So the recipe was perfect. Start with genetics, add a lot of loss and a lot of turmoil. What you end up with is a classic manic-depressive.

I wish I had more information about my family history. I know that my mother and father grew up in the same neighborhood—Kips Bay—then a mostly Irish-Italian section on New York's East Side. They met when they were nine or ten, but didn't start going together until after grammar school. My mom says that her sister Anna was going with dad's brother Michael, and that her brother Willie went out with my dad's sister Anna. But she was the only one who got the guy. My parents married on June 21, 1937, and my sister, Carol, was born a year later. They certainly look happy in their wedding picture, which I still proudly display. But their marriage, as I remember it, was always chaotic. I know that Dad was one of seven—could be nine—children. By the time I came along, most of his brothers and sisters had moved to other parts of the United States. People didn't get around so much then, so I never saw them. Until recently there were uncles I hadn't seen since I was six months old.

Daddy was very close to his older sister Anna, who, as I understand it, became the matriarch of the family. I don't know when my grandmother Duke died, but I think there were many years when Anna was still single and was running the household. From what I was told, Daddy didn't have much education. He went to school through the eighth grade and then he had a number of jobs—a parking lot attendant, a handyman, a cab driver. He always drank, and he was a happy drunk who loved parties and dressing up in spiffy suits and dancing and having fun.

It troubles me that I really know so little about Daddy except from now-distorted childhood memories. I was only six when he and Mama split up. Nobody really talked about him in the family except in very general and very glowing terms. People would say things like, "He was always a gentleman. He was always well dressed. He was always clean." In that era, it seems, the real criterion for good character was whether people kept themselves clean or not. It was always the unspoken—"He did all those naughty things, but he was really a good guy."

55

I remember my dad as being very little, very thin, with a red face and blue, blue eyes. He almost always wore dress clothes—clean white shirts, shiny, shiny shoes—and he always wore a hat, usually a gray fedora. When he walked on Second Avenue, he would tip his hat to the ladies.

I barely knew Daddy's father, Granpa Duke. I hve a very clear visual image of him: shocking white hair and red face. Very Irish. He was a bartender, and Daddy used to take me to where he worked, where I would be stood up on the bar to recite the Pledge of Allegiance and "The Night before Christmas," and get pretzels. I do remember feeling that Grandpa Duke was somebody to be feared. I don't know whether he ever did anything to anybody, but that's the kind of imposing figure he was. My mother certainly was afraid of him and she hated it when my father would get drunk, go over to his father's place, and stay there. Grandpa Duke would give him a safe harbor. I think Grandpa Duke drank, too.

My father and Aunt Anna stayed somewhat close until Daddy died. But my basic perception is that my father was a loner in the years after he and Mama were separated.

Whatever anyone says, my recollections of my father are basically good—melancholy but good, and probably idealized. My remembrances of his bad behavior are so limited. When I was a little girl, I don't think it bothered me that he was drunk—until it bothered Mama and got her mad and she erupted in a scene. The fact that his drinking created fights at home bothered me. But Daddy was sweet to me, so I didn't see him as the villain. I remember bits of things: sitting on his lap while he watched a ball game on television, reading the funnies with him, smelling the Camel cigarettes he smoked and the Old Spice he used, hearing him call me Ree-Ree (for Marie, my middle name). He had a little wooden soap dish which I kept after he left, and I held on to that dish until Mama in an outburst one day tossed it in the trash. But I still clung to the memories, maybe even embellished them a little. I thought I knew Daddy better than I really did. Now I've begun to wonder about his illness in broader terms. Was there a genetic predisposition to alcoholism? And if he didn't drink, would he have been okay, or was his alcoholism merely one symptom of something deeper?

I saw him only a couple of times after he moved out. The time frame is distorted for me. I know that I saw him once when he was in Bellevue Hospital for what might have been bleeding ulcers. He was very ill, and I insisted on bringing him rice pudding because I knew he liked that. That may have been the last time I saw him. Between then and the time he died when I was seventeen, I had no contact with him at all. None. He may have tried to get in touch with me, I don't know, but I think he was also intimidated by the Rosses with messages brought to him through other members of the family. My mother tells me that a couple of times when she answered the phone at the Rosses—when she was doing their laundry or some other chore—she recognized his voice. When he heard hers, he left no message.

Even though his death certificate states that his death was caused by "coronary thrombosis and cirrhosis," in my opinion he died of alcoholism. He was fifty years old. He was ravaged. If he didn't die directly from alcohol, certainly the noose was knit from all those grains he had ingested. He was living in a rooming house in the same old neighborhood, but apparently nobody missed him. That has to tell you how much of a loner he was. Since identifying his body, my brother, Raymond, has not drunk a drop.

Just a few months ago, I bought a memorial stone for my father. Even though he is buried in a V.A. cemetery in New York, I wanted some symbol here where I live that my dad existed. So I ordered this small stone with only his name—John Patrick Duke—his birth date, and his death date on it. We've put it out in the woods at our farm in Idaho. It's a nice place to spend a moment.

Unfortunately, I don't know a lot about my early family connections on my mother's side either, but I'm insatiably curious. That's where the clues are that tell us who we are now and why we do what we do. But we were one of those families where folklore was very limited and where there wasn't much talk about grandparents.

My mother is one of eleven children, the youngest. Her parents died when she was very young—her father when she was nine months old, her mother when she was five years, of tuberculosis or complications from it—she doesn't know much about them. She knows her father had red hair, that's all she knows—and that he used to disappear from time to time. Isn't it amazing, that she should have so little information? That generation wasn't as curious as we are about our histories. I guess they were too busy making new history to be interested in who was so-and-so.

My mother was raised by Lizzie, her eldest sister, who, according to all accounts, was a truly wonderful woman—jolly and loving, and taking care of everybody. She had a two-bedroom apartment on Second Avenue, and in it lived her own five children, my mother, and another sister and brother. The tales I heard at family gatherings when I was a child were mainly the happy ones.

But there is one story about the way my grandmother died—a story I had heard throughout my life, but which I now think could have set the stage for my mother's depression. I had always heard that the day Grandma died, Lizzie was taking care of her. Grandma had been coughing and was apparently in some sort of distress that Lizzie was tending to. And, quite suddenly, Grandma died. That was as much of the story as was ever told to me. Then, twelve years ago, I brought my mother here to Los Angeles because she was in a deep depression. While she was in treatment I went off to fulfill a movie contract in Canada. One night she and I were talking on the phone, and I asked her to tell me the story about her mother's death.

It seems that while Aunt Lizzie was taking care of Grandma, my mother, Frances, was down on Second Avenue playing. When she rang the doorbell to come back inside, Lizzie left Grandma and went to the window to see who was ringing the bell. When she saw that it was Frances, she went to buzz her in. And in those few moments, Grandma died. As soon as Mama told me that, a light went on in my mind.

I said, "Mom, I don't remember ever hearing the doorbell part before. Did you think it was your fault that your mother died?"

She said, "Well, if I hadn't rung the bell, then Lizzie would have been there with her and she wouldn't have choked."

I just sat there on the bed in a hotel room and the impact was unbelievable. For sixty years this woman thought she had killed her mother because she rang the doorbell.

I said to her, "Mom, now you don't have to believe me if you don't want to, but it's a pretty safe guess that she was going to die anyway. And you've got to let go. After all these years, you've got to recognize you didn't kill her." After I hung up the phone, I remember pacing around that hotel room, trying to imagine being back in 1918 and what it must have been like in an Irish Catholic household on Second Avenue the day Hannah McMahon—Grandma—died. And the drama of it became very real to me. I imagined the little girl coming in. Then the older sister went to see how the mother was doing. "Oh, my God, she's dead!" There was an incredible flurry of activity. Who knew that you should pay attention to this child? Maybe Frances was sent like a messenger—"Go get so-and-so, go get so-and-so." So this little kid is running around the streets of New York gathering family members, all the while trying to deal with her mother's death.

In those days the body was laid out in the house. I could imagine myself as that little girl—remember, she hadn't had a father since she was nine months old. My acting ability came into play: that little five-year-old, shorter than everybody else, all of them talking over her head and drinking, telling the story over and over and over again about how the doorbell rang, and when Lizzie went to answer the door, Grandma died. And probably nobody noticed this little kid. Every time she heard the story about the doorbell, it reinforced her belief that if she hadn't rung that doorbell, she wouldn't be an orphan.

Would Frances have been depressed all her life anyway? Maybe. But it seems to me something as simple as that can have a lifelong impact. It gave me a very, very clear vision of how a depression could be triggered.

59

In my generation, depression is not an unfamiliar condition either. I think that my brother, Raymond, who's four years older than I, has experienced depressions of one sort or another from time to time. I tend to think they were more environmentally caused than genetic, but I don't know. He has wonderful, original ideas—things just pop into his head and he's able to take them and go with them. My mind doesn't work that way. I think he has put aside his bitterness born of not having the career that was promised him by the Rosses. I think he felt duped and lied to. His marriage and his children, which are wonderful, are the cornerstones of his succcessful adjustments to those disappointments.

My sister, Carol—she's eight years older than I am—seems to have escaped our family history. Certainly there have been times when she was depressed—when Mama was ill and she was carrying the full responsibility for her care. But to my knowledge she has never had the stay-in-bed, hide-from-the-world depressions that I did.

But for me, not having my brother and sister as part of my life was another tremendous loss. And I think I feel it more today than I ever did—maybe because the concept of time passing has become so very real to me. The fleeting nature of time—I see it, I feel it, I touch it, and I want to use it. When I see people squabbling with each other over some absurd thing, I have the urge to say, "Please, don't do that. In five months you could be dead." When you've come through "the fire" you have a healthy kind of hunger to use your time to the best of your ability.

But as a very young child, I don't think I was aware of suffering. I was certainly aware that our family was very volatile, but I don't think I was unhappy.

I grew up in a tiny, tiny four-story walk-up in a tough neighborhood on New York's East Side. All of us—my sister, my brother, and I—had street smarts. You had to. It was the kind of neighborhood where kids played stickball in the street and people yelled out of windows at the top of their lungs.

There was a lot of screaming and yelling in our house. Most

of it was not directed at me. Usually it was my sister and brother fighting with each other or Mama exploding at Raymond. She was very physical, and when she got out of control, he got hit. He got hit a lot.

All of my recollections about Mama, from my earliest memories at three or four years up to about ten or twelve years ago, are of someone who was just tortured. She was either crying or angry or yelling or hitting. And she was totally unpredictable. Sometimes she would throw things across the room and have these incredible temper tantrums where she would literally beat herself up. She would pull her hair out—she had salt-and-pepper hair as far back as I remember. Then there were times when she was affectionate, and she would hold my hand tightly in hers. I remember her wearing blouses and straight skirts and a half apron, but always high heels. She had a thing for shoes. But never any jewelry, only her wedding ring. As a young woman, she looked just like I do now.

Mama was always threatening suicide, and one day someone came to our apartment and took her to Bellevue. I don't know who it was who took her or who called someone to come get her, but I remember that she was gone for about a week. When she came back, she was still depressed, but more subdued—not as many wild outbursts.

Mama was a woman who could not be pleased, no matter what. I have a few scattered memories of her laughing, at someone's birthday party or something like that, but on a daily basis she was in misery. The strain was always apparent in her face. There were moments, short spans of time, when she seemed a little more relaxed, but I think we were always waiting for the other shoe to drop. If you asked her what was the matter, why she was sad, she couldn't tell you. Sure, occasionally she could say there was some problem with my father or money problems, and she was appropriately sad. But that's separate from this sort of general personality that was in anguish all the time.

I'm told that as a younger person she did have a lot of fun, that she had girlfriends and that there was laughter in her life. But I have also heard her characterized as selfish and childish. At times, it seemed, she might be purposely setting out to make everybody's life miserable. She certainly succeeded in isolating herself. I can even recall hearing myself say, not that many years ago, "Well, she's alone because she arranged it that way. Who wants to be with her?" as though she had indeed done this on purpose.

I don't know that my mother had mania going for her at all. I tease her now, that she didn't have the good side, the exciting side, of the illness. At the same time I remember her being very agitated, but not in the euphoric way. She as agitated in an angry, violent, unpredictable way. In fact, you could take some of my behavior and fit Frances Duke's next to a lot of it because they're very much the same. That's one of the reasons I can understand how painful it must have been for my kids, because I remember how painful it was for me—never knowing what it was you were going to say that touches this thing off, but assuming, of course, that it's always you. Now I can see that it had little or nothing to do with my brother and sister and me.

My brother also remembers my mom as a woman who was always hysterical and carrying on. He still thinks about all the nights she made us sit on a cedar chest for hours just to get even with my father for something he did. And my mother and my brother were always at odds with each other. If my mother had a fight with my father, she would take it out on my brother physically. And, naturally, to us as kids, she seemed mean and embarrassing. You certainly didn't want to bring anybody home to play.

It seems to me that the choices she made for me—particularly sending me to live with the Rosses—were affected by her depression. Depression had to be a major contributing cause of her insecurity, her feelings of inferiority and confusion about how one is supposed to conduct one's life and the lives of one's children.

She was frightened, frightened of any kind of authority figure. I have chosen to believe, and I think that I'm right, that had she not been plagued with this depression all of her life, she could not have been manipulated into giving me up to live with the Rosses.

She is instinctively intelligent, with a mind as sharp as a razor, but not learned. But even her basic intelligence was marred by the depression. When I think about the times I spent so depressed and not able to make a decision about putting on my slippers, I can relate to what happened to *her* when the Rosses said to her, "We can give this little girl what you can't. If you really love her, give her this opportunity." I think even people standing on firmer ground than my mother might be seduced by something like that. Certainly someone as bereft of self-esteem and confidence as she was was an easy mark. And giving me up also helped her fulfill her depressive self-image. She felt she got what she deserved. After all, what kind of mother gives her kid away?

But she thought she was doing the best thing. And in some very surface ways, it seemed to be. There was more life at the Rosses'. They laughed. And in the beginning it seemed like a house that was much more fun than my mother's. But that never outweighed the wrench. When my mother sent me to live there, this child was miserable. I can still look back at that hopelessness, my own feeling of abandonment, my own fear that froze the words "Mommy, Mommy, don't leave me here" in my throat. That's what I wanted to scream. Instead, I just accepted what was happening to me. I didn't think I had the power to change it.

I have heard people talk about how abused children still choose the abusing parent over any other living situation. I understand that. I don't think of myself as an abused child, but for all the embarrassment my mother was to me, and for all of her inadequacies, when I was seven and eight and nine and ten I preferred her. The bond was that great. It is almost a physical sense. I would have preferred riding the bus with my mother at four in the morning when she couldn't sleep to going to the Embers jazz club with the Rosses.

Fear was the most oppressive thing about living with the Rosses. Fear of whatever the mysterious reprisals would be if I did not do what they wanted me to do. Fear of expressing an opinion—from what I wanted to eat or where I wanted to go to school to wanting to be with my mother. It was also connected to wanting to be a good girl and do what my mommy wanted. I think Mommy didn't know what she wanted. Maybe she even thought this was what *I* wanted. A lot of what happened to me happened because nobody told anybody how they felt. And nobody was able to read anybody.

Then the fear changed. The alienation from my mother became successful in the Rosses' terms. And my new fear was that I might be sent back. They used to tell me, "If you don't want to cooperate, we'll just drop you." And I would hear them say that about other people, and I would see that they did drop them. What does that mean but abandonment? If they dropped me, where would I go? I couldn't go back to my mother—the alienation from her was so final. So where was I to go? I was maybe twelve, thirteen years old.

I paid a great price in later years for my switch of allegiance from my mother to the Rosses. For a long time I questioned my ability to have loyalty to anyone. There was a time when I loved the Rosses—never the kind of love I felt for my mother, but an attachment coming out of my need to survive. While the switch of allegiance was happening, I did envy Ethel and admire her. I began comparing her with my mother. Ethel was smarter and Ethel was taller. Ethel wore makeup. Ethel smoked Parliaments. Ethel drank martinis. Ethel listened to jazz. It seemed necessary for me to demean my mother because it fit right in with what the Rosses wanted. But after a while they didn't have to do anything—it just happened.

One of the things that confounds me now is that it never occurred to me to pick up a telephone to call my mother or to try to find my father or to call a cousin or an aunt or my sister and say, "Look what's going on here." That just didn't exist as a possibility for me. I hear stories of people who are abused, and I think, "Why in the hell didn't they call somebody?" And people have often asked me the same question, and perhaps doubted my version of what went on, because it is so difficult to accept that someone would not make an attempt to call for help. Even my children don't understand it. All I know is that I was powerless.

The ability to think or consider other possibilities was totally inhibited.

Often I wish there had been one other person—ideally, an adult—to observe the Rosses, because I would love to hear another perspective about what made them tick and what made them both so stupid and so brilliant at these manipulations. In later years, when I was grown and had kids, I learned that no one ever called me because my mother did such a good job following the Rosses' edict that my family must leave me alone. She made it clear to my brother and sister that they were not to call me. The implied threat was "If you open your mouth, if you call, if you do anything, you're going to ruin this girl's career. And so you'd better not interfere." My Aunt Anna, my father's sister, told me much later, "We never called you because we were told, 'Stay away. Mind your own business.' My God, if we had known, we would have done something." And I believe they would have.

The Rosses also had this celebrity caste system working for them. My family felt it wasn't good enough to start with. And here was this awesome, unbelievable situation, where one of us had broken out and become famous. And people are intimidated by celebrity. They don't talk to you in the same way. They talk to their perception of you as a star. You almost overcompensate to prove you're just a "regular guy."

I think a lot about my family background and the kind of life I led for so many years, and I understand more now about the things that worked together to exacerbate my illness. Not long after I was diagnosed, I remember browsing through a very scholarly book about manic-depressive illness. I came to a chapter about the genetics of the disease and how loss early in life plays into that. I thought to myself then, "Well, this is my autobiography."

But, of course, my autobiography is far from complete. There is still a giant question mark, the real biggie. I have given birth to two sons. Will I pass my genes on to them? It's something I think about, but I don't focus on it anymore. When I was first diagnosed, we talked about it, the children and I, but the boys didn't seem too concerned. Sean was eleven and Mack was nine, so I'm not sure the impact of what I was saying really hit them. But I was sure to tell them there was a treatment for manic depression, so, even if they inherited it, there was something that could be done about it. I think that made all the difference.

At that time, the most important thing to them was my behavior because that's what affected them most. The long-range implications for them were just too far into the future for them to take seriously.

In the first month after I began to take lithium and we saw some changes in my behavior, we had a few more scattered conversations about the genetics of manic depression. This is a very expressive family I live in. The boys say a lot of what's on their minds. And I certainly say what's on mine. Never did either one of them straight out say that he had any concern about himself because of the genetic connection.

After I started to talk in public about my illness, someone in the audience would almost always ask how my boys felt about their vulnerability. A few times that stimulated me to go home and talk about it. On one occasion, when Sean was about sixteen and Mack fourteen, I asked them directly if they worry. Sean answered a straight out "No." But Mack said, "Yes." Apparently Mack was the victim of an elder sibling who sometimes needed a weapon. When Mack would have a tantrum or behave in a way Sean didn't like, he would occasionally tease Mack, as boys do. "Oh, look, you're just like Mom. You're out of control. There you go. You want some lithium?" And it did strike some fear in Mack. Were his tantrums because he was mad at Sean, or *was* he out of control? When I pressed him, he got very teary, but as we pursued the conversation, the bottom line was that it didn't frighten him, because he had seen the success of lithium and therapy. His intellect is so great; he is a thinker. I wonder: Does he suspect an affinity to Mama's personality in terms of intelligence and creativity, and does that mean that the mania goes along with it like a package?

Dr. Arlen told them and I told them that up to now they have certainly shown no symptoms. And that in any case we were a few steps ahead of some other folks because we already had a guinea pig—me—and so we do know a bit more than others about what to notice should symptoms start to appear.

Does either of the boys worry that we'll have a throwback when grandchildren start coming around? Of course, both of them prefer that didn't happen, but because of my experience I suspect that they have no real worry that it couldn't be rectified.

Many people—mostly strangers I meet at the theater or when I'm giving a talk about my illness—ask me whether I would have had children had I known I was a manic-depressive. The part of me that is progressive and a solid citizen wants to say I would not have. The other part of me says I would have gone right ahead and had them anyway. I worry about making choices about procreation based on a potential—and fixable—illness. But I'm sure glad I have a choice. I suspect that the part of my psyche that demands every piece of immortality that I can find would have insisted that I have children. With expert medical assistance, of course. I'm not sorry.

CHAPTER FOUR

WHO GETS MANIC-DEPRESSIVE ILLNESS?

Until the early 1960s, mental illness was considered to be rooted in psychological trauma—indifferent, cold mothers were blamed for their daughters' schizophrenia; an unhappy childhood could condemn a person to lifelong depression. It was presumed that a thorough cleansing of the psyche, through psychoanalysis or long-term psychotherapy, was the way to exorcise the ghosts of the past.

Today, Freudian thinking has been jostled, if not replaced, by newer theories that link mental illness to faulty body chemistry. The shift came about largely because of the introduction of drugs that have, in many cases, brought rapid, almost magical relief to those tormented by mental illness. Mood disorders have been particularly responsive.

While the nature-versus-nurture debate is not yet settled, there is little doubt among mental health practitioners that certain forms of depression and manic depression are surely biochemical illnesses. They cannot be willed away any more than diabetes or congenital heart disease can.

The experts don't have all the answers, but they are getting closer. They know that manic-depressive illness runs in families. They believe that its mystery is encoded in the genes. And they surmise that there may be some relationship between genetics and environment that allows the disease to flourish. Even Sigmund Freud said, more than a century ago: "Endowment and chance determine man's fate—rarely or never one of these powers alone."

◆

FAMILY HISTORY

Studies consistently show that people with manic-depressive illness—no matter which form they have—come from families rampant with mood disorders and other psychiatric conditions. They are two to three times likelier than someone without that family history to get a mood disorder, either bipolar or unipolar. And the increased risk to a first-degree relative—mother, father, sister, brother, child—is approximately ten times that of someone without that history, about the same as for schizophrenia.

Although Patty Duke doesn't know much about the rest of her family, her mother was diagnosed as having unipolar depression and her father suffered from alcoholism.

Most people with manic-depressive illness, if they dig deep enough, will find other family members who, even if they were not diagnosed as being mentally ill, exhibited strange behavior. It may be a grandmother who was confined to a dark room for weeks with a mysterious headache that wouldn't go away. Or a cousin who vanished from home when he was in his twenties, never to be heard from again. Or a great-uncle that was whisked off to a hospital for three weeks and returned with his memory impaired. Sometimes there was a suicide that was banned from discussion or a brother dismissed from the family because he was the town drunk.

Jennifer, one of Dr. Jay Amsterdam's patients, says that when he took her complete family history, she realized it was a "doozie." In retrospect, she says she should have been suspicious about her illness—a series of depressions and elations, though never full-fledged manias—all along. There were so many clues. But, as Dr. Amsterdam explains, clues are meaningless to people not tuned in to the importance of family history.

"Now it all seems so clear," Jennifer says. "From my great-grandmother on down. There would be certain times of the year when my great-grandmother would suddenly whack out. They'd chain her to a bed in a hospital, and eventually she'd come out of it. She'd be back home, work the farm, get through a few months, and the next spring it would happen again.

"Three of her daughters have the same thing—we're talking manic! These women, my great-aunts, used to bake all night, clean all night, spend every dime they could get hold of, buy gifts for everybody in the whole town. No one knew what was wrong with them. They'd just put them away for a while. I'm not sure where. I presume it was in some institution.

"There's a lot of alcohol abuse in the family, and there's drug abuse. My father's sister committed suicide at twenty-seven. And my cousin who is fifty has been manic-depressive for years. 'Crazy Katie' they call her in the neighborhood. She's extreme. Once she set her car on fire because she said her kids had drugs in it and she didn't like it. Of course, she was right about the drugs, but the fire . . . ?

"When I began filling in my family tree with Dr. Amsterdam, it became pretty obvious. But I had never associated any of that with what was wrong with me."

Jennifer's situation is not unique. It is not unusual to look at a huge family tree and see people with a mild form of manic-depressive illness, and other people who have had hospitalizations and committed suicide before the age of forty. Dr. Anthony J. Rothschild, assistant professor of psychiatry at McLean Hospital and Harvard Medical School, describes a family of prominent brothers, of whom one heads a major corporation, one is an inventor, the third is a successful musician. All three appear to have a mild, never-treated form of the illness. One of the brothers has four children, and three of the four have full-blown manic-depressive disease.

NATURE OR NURTURE?

The struggle to untangle nature from nurture often focuses on twins and on children who have been adopted away from their families. Adopted children make ideal subjects because their environments are shaped by their adoptive families while their genes reflect the biological inheritance from their birth families.

In a significant study in Belgium, for example, 31 percent of birth parents whose adopted children had manic depression had a history of mood disorders. Among the adoptive parents of bipolar adoptees, the prevalence of mental illness was 12 percent. And when their illness was unipolar depression, it almost always developed after their adopted child had shown signs of manic depression, so it could have been a reactive depression rather than having anything to do with genes. When adopted children did not have manic-depressive illness, only two percent of their birth parents had a mood disorder.

While adoption studies are significant, they cannot rule out, unequivocally, that environment may play a role. It is the studies of twins that offer the most compelling evidence that genetics and mood disorders go together.

Identical twins have exactly the same genes and would be expected to inherit the same propensity toward an illness. Nonidentical twins, on the other hand, are no more the same genetically than are any brothers and sisters. If it is assumed that environment would have the same impact on both types of twins, any difference in the way they develop an illness would point to something in the genes that is causing it.

Results of twin studies where one identical twin had manic-depressive disorder have shown that in approximately 60 percent of the cases the other twin also developed it. For nonidentical twins, the figure was only 18 to 20 percent.

No one knows, for sure, why *all* identical twins do not share the disease when one shows symptoms, but nongenetic factors may figure—diet, infection, exposure to chemicals, as well as, perhaps, the impact of life experiences.

◆

THE SEARCH FOR A GUILTY GENE

Researchers are convinced there is one—probably more than one—gene responsible for causing manic-depressive illness. For more than twenty years they have been struggling to pinpoint it. Each time they take one step forward, they take a half-step back.

Genes—each of us has 50,000 to 100,000—are the hereditary units that occupy a fixed spot on one of our 46 chromosomes. Each chromosome contains DNA, the units of heredity, for thousands of our individual genes. It is hoped that, through the examination of DNA, the guilty gene will be isolated. Screening and analyzing DNA is tedious and painstaking. Dr. Janice Egeland, a medical sociologist at the University of Miami School of Medicine and one of the field's major researchers, describes it like "stepping through sesame seeds on a bread stick."

Some studies have come tantalizingly close to zeroing in on the guilty gene, but their results have not been replicated by other researchers, or flaws, uncovered later, seemed to invalidate their findings. Nonetheless, some researchers believe that a link to the X chromosome may figure in some people. The X chromosome is sex-related—women have two and men have only one—which could explain the absence of father-to-son transmission in some families.

THE X-CHROMOSOME CONNECTION

In a 1969 research project at Washington University in St. Louis, researchers found that in two families everyone who was color-blind also had manic-depressive illness. This was too much of a coincidence to be explained by chance. Since there was no reason to associate the conditions, the researchers concluded that the gene for color blindness, which is located at the bottom of the X chromosome, must be very near a gene for manic depression, near enough that when the genes are shuffled, these two seldom get separated.

Findings from a study of five large Jewish families in Jerusalem corroborated the X chromosome connection. In forty-seven people who suffered from manic depression or related conditions, the location of the faulty gene was pinpointed to an area near one tip of the X chromosome because it was often inherited along with one of two other conditions located in that region of the chromosome—color blindness and anemia. This does not mean that someone who is color-blind or who has anemia is at greater risk of having manic-depressive disorder. And it does not suggest that Jewish families are more at risk than others. It means, merely, that specific families are more prone to the condition. Dr. Neil Risch of Yale University School of Medicine, who was one of the investigators, says that a substantial number of the cases of manic-depressive illness are probably linked to a defect on the X chromosome. Such a defect is not guaranteed to produce the condition, but the risk may be dramatically increased.

The X chromosome connection has not been refuted, but it has not been proven, either. In any case, the culprit gene, the specific one that produces manic-depressive illness, has not been identified.

THE TANTALIZING AMISH STUDY

Dr. Janice Egeland will always remember the incident that piqued her interest in manic-depressive illness. Dr. Egeland was a graduate student at Yale, headed toward a career in cancer research. She was living with an Amish family in Lancaster, Pennsylvania, while gathering information on health beliefs and behavior for her doctoral dissertation.

"I knew that one of the women in the family had manic-depressive illness, but I knew nothing of the condition," Dr. Egeland says. "One morning, I saw this woman doubled up in pain, moaning and sobbing. When I asked her what was wrong, she responded, 'I don't have a physical pain. It's the pain of the thoughts I'm having that is doing this to me.'

"It made such an impact on me that I shifted gears right there—that was about thirty years ago—and said, 'That's it. My life's work will be with this condition.'"

In 1987 Dr. Egeland announced the astonishing results of a study among the Amish in Lancaster that rocked the field of manic-depressive illness. At last it seemed as though the mystery was solved. The study, which she conducted with the Miami University School of Medicine, the Massachusetts Institute of Technology, and Yale University, concluded that an identifiable defect near the tip of the eleventh chromosome was responsible for predisposing a person to manic-depressive illness.

Included in the research were families with mood disorders spreading through three generations. Of the eighty-one people who participated, fourteen had some form of manic depression, five had severe depression, and sixty-two had neither.

Because of its humanitarian spirit, this group of people, whose members place a premium on maintaining the community's privacy, cooperated with research scientists and particularly with Dr. Egeland (who calls herself "the Margaret Mead of the Amish") because they had come to know and trust her.

The Amish experience manic-depressive illness at the same rate as other populations, but their unique history makes them perfect for such research. The community is stable and homogeneous, so some of the social and psychological factors that influence and complicate such studies on the larger American society are eliminated. In addition, the Amish, because of their religious and moral traditions, have almost no crime, violence, drug use or alcoholism, marital separation or divorce—behavior that could compromise the purity of research. In the general population, any study must consider environmental factors that could influence its results.

Even educational levels among the Amish are remarkably similar. Their families tend to be large—ideal for genetic studies—and detailed genealogical records are available for most of them. Perhaps most important, the population is "pure" in that the group was founded by a small number of pioneer couples with few outsiders marrying in and introducing multiple genes that complicate research.

Moreover, it is rare to find a flamboyant—or deeply withdrawn—personality because "the Amish do not want to stand out against the social landscape," Dr. Egeland says. Someone who took off for a vacation in California or bought a fancy new car or went into the next town for a beer would stick out in this community. The Amish have long maintained that such peculiar behavior is *siss im blut*—in the blood.

Through analyzing DNA from blood samples of those who participated, Dr. Egeland and her colleagues had hoped to turn up the specific gene that causes manic-depressive illness. Their happy results—that nearly 80 percent of those with an identifiable genetic defect near the tip of the eleventh chromosome had manic-depressive illness— were reported on the front pages of newspapers and magazines everywhere.

It was a wonderful time for Janice Egeland. "To those of us in research, a genetic study sometimes feels so sterile," she says. "A disease is just a set of symptoms. But when you have lived through this experience with someone and seen the effect on the family—nothing invades the family quite as much as an illness like this one—it feels so good to be part of what might be an answer."

Dr. Egeland's meticulously crafted project was replicated by a team from the National Institute of Mental Health, reinforcing its findings. However, in 1989, just two years after the results of the breakthrough Amish study were hailed as a major advance in understanding the origin of manic-depressive illness, new evidence cast serious doubt about the eleventh chromosome link.

As the Amish study continued, after 1987, and expanded to include more family members, the researchers themselves recognized that their earlier findings might have been a false positive. In one shift, two people from the original group who had shown no signs of manic-depressive illness and were not expected to develop it subsequently did. This was a major blow to the theory that the gene defect exists on chromosome eleven.

Still, Dr. Egeland isn't quite sure. The strict criteria of her study called for including anyone who suffered from depression or mania, whether or not their illness was cyclical or recurrent, two critical features of manic depression. It did not provide any way to identify someone who may have suffered from a depression that was situational or reactive, caused by some trauma in his or her life, not by inherited tendencies.

The forty-two-year-old man who became depressed despite the absence of an eleventh chromosome connection had taken over his father's farm and had been working long, difficult hours. Then his father died. He may have been going through a perfectly understandable reactive depression, having nothing to do with genetics. If that was true, would the original study be tarnished? Dr. Egeland says that only time will tell. If the man's depression recurs, the eleventh chromosome connection will become flimsier.

The second person who cast doubt on the study's conclusion is more difficult to explain. He came from a complicated family with a lot of manic-depressive illness among its members. But he had so many younger siblings who had not yet shown signs of the disease (but might develop it later) that the mathematical calculations that would prove the eleventh chromosome link were not convincing enough.

Some scientists now think that more than one gene may be involved or that the culprit gene is in a different location. A 1989 report, published in the scientific journal *Nature*, reexamined the original Amish study and offered convincing evidence that the gene that had been originally indicted may not be involved at all.

The Amish study continues, now expanded to cover 120 subjects in 11 families, but Dr. Egeland agrees that confidence in its original findings has been shaken. She and her colleagues grope for answers, and Dr. Egeland still has sleepless nights. "Sometimes I lie in bed thinking there must be some gene on chromosome eleven that we cannot rule out. Other days I think there must be another gene for new people we are testing. But I know that in this decade we have the technology to track the pathway in the brain. Maybe what we found before was just some weird association. Or maybe there is a modifier gene for chromosomes X and eleven. But we have to wait before we have a final answer. We are in a holding pattern."

WHAT LIES AHEAD?

The ultimate answer to the riddle of manic-depressive illness may come from a promising project, the Molecular Genetics Initiative, sponsored by the National Institutes of Health. Investigators there and at three other institutions—Johns Hopkins University, Washington University in St. Louis, and Indiana University—have initiated a multiyear study of approximately 266 families with a history of manic-depressive illness. Psychiatrist Raymond DePaulo, director of the affective disorders clinic at Johns Hopkins, who is participating in the initiative, is optimistic that the NIH project and his own research could eventually unravel the puzzle.

Dr. DePaulo, who calls himself a "country doctor," is using advanced molecular techniques to take a close look at the human chromosome and track what is inherited through any family. He hopes to isolate *not just linkages* but the *actual genes* for the illness, determine which ones cause which variety of the disease, and learn which medication each type responds to best.

His study works this way: a person with suspected manic-depressive disorder presents himself as a research subject. Dr. DePaolo's group draws a blood sample, takes information about family members, interviews as many of them as possible, and draws blood samples from them also. His collaborators in Baltimore clip up the chromosomes in the blood samples, label them, and study their inheritance through the family. As part of the clinical assessment, Dr. DePaulo and his team determine who in the family they think is affected and who is not. That information is fed into one side of the computer; the information gleaned from his collaborators goes into the other side, and the computer reveals whether there is a "match."

Dr. DePaolo's short-range goal is to pinpoint the offending gene or genes, and to develop reliable diagnostic tests for manic depression. He suspects that the location of the gene, which will be different for different people, will dictate the long-term prognosis and the appropriate treatment.

His long-range goal is prevention. Since the gene must be present at birth, something keeps the illness from emerging until later in life. Dr. DePaolo wants to know why. What slow process is going on that crosses some critical threshold in adolescence or the early twenties? Can it be prevented? How?

SPEEDING UP THE PROCESS

In November 1991, three dozen prominent researchers met at the Banbury Center of the Cold Spring Harbor Laboratory on the North Shore of Long Island, New York. Their think-tank session, sponsored by the National Institute of Mental Health, was called "Genetics of Psychiatric Disorders" and focused on gene research for manic-depressive illness and schizophrenia.

A proposal made there—that major investigators of the genetic link to manic-depressive illness pool their research findings—if acted upon could speed up significantly the race to pinpoint the culprit gene through the wizardry of molecular biology.

"In researching this illness, the peaks of science are like the peaks of manic depression," says Janice Egeland. "We think we're on to something and we're euphoric; then our results cannot be repeated and we get deflated. Then there is the level time when we're back at the drawing board.

"Because several of us are doing the same thing—taking families and systematically looking at all of the markers spaced

through the human genome, our complete set of chromosomes—
it makes the most sense for us to talk more and share more. Each
of us wants to be the one that is on the edge of discovery, but
instead of our sitting in our labs and keeping our work under
cover, collaboration would give us a way to quickly test out our
findings. In the interest of those who are suffering with manic-
depressive illness, this is something we should be doing." Dr.
Egeland is optimistic that such cooperation could cut ten years
of research to perhaps four or five.

PERSONALITY AND GENES

Unraveling the riddle of manic-depressive illness is even more
complicated than the tedious task of finding a faulty gene. Because it is a disease that manifests itself largely through excessive
behavior—either manic or depressed—it is impossible to know,
with certainty, whether someone's strange symptoms result from
manic-depressive illness, temperament (genetically or constitu-
tionally determined tendencies), or personality (one's style of
self-expression). Clinical descriptions of manic-depressive illness
that sound so clear in the literature may be a lot fuzzier in real
life, where so many factors impact on the way people behave.

Research has established that personality has a hereditary
basis, but it is not clear how that genetic influence works and
how extensive it is. In a person with manic-depressive illness, are
personality traits a complication of his or her mood disorder? Or
does personality come first, and the mood disorder follow? Is personality determined by innate temperament? Is temperament a
player in manic-depressive illness? When someone who is manic-
depressive is controlled by medication, does personality change,
too? Does he or she become a different person?

These are complex questions for which there may never be definitive answers. But an intriguing theory about the way manic-
depressive illness develops comes from the National Institute of
Mental Health's Dr. Hagop Akiskal.

In the mid-1970s, when he was director of the University of Tennessee Mood Clinic and worked with its affiliate Lakeside Hospital, Dr. Akiskal was confronted with large numbers of patients who were moody, impulsive, erratic, and volatile, but who did not have the symptoms of classic manic-depressive illness.

They came to the clinic primarily because of social failures—broken romances or unhappy marriages—and because they had been labeled by former therapists as passive-aggressive, as antisocial, or as having borderline personalities. They had a history of promiscuity, frequent changes of jobs and locations, uneven work records, brief affiliations with cults, and episodes of alcohol and drug abuse. They often used the terms "high" and "low" to describe themselves and said that their changes in mood were sudden and had little to do with personal or business pressures. If anything, their personal crises seemed to come as a result of rather than as a cause of their instability. The family histories of these people were identical to those of a control group who had classic manic-depressive illness.

Today, after almost twenty years of immersing himself in the study of personality and mood disorders, Dr. Akiskal suggests that *it is not a gene for full-blown manic-depression that is inherited, but a genetic tendency toward temperamental instability that makes a person vulnerable to developing the illness later.* He identifies three predictor temperaments.

THE HYPERTHYMIC

The *hyperthymic* is optimistic, self-confident, arrogant, and extroverted, and has high energy and a powerful drive—"always on the go." These are the people who run the world: their self-assured entrepreneurial bent often places them in leadership roles where their aggression is tolerated.

Although their intensity tends to drive people away, it is balanced by their exuberance and people-seeking behavior. They are habitually short sleepers—two to three hours a night—and have the notion that there is very little time to do all they want to do.

Hyperthymics often came to Dr. Akiskal's attention through the Baptist Hospital Sleep Laboratory, of which he was research director when he was at the University of Tennessee. They were urgent about finding a way to condense their sleep even further. Some of them said they would be willing to invest money in Dr. Akiskal's work if he could find a way of manufacturing sleep in a package so that one hour would meet all of their needs. Dr. Akiskal suggests that their driven work habits may actually overcompensate for depressive tendencies.

THE IRRITABLE TEMPERAMENT

The second type, the *irritable* personality, is angry and impulsive, snaps at the slightest provocation, curses a lot, and is generally unpleasant. These personalities have a tendency to brood and are hypercritical and complaining, yet can't tolererate being criticized themselves. They believe there is only one way to accomplish a task—their way—and have little tolerance for the differences in people. Those with irritable temperaments can hurt others deeply, then feel incredible remorse and guilt. They may apologize and promise themselves that they will change. But they can't control their behavior.

THE DEPRESSIVE TYPE

The *depressive* or *melancholic* type tends to be gloomy and pessimistic, has little energy, feels inadequate, and needs lots of sleep. This type of person is usually passive and dependent and remembers that he or she has "always" had depressive tendencies. These types will sometimes say, "I was born unhappy."

In the work world, they do well with jobs that require attention to detail and selfless devotion, but they are unable to enjoy leisure, and their gloom usually drives people away.

Not everyone with these temperaments is a potential manic-depressive, but Dr. Akiskal's meticulous investigations of adults

81

with bipolar I and II show that these temperaments frequently preceded exacerbation of the disease.

In most cases, they were there before the age of twelve, often since birth. Mothers will sometimes say, "I could tell before she was born that she was more restless. For the first six months, she barely slept . . . " Or, "He has always been moody and snappish, ever since he was a little boy . . . "

Drawing on two decades of observations, Dr. Akiskal believes that establishing the relationship between these temperaments and the origin of manic-depressive episodes will require a greater commitment by physicians to scrutinize patients and their relatives with "softer forms" of manic-depressive illness. Their examination will need to focus, particularly, on behavior during the transition periods between childhood, adolescence, and early adulthood. He suggests that psychiatrists and behavioral scientists working together in specialized mood clinics, of which he has long been a champion, can best conduct such studies. This line of thinking is catching on, and such centers are springing up in this country, Canada, and Western Europe.

TEMPERAMENT AND LOSS

Are there substantial numbers of young people with these kinds of temperaments, ready to tip over into full-blown manic-depressive illness? Dr. Akiskal says it depends on the environment—sometimes a reaction to a loss early in life, usually the loss of a person.

Attachments are critical to people, and the disruption of a meaningful relationship can have lifelong repercussions. Loss affects everyone—it is a staple of our environment Most people grieve for their losses, even the loss of someone dear to them, and go on living. In these vulnerable people, however, such a loss can precipitate depression or, in some cases, an "excited fugue," marked by agitation and hyperactivity. Social and psychological stressors, such as the illness of a close friend or starting a new job, may stimulate additional episodes; finally, mania or depression can occur on their own, not precipitated by any external cause. In fact, if the disease continues to cycle through its typical series of remissions and relapses, it tends to worsen with each succeeding episode. Keeping that from happening may depend on appropriate treatment of the illness when the first symptom appears. And preventing it may depend, ultimately, on identifying someone's vulnerability before he or she has any symptoms.

Research by Dr. Robert Post, chief of the biological psychiatry branch of the National Institute of Mental Health, suggests that psychological and social stressors not only affect neurotransmitters in the brain and the endocrine system, but also alter the way genes are expressed and cause a long-lasting change that results in vulnerability to manic or depressive episodes.

Betsy: Loss and a Depressive Temperament

Betsy's father died in 1973, when her sons were nine, fifteen, and seventeen. She had always been close to him and, perhaps because she was the oldest child, took over the burden of handling his affairs and helping her mother rebuild her life. That was when her debilitating depressions began.

But as far back as Betsy can remember, she had depressive tendencies. "I wasn't bleeding and I wasn't crippled," she says, "but I was very, very sick. All my life I kept waiting for the other shoe to drop. When my father died, it did."

Before her father's death, her depressions were private, known only to her. She had friends, she played bridge, car-pooled her children. But the underlying feelings of depression—"insidious" depressions, she calls them—were always there. "When you are so bad that you're slitting your wrist or you're bananas high, everyone knows you are really sick. What I had was just an all-consuming misery."

But Betsy didn't know she had an illness. She pushed to go to her part-time job or take care of her family. Often it was difficult to be with people because she didn't want anyone to know her secret. "If someone gave me a million dollars, it couldn't have made me happy," she says. "Happiness just wasn't something I was capable of.

"When I was depressed, I felt like I was looking at myself from the outside, like I was in this little glass bubble, not really touching what was around me. I functioned, but I felt like I wasn't really there."

The symptoms Betsy describes, in the absence of the mania that came later, are what has come to be referred to as dysthymic disorder, or the DDs. People with this condition insist that they have felt this way all their lives. They don't know what being happy means. The word "joy" does not appear in their dictionaries.

If not for her father's death, which prompted a deeper, different kind of depression, Betsy would not have sought help. Soon after she did, she experienced her first hypomanic episode.

It came on suddenly, a dramatic switch from her familiar despair. She felt "beautiful, clairvoyant, full of self-confidence." After a lifetime of depression, this felt fantastic. All of her creative juices were bubbling. She slept little and began to write a book. The wonderful mania lasted for three months before the depressions reclaimed her. Since then she has experienced recurrent mood swings, which are controlled, but not eliminated, with medication.

Barbara: Loss and a Hyperthymic Temperament

Barbara's symptoms came the day her oldest child left for college. Until that time, she had the kind of personality Dr. Akiskal describes as *hyperthymic*. She had worked full-time, raised three children, gave family dinners for thirty every month, planned the neighborhood block parties, and survived on little sleep. She was witty, bright, and always "up."

The day she settled her oldest child in college, Barbara became manic. She shuffled through catalogs that arrived in the mail, and ordered things from every one of them—dresses, toasters, furniture. Within three weeks, seven different-style toasters arrived by parcel post. She wanted to go dancing every night—if her husband wouldn't join her, she said, she would go alone. Her taste in clothes changed, from perky but always appropriate suits and dresses to plunging necklines and short, tight skirts, even for a trip to the supermarket.

Then without warning, on a sultry Monday in July, she stopped shopping, dancing, and ordering from catalogs. Each day she would do less and less, and she finally reached a point where she couldn't leave her bed. One morning, she tried to kill herself with pills.

The psychiatrist in the hospital didn't know about Barbara's highs. He never asked. He treated her for unipolar depression, and a month later she was discharged with an ample supply of antidepressant medication. The next week, she became manic again. She was bursting with confidence and had visions of becoming a millionaire. But she was agitated, too, running around in such a frenzy she would collapse on the floor from exhaustion. This time, the psychiatrist realized she had manic-depressive illness.

MANIC-DEPRESSIVE ILLNESS: A MATTER OF DEGREE

Family histories of patients with the temperaments Dr. Akiskal describes and those with full-blown manic depression often look similar, he says. This suggests to him that the predisposing temperaments and the illness itself, even in its most explosive and destructive form, have the same origin. It is only the degree that varies. This became particularly evident in his work with children and young adults who did not have symptoms of manic-depressive illness when he first saw them, but who developed them later.

CHILDREN AND YOUNG ADULTS

Since most people with manic-depressive illness don't get diagnosed until they are adults, it is rare that clinicians have the opportunity to track a child's behavior before he has had specific symptoms. But in 1985 Dr. Akiskal and his colleagues reported results of an investigation on sixty-eight children or younger siblings of adult bipolar patients. They ranged in age from six to twenty-four.

Forty-four, all under eighteen, had been previously seen by child psychiatrists, psychologists, social workers, or school counselors. Their diagnoses included a medley of ailments such as character disorder, borderline personality, emotional problems caused by family or peer conflict, attention deficit disorder, schizophrenia, school phobia, overanxious reaction, and mental retardation. None had been called unipolar or bipolar even though their records were crammed with symptoms associated with those disorders. Eleven patients were referred to him because of "bizarre" behavior of psychotic proportions, including seclusiveness, odd ways of communicating, aimless wandering, or assaultiveness.

One was a sixteen-year-old boy who had attempted to take hostages in a bank, hoping to be killed in the process. Drug-related problems accounted for seven referrals, while eight other children were considered to be moody, temperamental, impulsive, unpredictable, or unusually touchy or sensitive. Six children, all under eighteen, had tried to commit suicide through drug overdose, swallowing household poisons, drowning, hanging, or, in the case of a nine-year-old boy, a self-inflicted gunshot wound. Unexplained scholastic failure that seemed to occur in phases prompted referral in six cases. And in five children, philosophic "brooding" about the meaning of life tormented them. Dr. Akiskal describes a fifteen-year-old boy who was referred by his school principal.

The boy had little interest in communicating with family members and peers because he said they didn't understand that "my mind is growing too fast—I am not sure I can handle it—I think strange things. Why are we here? Has everything I dreamed existed before? Where did God come from? What is beyond space?" He said he could not control the flow of his thoughts and emotions. He would be happy for a few days and then, for no reason at all, "sink into dark thoughts." He had moved from thoughts of suicide to embracing religion and feeling he had been "saved." At the time he was referred, he was undiagnosed.

A nine-year-old boy had been restless for almost a year. His behavior was unruly and he would feel so energetic he would jog in the middle of the night. He angered easily. After four or five days, he would move into a quiet period, followed sometimes by a sluggish time where he skipped school and slept sixteen hours a day. A week or two later he would shift back into high gear.

The study's main finding was that acute depressive episodes (perhaps exacerbated by living in a disturbed home) and cycles of depression and cyclothymia are the most common symptoms in the younger siblings and children of manic-depressive patients. No cases of full-blown manic depression were seen in children under thirteen, but they did have hypomanic features. Minor mood swings, personality disturbances, and substance abuse that had a cyclical pattern were common, and many of those children were felt to be cyclothymic. Seven of ten adolescents who later exhibited bioplar I or II had a history of cyclothymia.

Half of the sixty-eight children Dr. Akiskal studied, no matter what their reason for referral, went on to develop more clear-cut symptoms of bipolar illness within three years.

Studies by Dr. Donald H. McKnew, clinical professor of psychiatry at George Washington University, reveal that signs of mood disorders and even manic-depressive illness can be picked up in children under the age of seven.

In fact, his two studies of one-year-old children with at least one manic-depressive parent showed that they already had precursors of mood disorders—poor attachment to their mothers and episodes of sadness, anger, or frustration when faced with a difficult task. These disturbances were particularly striking in children whose parents were severely ill—those having psychotic episodes and being frequently hospitalized.

Children of more moderately ill parents did not show such dramatic signs of mood disturbances. But they did have some difficulty in attachment, and their parents could discern mild behavioral troubles.

By the time the seven children with the gravely ill parents reached the age of six, all had marked problems in their general life and five had clear-cut mood disorders. Thirty percent of the children from the more mildly ill families by the age of six also showed some form of mood distress.

For the past year, Dr. McKnew has been treating two four-year-olds whom he diagnosed as having manic-depressive illness with lithium. Both come from families where one parent has bipolar illness; both have been stabilized on the medication.

"We've been doing this work for twenty-three years now," says Dr. McKnew, "and it is clear that there are precursors by the age of one, and that by age six you can very straightforwardly diagnose a manic-depressive illness in a child. There are a lot of children who have mood disorders. And by the time they reach adolescence, they represent a very major source of illness. Manic depression doesn't get diagnosed often because doctors don't know what to look for, and they wouldn't believe it if they did know. People just don't want to believe children can have illness this serious."

"PENETRANCE" OF THE GENE

Dr. Joseph Mendels, medical director of the Philadelphia Psychiatric Institute and professor of psychiatry and pharmacology at Thomas Jefferson University College of Medicine in Philadelphia, maintains that the way manic-depressive illness develops depends on the "penetrance"—the strength—of the manic-depressive gene, whatever it turns out to be. Dr. Mendels compares manic depression with conditions such as diabetes or high blood pressure which are partly genetically determined, but which manifest themselves to different degrees in different people and can be induced by stress or other environmental factors.

"In manic depression," he contends, "if you don't get the gene, you don't get the disease. It doesn't matter what happens to you in life—no matter how stressful your environment, no matter how difficult your childhood may have been, a person will not become a manic-depressive without having the gene (or genes) for it."

On the other hand, if you have a powerful gene, you get the illness no matter what—it will come bursting through. It is something like childhood diabetes, a severe form of the illness, where the gene is so powerful that it looms early in life. But in some people, the genetic tendency toward manic depression is less powerful, and the illness might be exacerbated only in the face of factors such as environmental stress.

High blood pressure is another example. Some people may have a genetic predisposition to the condition, but may not have high blood pressure readings—until they gain weight, eat cholesterol-laden foods, stop exercising, or undergo serious stress. Then the blood pressure starts to climb. Someone who goes through the same things, but who does not have the genetic predisposition, will not develop hypertension.

Evelyn, who was diagnosed with manic-depressive illness twenty-five years ago, when she was twenty-seven, agrees that her "gene" must have a mind of its own. She insists that her seesawing moods are precipitated by nothing. A series of events that would send even the most stable person reeling might leave her unaffected. And times where life was going very well would be interrupted by unexplainable depression or mania.

"There was a time when I was under incredible stress," says Evelyn. "My younger son was being Bar Mitzvahed. My father died the night of the Bar Mitzvah. I was scheduled to go into the hospital two days later to have a lump in my breast removed. The following week, my older son was hospitalized for a cardiac catheterization. All of this happened within three weeks, and I was fine. I was neither manic nor depressed. I just functioned and handled everything. Other times, I was sitting on top of the world, and I'd do something crazy."

ASSORTATIVE MATING: STRANGE BEDFELLOWS

Why does a major psychiatric disorder such as manic-depressive illness tend to concentrate in a relatively limited number of families? And why do those families have a history so crammed with people having some form of mental illness?

Dr. Elliot Gershon, chief of the clinical neurogenetics branch of the National Institute of Mental Health, says it may have to do with "assortative mating," the tendency for men and women with psychiatric conditions to be attracted to and marry each other.

No one understands totally what it is among patients with mood disorders that attracts them to each other, but Dr. Raymond DePaulo and his colleagues at Johns Hopkins University found that more than 30 percent of bipolar patients admitted to their clinic had family members on *both sides* with mood disorders.

MANIC-DEPRESSIVE ILLNESS— A WHOLE BODY DISEASE

Anyone who is familiar with mania or depression knows that it is more than mood and behavior that is affected. There are sleep disturbances, changes in eating patterns, and sharp variations in energy levels. The University of Pennsylvania's Dr. Jay Amsterdam calls it a "whole-body disease" that reflects defects in the hormonal system that regulates body function, in the brain neurotransmitters that send messages from cell to cell, and in daily body rhythms. The hormonal relationship shows up especially in women, whose hormone levels naturally fluctuate more than those of men. A substantial number of women correlate their worst symptoms with specific times in their menstrual cycle. Abnormalities in the production of the thyroid hormone thyroxine often play an important role, especially for those tormented manic-depressives who are rapid cyclers. And depressed people frequently have elevated blood levels of the hormone cortisol—associated with stress— which almost always decreases when the depression is over.

"We're not sure, however, what all of this means," says Jay Amsterdam. "And it is incredibly complicated. Even when you see abnormal variations in hormone levels, you're not sure what you're looking at. Do they cause the mood disorder, or are they caused by it? Are they related to the depression, or do they reflect something else, like polycystic ovaries, for instance? If your patient is a woman, test results could be different depending on when in her menstrual cycle she is being studied.

"We tend to think compartmentally. We are looking at gray areas and we want to pull out black and white. We can't do that yet."

To make his point, he describes Helen, a thirty-two-year-old woman, who had been diagnosed by her psychiatrist as having manic-depressive disorder.

Since her early twenties, Helen had had mood disturbances that cycled. Three weeks out of the month she was gloomy and depressed. The fourth week she felt marvelous. She was busy and full of energy, redecorating her house, preparing fancy dinners, and making dresses for her three daughters. Then she would crash.

In a fine-tooth combing of her background, Dr. Amsterdam found nothing that would point to manic-depressive illness. No thyroid problems. No postpartum disease. No depression in family members. No suicide attempts. No alcoholism.

He finally diagnosed her with PMS, which, because of something in her physiology, lasted longer than it does for most women. So she felt awful for three weeks out of the month. During her one week of feeling good, she would run around frenetically trying to get everything done. The combination made her look bipolar. But she wasn't. She was treated successfully with birth control pills.

While the specific pathways to manic-depressive illness are not known, some things are clear:

- In women, there is a definite hormonal component of manic-depressive disorder. In some cases, the symptoms of premenstrual syndrome are similar to those of manic-depressive illness. The nadir of depression may come when they are premenstrual. Pennsylvania psychiatrist Steven Secunda, formerly with the National Institute of Mental Health, says that over time such women will probably have fewer manias and more depressions. By the time they reach menopause, there may be no more highs, just lows.

  And Dr. Amsterdam says that all postpartum depression—except for the transient "blues" that follow birth and vanish within two weeks— must be considered manic-depressive illness unless proven otherwise.

- The thyroid hormone thyroxine produced by a horseshoe-shaped gland in the neck, affects the brain; when the body produces too little, it can bring on behavior changes that show up as the dramatic mood swings of the rapid cycler.

  Dr. Peter C. Whybrow, chairman of the department of psychiatry at the University of Pennsylvania, who specializes in treating rapid cyclers, says that there is a connection between thyroid hormone and catecholamines, a type of brain chemical that carries messages between neurons— messages that dictate how our bodies and our minds behave. The thyroid hormone may enhance those messengers or act as a messenger on its own.

  While thyroid disease and manic-depressive illness are two entirely separate disorders, and one certainly does not cause the other, there is undoubtedly a connection in some people.

- Changes in seasons precipitate symptoms in many manic-depressives. They complain that their symptoms match the weather, often growing worse in the dim, chilly days of fall and winter.

At those times, they may crave sweets and other carbohydrates, lose interest in sex, and want to hug their blankets and sleep the day away. They may have difficulty concentrating and initiating tasks, and often withdraw socially from their friends and families. Women often complain of premenstrual mood problems. The degree of impairment varies, but can be severe enough that the patient contemplates or tries to commit suicide.

Psychiatrists at a Long Island clinic for bipolar patients found that within two weeks after Hurricane Gloria passed over Long Island in the fall of 1985 and cut off electricity for several days, ten of their patients had relapses. Half experienced manic and half experienced depressive episodes. Three needed to be sent to the hospital. Since five of the ten patients usually became manic or depressed at one-year intervals and this time relapsed so much sooner, the storm seemed to be the only possible explanation.

Millie: Victimized by Winter

Millie, a forty-two-year-old mother of two, responded to a newspaper advertisement recruiting volunteers with winter depression to participate in a treatment program. Millie was raised in the Pacific Northwest and said that she recalled seasonal changes in her mood dating back to her school years. They became worse when she moved to Fairbanks, Alaska, as a young adult.

This was her typical pattern: in late August, she would begin to get a sense of foreboding. By October, she would cut back on her hours at her job as a counselor, drop out of her fitness program, and change her diet to include more pasta and red meat. She would gain weight. By early December, her gloom intensified and she developed crying spells, became irritable, and was unable to experience any pleasure in life. She was not, however, suicidal. As the winter wore on, she lost interest in sex and her premenstrual mood swings would worsen. By early March, her energy would return, her outlook brightened, and she was able to resume her regular work schedule. By late spring, she was back in her fitness program, chose salad and chicken over spaghetti and steak, and lost a few pounds. June brought a great surge of energy, and she could work until midnight in her garden after having spent a full day at her office.

She was treated her with phototherapy (bright light), which adequately relieved her symptoms.

This kind of seasonal mood swing in persons not having manic-depressive illness is called seasonal affective disorder (SAD), but it is not clear whether those suffering with SAD are really experiencing just another variant of manic-depressive illness.

Not every bipolar patient becomes gloomy in the winter. There are some whose doldrums come in the bloom of spring and summer. Researchers in the Washington, D.C., area described twelve patients, eight of them women, whose depressions started in the spring and ended with the crispness of the fall. Many thought that high temperatures and humidity augmented their symptoms. One woman made dramatic improvement after spending five days in an air-conditioned house and taking several cold showers a day. But she relapsed nine days after stopping that treatment.

Geographical location, too, determines at what time of year a person will experience a sharp mood change. In Alaska, for instance, the peak time for depression is usually late August or September, with remission around spring equinox. Then a hypomanic phase begins, marked by more creativity, a general sense of well-being and loss of the excess weight picked up during the seasonal episode. Some patients slide immediately into full-blown mania.

Changes in **sleep patterns** are an early giveaway of manic-depressive illness. Because they are so pervasive, some doctors suggest that sleep disturbances may be more than just a symptom. They may indeed trigger the illness. Studies on sleep patterns of bipolar patients are astonishingly contradictory, but it is widely accepted that total sleep deprivation and partial sleep deprivation in the second half of the night can bring about temporary remissions in unipolar and bipolar patients in their depressed state. The improvement rate among almost fifteen hundred depressed patients who took part in sleep deprivation trials is about 60 percent. However, after sleeping again, they usually relapse.

It seems to be the *timing* of the sleep deprivation that correlates with improvement. Losing four hours of sleep in the first half of the night does not make a difference; losing it in the second half or advancing the entire sleep period by six hours can reduce or eliminate depression.

It may have something to do with stages of sleep that are marked by the presence or absence of rapid eye movement (REM). Most people, when they fall asleep, go through progressively deeper stages of a non-REM period when blood pressure and heart rate slow down, muscles relax, and the eyes are still. Then comes REM sleep, the period when pulse and blood pressure rise and fall and respiration becomes irregular. It is at this time that we dream and our mental activity speeds up. REM sleep is most concentrated just before waking up. Interrupting REM sleep, in some mysterious way, seems to short-circuit depression.

Doctors caution, however, that sleep deprivation for someone who has bipolar illness is risky because it can precipitate mania. This has powerful implications for the 50 to 60 percent of manic-depressives who are sensitive to losing sleep, says Dr. Thomas A. Wehr, chief of the psychobiology branch of the National Institute of Mental Health. Emotional reactions—grief, joy, infatuation, fear, and anger—to life events frequently cause insomnia and might thereby trigger mania. These events can include shift work, travel, noise, the demands of caring for a new baby, or a death in the family.

"It may seem paradoxical and inappropriate for the euphoria and optimism of mania to come as a reaction to the loss of a loved one," says Dr. Wehr. "But a manic response to grief is not so surprising when one considers that grief very often causes insomnia and that insomnia in turn may precipitate mania. In cases like this, mania is not so much an inappro priate emotional re-

95

sponse to loss as it is an unfortunate complication of an appropriate emotional response."

He cites a case described in the psychiatric literature: After her eighteen-year-old son was seriously injured in an automobile accident, Mrs. A, a forty-one-year-old widow, went into a "shock-like" state and showed almost no emotion. When word of his death reached her two days later, she threw herself on the floor and screamed incoherently for several minutes. For the next two days, she ate practically nothing and slept only two or three hours a night. After the funeral, instead of becoming depressed, she became extremely manic and had to be admitted to a psychiatric hospital. For the next two weeks, she was almost entirely manic. She was coy, seductive, and manipulative with her psychiatrist; with others, she was happy and gleeful. She slept hardly at all except when she was heavily sedated.

Dr. Wehr suggests that sleep deprivation might even induce mania in someone who is genetically predisposed to mood disorders but has not, up to that point, shown any symptoms. He describes such a situation.

A thirty-three-year-old attorney, married and the father of two children, held a high-level job with a major company. He was a stable, responsible person and had never been physically or mentally ill. However, his family background was rife with mood disorders. His paternal grandfather had had violent manic episodes; an aunt had been hospitalized and treated with electroconvulsive therapy; a cousin had been hospitalized several times to treat mania and was taking lithium.

The attorney was working on an important case and needed extra time to prepare it for court. So the night before trial, he decided to work through the night. The next morning, he became very talkative, impulsive, and euphoric. His thoughts raced and he felt he could become a negotiator between nations and solve the world's problems. When his wife questioned his judgment, he struck her. As his mania increased, he needed to be taken to the hospital and involuntarily committed.

The patient's history suggests, says Dr. Wehr, that the attorney was genetically predisposed to mania. It is conceivable that he might never have shown symptoms had he not decided to forgo sleep.

Dr. Wehr warns travelers to be mindful of jet lag, and to compensate for lost sleep as they fly from one time zone to another. He also tells new mothers who traditionally lose sleep when they bring their infants home from the hospital to take daytime naps so they are not jolted into a manic episode.

◆

ENVIRONMENT: A MINOR PLAYER?

There are more reports of manic-depressive illness among people born after 1940 than before that date, and psychiatrist Elliot Gershon, of the National Institute of Mental Health, blames the environment. He speculates that the increased use of alcohol, tobacco, and illicit drugs may interact in some way with a genetic vulnerability.

But virtually no mental health expert, including Dr. Gershon, believes that environment alone causes manic-depressive illness. In fact, Dr. Paul Fink, past president of the American Psychiatric Association, calls manic depression the perfect "bio-psycho-social disorder." It is familial, probably genetic, and responds to specific medications, but the psychological development of a person counts, too. Stressors early in life may even have an effect on body chemistry—they may change the metabolism and influence the way the brain functions.

Some practitioners still believe that family background and environment cannot be eliminated in determining the cause and course of manic-depressive illness. For instance, three patients studied at Yale University School of Medicine demonstrate the environmental connection. All were treated successfully for manic-depressive illness; all relapsed after they experienced failure and frustration in their efforts to achieve certain goals in life.

And research at the National Institute of Mental Health noted that in addition to whatever genetics are at work in perpetuating manic-depressive disorder through the generations, certain patterns of family behavior may contribute. They include:

- the use of denial to manage hostility and anxiety
- family members having unrealistic standards of conformity and self-expectation
- difficulties in initiating and sustaining intimacy outside the family
- transmittal of low self-esteem from parents to children
- fears about the heritable aspects of psychiatric illness within the family.

The NIMH investigators also suggest that the absence of a father or an emotionally distant father during critical stages of development was an important factor in the families they studied. They say that most families are similar from one generation to the next; issues and problems that don't get resolved as they come up often pop up in successive generations.

Until research teases out an answer, the precise cause of manic-depressive illness remains elusive. But that doesn't mean that those with the condition must continue to be tormented. The diagnosis, while often tricky, is being made more often as physicians gain knowledge about this peculiar and fascinating mental illness. Once diagnosed, it can be treated successfully.

CHAPTER FIVE

MY LITTLE BEIGE PILL

I have been taking lithium every day—two times a day—since 1982, when I was diagnosed. I'm one of the lucky ones. For me, lithium works. It began to work within three weeks after I took the first pill. I think I expected that something dramatic would happen to me, that suddenly I would feel very different. And that isn't the way it happened. I just felt a calmness I had never known. I felt easier—what most people might call "normal." It was easier for me to get up in the morning. Easier to have a conversation with a friend. Easier to choose what to wear or what to make for dinner. Easier to go to the supermarket.

Once I heard from Dr. Arlen that there was a treatment for this thing I had—whatever it was—I just knew my life was going to be different. Even when I was at my worst, running around breaking the dishes or figuring out how many pills I would need to make the pain end, I always believed that somewhere, sometime, there would be something—I truly envisioned a little pill—that would make all of this go away. Finding it seemed like some kind of a miracle.

It's so simple. This little beige pill—one in the morning and one at night. With water. And it keeps me even. I wasn't at all fearful about taking it. To me, it was the answer to a prayer.

That, together with the therapy I needed to mop up the debris in my life, made all the difference. I do have to admit that in the beginning I was a little embarrassed about taking a pill in front of anyone. In my business, we're always being accused of being dope addicts. And I was not used to taking pills, not on a regular or regulated basis, anyway. So I started collecting little pillboxes. I must have upward of forty of them. Mike needlepointed the tops of some of them. I love them, and I play with them like toys. I'll use one for a few weeks, then I'll switch to another. Taking my medicine is a very pleasant experience now. I open my pretty little porcelain pillbox and I take my pill. And I don't forget because it's become a nice little ritual.

I experience only the mildest of side effects. Occasional nausea, but I remember having that before I took lithium. And my eating habits are just dreadful. I don't eat in the morning. I would feel nauseous far less often if I would eat a little something first. Once in a while I'll have a stomachache. And almost invariably I can track it back to having taken my pills too close together. I may have taken my nighttime pill around one in the morning and my morning pill at around seven. That'll do it. There was a brief time when I had a blurring of vision. But no one could be sure whether that was a side effect of lithium or being over forty and needing stronger glasses. I got the stronger glasses, they worked, so I'm not worried about it (the vision that is, I worry plenty about being over forty).

Every so often, maybe once every six, eight, or ten months, I get a metallic taste in my mouth. It's an indication of something—maybe that I've been working outside on location and it was hot, or I've been doing something strenuous and I've been sweating, so that the lithium concentration has become more intense. I drink water and it goes away. I am aware enough of what's going on with my body to recognize signs that I might need to do something, even alter my dosage of lithium.

About a year ago, I was feeling a little like the motor was running. I called the doctor and told him. After taking blood tests that showed my lithium level was down, he decided to up my dosage from 450 milligrams twice a day to 450 milligrams three times a day. I did that for about two weeks. Then I began to get a very metallic taste on a daily basis, and that was the clue, besides more blood tests, that we needed to take it back down. Now we alter the dose as I need it.

I've noticed hand tremors in others. I don't have that. And weight gain—this is one that really ticks me off. I've heard so much from women who say they don't want to start the medication, even though they need it desperately, because they know they're going to gain weight. It could be a smoke screen for other fears that keep them from wanting to take the medication. I know that old saw. I was a smoker, and I claimed I didn't want to stop smoking because I would gain weight. Well, I have not gained anything since being on lithium. Not only that, I have maintained the same weight except for a time, about five years ago, when I specifically wanted to lose a few pounds. This never happened to me before in my life. I was always up and down like a yo-yo. I know some people do gain weight—four, five, or six pounds. But eventually—if you stick with it—the weight gain levels off and the trade off has to be worth it.

I've experienced one other side effect—and this can be annoying, but I think it's a small trade-off: frequency of urination. I used to be like a camel and now, when I gotta pee, I gotta pee. And often. It's just something you adapt to. We travel a lot, and I'm starting research for my third book—*Patty Duke's Pacific Northwest Pit Stop Guide*. I know that if it should become more frequent than it is now, I'd need to check and make sure everything's okay with my kidneys and bladder.

Right after I was diagnosed, for a very short period of time, I had my blood checked every week. Than it was every month for about six months, then every three months. I was very naughty last year. I should go once every four months minimum, and I found myself sort of slopping over into five or six. When I realized I'd become a bit cavalier about it, I dug into my discipline bag and got back on track.

Taking lithium, however, was just the beginning of my journey back to health. I did need to clean up the debris I had left in the wake of my manias and depressions. There was a lot of mopping up to do. I needed to ask forgiveness for those things that I did that were cruel, thoughtless, and hurtful. My children came first. The starting place was telling them, "I'm going to take this medicine." And making true apologies, using the words, "I'm sorry." Then living it. I don't like to do auditions to prove I can act, but the kids needed proof, and the only proof was changing my behavior.

It took a while for them to feel reassured that they trusted me—maybe for the first time. I tried to do things they weren't even aware I was doing to reassure them. For a long time I left the bathroom door open. Their experience had been that when the bathroom door was closed, there was a suicide attempt going on. I can remember their showing, in the beginning, a certain trepidation about telling Mom certain things, an uncertainty on their part about whether this would last. They did a little testing. Will this set her off? I think they were used to certain dynamics, and they had to find out whether they could get me to act that way again. The turning point with me came when someone asked Sean, "What is so different about your mom?" He said, "You can count on her now. It doesn't mean we always get along. But I'm more free to express my opinions now."

With other people I tried "cleaning up" by the way I was living my life. I didn't run around begging and pleading for forgiveness. But when the opportunity presented itself, I would say, "I know you were hurt by this."

My mental illness is not an excuse. I didn't say, "Look, I did it because I was mentally ill." But I had hurt people and I had to let them know I didn't mean to. By the way people responded, I knew the message had been received and that the forgiveness was there.

Sometimes I sent my apologies indirectly. Desi, for instance. So much time had passed and he had his own life, but whenever I had the chance—when I ran into his sister or someone who knew him—I let them know I realized how awful it must have been for him and that I wished it had been different. My first book was helpful in doing this with people I couldn't find.

Then I had to make the choice to forgive myself. I had done so many embarrassing things, so many unkind things. But I had to stop beating myself up about them. It was very personal—sort of a spiritual high colonic. And once I had done it, I was able to work more honestly on forgiving those who had hurt me when I was younger.

Some people I needed to deal with were already dead. So I had to be my own confessor and absolver. Let's say with the Rosses. Now, people who knew my history with them said, "She thinks *she* needs *their* forgiveness?" Well, I did. I needed their forgiveness for my hatred of them. So I made up conversations with them in my mind that could be considered psychotic, I'm sure, but they weren't because I understood what I was doing. It was a little exercise I had. Sometimes I would do it in Dr. Arlen's office, and sometimes it was when I was driving in the car by myself. And it took practice.

I did the same thing with my father.

But the dynamics with my mother were especially delicate. For one thing, it's hard to imagine that you're mad at your mother, that you hate your mother, that you hate her for something she did or whatever. To me, that's not a noble way to feel. Once I was able to accept that, yes, as a little kid I was mad at her, and she did a bad thing, she did a stupid, stupid, bad thing, and that if she'd known better, she wouldn't have done it, how could I hate her for that? And since I need her in my emotional life, I must forgive her for that stupid, bad thing she did.

I believe that bitterness is counterproductive, so in an almost selfish way it was important for me to forgive—to truly forgive. And I honest-to-God believe that I would be dead if I had hung on to all of the rage and bitterness that it was possible for me to have. There is this little trick I have that works most of the time. I assume that the person who hurt me really wasn't capable of malice. Maybe he or she was sick like me, only in some other way. Then I can let my anger go.

My forgiveness of my mother sort of evolved. She never told me straight out, "I did wrong to you." She did say, "I made a terrible mistake in sending you to live with the Rosses, but I didn't know what else to do." We've never had long talks about it, and one of the toughest things about my relationship with my mother is that I had forgiven her for years and she wouldn't accept the forgiveness. She wouldn't let herself off the hook. Until very recently, she carried the guilt and the pain because she just couldn't forgive herself.

I don't feel that way about myself anymore. When I talk about cleaning up the debris after the manias, I mean that once I've done that, then I've done it and I've done the best I could. There are moments, certain times during the manias, that I still find embarrassing, but they were just that—embarrassing—and like anyone else who goes through life with a "was my face red" story, I don't live there and I don't harbor that pain.

To be honest, I kind of like the position of being the fair-haired savior of my mother. The truth of the matter is that the person who has been most attentive to her this year has been my husband. He'll go by with Kevin to see her in the afternoon without saying a word to me. I ask him, "Why do you do that?" He says, "I like her." She happens to be fun now. She wasn't fun before. So he gets a kick out of her with her New York accent and her funny asides. I pray that we can pass that attitude—that attitude of forgiveness and caring—on to our children.

Now, I didn't get to this point all by myself. Once I became stabilized on lithium, I began to benefit and even like the process of psychotherapy. Actually, I don't believe anyone with manic depression can truly benefit from talk therapy until the chemical imbalance is fixed. If that doesn't get taken care of, you can talk till you're purple in the face, you can spend billions of dollars, but you'll never be helped until someone says to you, "You're manic-depressive. Take your medicine, clean up the messes you've made, and get on with your life." Before taking lithium, trying to participate in therapy was like trying to fly a jet without ever having been on a plane. There was nothing wrong with the intellectual part of my brain. I understood the words the psychiatrist was saying. They just didn't compute.

I was swell at the jargon of psychotherapy. I could sit around with other people who'd been in analysis and we could just jargon ourselves to death. It didn't change a thing.

All those years, when people had told me they loved being in analysis, I thought, "They're all nuts. What's to love about this? It's terrible." And then I found myself looking forward to going, to talking to Dr. Arlen, to sorting things out. But that was not until after I felt I had the tools to do it, the tools to even organize my thoughts.

Today, I think that many doctors tell patients like me that they don't believe prolonged psychotherapy is necessary. But there is that "cleanup" work to do, and then you are better able to use the therapeutic methods that eluded you before. The balance that I got from my medicine allowed me to be able to interact with Dr. Arlen even in an unpleasant conversation or a defensive conversation or an angry confrontation without being afraid that he was going to think I was crazy. All of that fear got left behind, so I could begin to interact with human beings.

Like many people with undiagnosed manic depression, I had more than my share of mental hospitals that didn't work and of psychiatrists, none of whom could help me in the least. Neither could well-intentioned relatives and friends who urged me to go through psychoanalysis or gave me advice I was utterly incapable of following, like, "Pull yourself up by your bootstraps."

Not that I was a great patient. For one thing, I was adamant about never going to a psychiatric hospital. I didn't think I needed one. And I believed that going to such a hospital would ruin my career. So I made Harry Falk, my first husband, promise that he would never commit me. Even when my behavior was atrocious, he tried to keep that promise.

It wasn't until I was anorexic—I weighed seventy-three pounds—and had just tried to kill myself that Harry took me to the psychiatric division of Mount Sinai Hospital in Los Angeles—it's now Cedars-Sinai. Once I was on the other side of that door, something snapped and I was talking like a lawyer. I said I had been taken there against my will, that I had rights, and that I wanted to talk with my attorney. I wasn't there forty-five minutes and I was so glib, so sure of myself, that I was let out, with the understanding that if I didn't behave myself I would have to go back. By the time I got to the car, I was back to my original state.

Where did it come from, that incredible energy and guile? If I were asked to do it now, I couldn't do it. But then it was just there. It was almost as if the illness itself had its own defense mechanism.

Within a short time, maybe a month, five weeks, or so, Harry took me to a psychiatrist. I didn't cooperate there either and I got sent home with pills. I seem to recall that they were Valium. Meanwhile, I picked fights with Harry, about what I haven't the vaguest idea. But nothing important, just things that I provoked. One day I had an angry outburst with him, ran into the bathroom, and took a whole bunch of Valium. Harry said I had to throw up. I said I wasn't throwing up. Of course, I finally did. But Harry still tried to make good on his promise not to commit me.

In an attempt to keep me out of the hospital and to keep all of this out of the papers, he hired a full-time psychiatric nurse. She made me get out of bed, made me eat, made me comb my hair and brush my teeth. But somehow I managed to find more pills, and I swallowed a whole lot of them. That was it for Harry, and it resulted in my second and longest hospitalization, at the Westwood Psychiatric Hospital.

At Westwood, I never knew what my diagnosis was. I do know that the treatment was ineffectual and probably inappropriate. I was prescribed Thorazine, Stelazine—in large quantities. These are big-time drugs used for schizophrenics, so I guess they thought that was what was wrong with me.

I spent six weeks in the hospital playing volleyball with other people because the doctors and nurses insisted on it, doing the Thorazine shuffle—basically out of it. Mostly I cried that I wanted to go home.

I felt totally abandoned. This was twenty-five years ago, and visits were very limited. I used to cry and try to find money for the pay phone. When I called Harry I would whimper and say, "I'll be good. Please take me home." He came every few days, and it was so painful for him. He knew that all we would do was work our way to my crying that I wanted to go home. I remember standing there sobbing, telling Harry I would never forgive him for this. Then he had to walk away by himself and go home and wonder if he had done the right thing. In a way, it must be far more frightening and mysterious for the families than for the people they leave in the hospital. They don't have the camaraderie of fifteen or sixteen other people pissing and moaning about how angry they are to be there. The family members are out there thinking, "I've got a breather now. That's nice, but God, what have I done?"

I hated the place. It was a little Spanish building that looked like it might have been a convent at one time. It was dark inside and it smelled like sweat. But when Harry came to visit he said it looked like a country club. I remember the intensive care wing. It was kind of a joke because the "wing" was about two rooms long. That's where you were really locked up. It was for people who had tried to kill themselves or who had been violent with others. You could hear screaming coming from there, and I remember being repulsed and terrified and fascinated by it—so much so that I tried to be bad and get myself in there once. It didn't work; I wasn't bad enough. But I had a couple of buddies that I developed in between crying spells, and they were always going back there. Sometimes they'd ask to go because they felt out of control. I didn't understand that. One of them was a lovely, small, dark-haired girl. She was eighteen—in, I was told, for LSD, bad trips. She'd play the guitar and we'd sing folksongs. I think we probably fancied ourselves prisoners.

There was a doctor there—Jack Lomas—whom I called Grandpa. He's dead now. A lovely, lovely man. But how was he going to deal with this person who did nothing but wail? I did love him. He was sweet. He would pat me on the head and give me medication. But I didn't tell him anything. There was a time he went away for a week and there was a substitute doctor, a Dr. Goldman. For some reason, I talked to him, and I made a little progress. We'd sit outside and I liked that. He asked me pertinent psychiatric questions, which I didn't answer. But I did say things like "Why, why me?" and I remember he said, "Of all the people in the world, why not you?" And it made me laugh. He brought me Gilbert and Sullivan records—*The Mikado* and *HMS Pinafore.*

The reason I remember this so distinctly is that recently I got a letter from a young woman who said that she and her mother had just been reading in *Call Me Anna* the part about the "rolypoly doctor." Her mother was convinced that this was her father, who died three years ago. And indeed it was. They sent me a little picture of Dr. Goldman and he looked much older, but there he was, a jolly, sweet, smiling man.

One day out on the volleyball court I got angry because I thought one of the attendants was mistreating a patient who was very out of touch with reality. Actually they were horsing around, but I didn't like it—I considered that he was ridiculing the guy—and I got mad. Now, I hadn't spoken to any of the staff for about four weeks. I hadn't spoken, just cried, "I want to go home, I want to go home." I wouldn't participate in occupational therapy or any of that stuff. Well, out on that volleyball court I started yelling and swearing, and I remember that all the patients cheered. That was the dramatic moment for me. I decided that I had had enough of this and I was going to get out of there. The only way to get out was to cooperate, so that afternoon I went to occupational therapy and made little clay birds and ashtrays. I started taking my medicine and stopped crying, and I was out in two weeks. And for all intents and purposes I felt better. I recall feeling I'd better keep it together or I was going to wind up back in there.

Well, I didn't go back to Westwood, not right away, but a year later, after my split with Harry, I landed in Cedars-Sinai Hospital to get my stomach pumped. I had taken an overdose, and my manager knew someone who got me into the hospital quietly, without fanfare. I was on the critical list for a week.

But inevitably I found myself back at Westwood in the spring of 1970. It was after my strange behavior at the Emmys when I really lost it, when I rejected my award and said I was going to become a psychiatrist. A lawyer friend finally convinced me that I needed help. At first I was adamant: there was no way I would go. But a few days later, when I felt I was totally coming apart, I said, "What the hell. I'm not doing anything else this week anyway."

Well, that turned out to be another time when I talked my way out of the help I so desperately needed. I wouldn't sign the forms they gave me. I said, "What's this about shock treatments? I never said anybody could give me shock treatments. I never said I would take these medicines." Three days later, I had a physical fight with one of the attendants, and, small as I was, I was powerful. I managed to escape from the building, and I just ran and ran until I saw a taxi. A week later I was back in the hospital, but again I wouldn't stay. I was completely unraveling and I was scared to death, but I was beyond anyone's ability to control, least of all my own.

I continued to swing between the depressions and the manias, and I made I don't know how many suicide attempts. The fan magazines and the tabloids all accused me of being a druggie and an alcoholic. That was murder for me to read. But no one ever suggested I was mentally ill.

I did go to doctors on and off throughout the years, and I would either be sobbing and crying and incoherent—I'd sit there and cry for an hour or three—or I'd be so lucid. I would be more lucid than the doctor. And charming. And in control. I never felt that I was putting that on. I call it the cleverness of the illness. It *is* clever. I never got caught.

After I married John Astin, he made endless pleas for me to go to a doctor, to talk to someone and get some kind of help. Mostly he got no response at all from me. Sometimes he got tears. And once in a very blue moon I would say, "Okay."

And I began going to someone Dr. Arlen, who was John's doctor, had recommended. A lovely man, I guess. I really don't know. A couple of times a week—though I was scheduled for five times, I showed up only maybe twice each week—I would go to him. I would start crying the minute I got into the car. And I would continue to cry until I got back into the car and we were going home. I almost never spoke to him. I had been going there over a year before I noticed the man wore a hearing aid. Or before I even saw what he looked like. If you asked me to describe him, I couldn't.

I didn't want to be there—that's what I was crying about. I was just putting in the time. In my head, I was doing this to shut John up. Okay, I'll go and I'll be tortured for forty-five minutes—that was my perception of therapy. It never occurred to me that somebody was there to help me.

I remember that occasionally somehow the topic of sex would come up, and it certainly wasn't generated by me. After that, I would not go back to him for three, four, five, six, seven weeks, until I was sure he had forgotten that question. Frankly, I remember having thoughts like, "What the hell does the way I feel right now have to do with whether or not I had sex last night?"

This went on—off and on, mostly off—for the first four years of my marriage to John. Once in a while, I'd eke out something about a dream, or I'd tell some sad story about how bad the kids had been, but I never really talked about what I was feeling. And God forbid I should stop crying, because then he would ask me what I was thinking, and that just paralyzed me. Sometimes I didn't feel anything. It's very hard for people to imagine how you cannot feel anything or not think anything. It is so hard to describe. You simply exist. It's like being in a holding pattern. You're told that the only person who can help you is you, and you just can't. It would be the same as though someone told me I could build an exact replica of the Empire State Building. It was that ridiculous to me that I could fix this.

After the sessions, I felt guilty because John and the doctor were both saying that it was up to me. I thought I was a bad person, that I must be lazy and selfish and no good because otherwise I would do what they said.

It was that kind of thinking which would eventually lead to the suicide attempts, to the high drama. Look, if I can't fix it and I can't do all these things you tell me to, then the only thing I know how to do is end it.

I've been asked if these were classic cries for help or if they were real suicide attempts. Well, I'm not so sure that I or anybody else knows the difference. And I worry about that. Anyone who puts up with a person who's always trying to kill herself can wear down so he—or she—doesn't take every one of those attempts seriously. I ache for the friends and family members who have to come to the aid of people who are always trying to kill themselves. I ache even more for the friend or relative who, at one time, says, "I can't go through this again." And then all of a sudden, their loved one is dead. I also know that if I had died, no one but myself would have been to blame. I think it is very important for the survivors of family members who commit suicide to recognize that there is a something—I don't know what the name of it is—that takes over, and there isn't anything you could have done.

Every so often John and I would go to Dr Arlen for marriage counseling, crisis-intervention-type meetings. But even then I thought, "Mm, mm, he has already decided how crazy I am." So those meetings were never very productive.

Then came that unforgettable night in 1977 when Dr. Arlen got to see just how crazy I could get. It was midwinter, in the middle of the night, and for some reason I couldn't sleep. My motor was racing, and I was running around the house like a lunatic, smashing lamps, scratching at John's face, running to the bathroom, slamming the door. The boys—Sean, who was six, and Mack, who was just four—had awakened from all the noise and just stood there watching.

John didn't know what to do with me, so he called Dr. Arlen. Now, Dr. Arlen wasn't treating me except for the occasional marital therapy because he was John's doctor then, but this was a real emergency. We ended up at Dr. Arlen's house in the middle of the night. We were there from two to six in the morning.

Since then Dr. Arlen has told me that I was as manicky as he has ever seen any patient. I was talking a mile a minute, at this unbelievable rate. My speech was so fast that night that I was saying everything that was coming over the radio, seemingly at the same time it was being said. It was as though I knew what was coming before I heard it.

I was also saying everything John said to me at exactly the same time, parroting him. I may have been a hair off in the timing, but it was freaky. My brother happened to be visiting us, and he witnessed it, too. I remember thinking to myself even then that this was really weird. I knew what I was doing, but I couldn't stop. John would say, "All right, okay, that's enough now," and I'd be saying, "All right, okay, that's enough now."

I was bursting with ideas and I kept interrupting whatever conversation was going on. I insisted that I had heard some messianic message. I couldn't sit still. I was expansive, elated, grandiose.

Dr. Arlen told me later that he thought I should have been hospitalized. But of course John and I both refused. No more mental hospitals for me. And no threatening my career. No, John would take care of me at home until I calmed down.

But, after that emergency visit, I felt a little more comfortable with Dr. Arlen, and I went to him by myself a couple of times. Then a few months would go by and I didn't go. Then I would go again. John had finished his psychoanalysis with Dr. Arlen by then, so there was no conflict there as there might have been earlier. And I thought it might be helpful to me that he knew so much about John. So in 1980 or '81, I began to go more often by my own choosing.

I was not in analysis. It was still crisis intervention, although the crisis might be smaller. You might be dealing with a divorce rather than a suicide attempt. I was able to talk more to him, certainly much more than I ever did with my previous doctor. But I never revealed the manic feelings I had. Once they were over, I didn't even want to think about them, and I didn't feel the need to discuss them. And some of the things I did were too embarrassing to talk about, so I would file them away.

And, of course, it's rare that anyone goes for help during mania or even recognizes a need for it. During mania, we own the world, we don't need anybody, we don't need anything. We're going to be millionaires, and we believe it. It is the depressions, I believe, that save us, because then we are more willing—or maybe it's just that we're more aware of our obvious disability—to go to anyone to make that pain stop.

I joke around a lot about the manic times because they're funny. We manics do outrageous things and it is part of our colorful nature, but the manias are at least as debilitating as the depressions and certainly, I think, more destructive to those around us. The spending sprees, for example, can wipe out everyone close to us. By the time most of us are willing to go for help, we can't afford it because we've blown all the money, and other people's houses are hanging in the balance. I would love to find a genius somewhere who could figure out how to entice someone in mania to go for help.

So mostly I would go to Dr. Arlen when I wasn't feeling good about myself, and we would talk about my sadness or my feelings of inadequacy, my not understanding why I couldn't feel better about the way I was functioning. Sometimes I was functioning very well, but I still didn't feel I was. I was never good enough or smart enough or confident enough. I'd go to Dr. Arlen a few times, and then when the deeper depressions came, I would disappear. So I can't say that I became a full-fledged cooperating patient until after I was diagnosed.

I know that religion has helped some people find their way back, but at the moment it is a confusing part of my life. In searching for some spiritual component to my life, I tend to get very busy with day-to-day stuff and get away from my reading of Eastern philosophies and Catholicism and Judaism. In my explorations, I would not be surprised that the most comfortable that I would be is with some form of Catholicism. I was raised

113

Catholic, but I have trouble with some of the politics of the Church, and I've gotten so intellectual that I can't quite separate them from the spiritual, ceremonial aspects. So I don't go to church regularly now, but I do enjoy an occasional visit.

If I have any message for others, it is to go for help early and not to be a resistant patient. And I don't mean that in the sense of "Now, be a good little girl and take your medicine." I mean cooperative in terms of asking questions, doing the best you can to express what it is you're feeling. Even if you don't have words for it, expressing whatever you can will tell the doctor something. And do the best you can to absorb the information coming back to you from the doctor, and use your motivation to get well, to allow yourself to trust.

If you're like me, and you're affected by lack of sleep or changing time zones when you travel, try to pace yourself. Allow time for a nap or just don't schedule yourself too heavily until you've rested.

And if you need to eat on time the way I do, make sure you do it. You don't want to be around when I'm hungry and the meal is taking too long to arrive. Now, if it's in a restaurant, I'll be gracious and charming and borderline regal. A waiter could drop a plate of soup on my lap and I'd say, "Oh, isn't that nice?" That's my training. But if I'm home and I miss a meal, I'm murder.

Once you get on a more-or-less even keel, don't panic about feeling a little wired once in a while or about the "down days." Everyone has them. I don't assume if I'm having a "down" day that I'm going into a depression. I don't discount the possibility. You never lose those memories. But I have no fear that I will ever go into one of those old-time depressions—for two reasons: first, I believe the medication is working, and second, I also believe that I now feel comfortable enough to recognize and deal with the symptoms of an onset if one occurs.

For instance, after I married Mike, there was a period for more than a year when I didn't work in a paying job—a real paying job. And we had some serious financial difficulties. It would seem to me that if I was going to be in a real depression, it would have happened then. All the triggers were there, the problems were real. But I never felt disproportionately "down." I also talked to Dr. Arlen, and I assessed with him whether my responses were appropriate to the crisis.

In fact, I did try to impose on myself for a couple of months a kind of false "up," but I realized it was counterproductive. What I was feeling was real. It was distressing not to have worked for a year and not to know why. But when I look at the cards that we were dealt that year, and I think back to how I might have responded to them nine years earlier—number one, I wouldn't be writing this book. I would be in bed, making all kinds of excuses.

Now, I have to tell you that during that time I didn't jump right out of bed every morning raring to go. I would wake up and turn on the TV, and I'd see other people with problems bigger than mine. Then I would ease myself out of bed and get in the shower. I think that even if you are on medication, you have to discipline yourself because life stays just as hard. Problems may change, but there are always problems. It has been reassuring to me to see that I didn't panic and that I didn't assume I was a worthless, terrible person, and that something in my brain didn't take over to tell me those things, either.

If I'm feeling a little down, sometimes I'll indulge myself. If I want to take a nap in the afternoon when normally I wouldn't, I say, "I don't feel so hot," and I take a nap. But I don't allow myself to stay in bed all day long or until the next morning. I get up and do something. It may not be a whole lot of something— maybe go outside to my garden and torture the poor roses, or go for a walk with Kevin or play with him or read the paper. I've become more of a physically active person now that we live in the Great Northwest with horses and trails in the woods and, of course, a three-year-old boy motivates you one way or another.

But still, one of my favorite exercises is to get in my car and drive around watching people. People are amazing to observe. I find it very stimulating. I have never been so fascinated by the

115

human condition as I've been in the last couple of years. So I'll drive around and make up little stories in my mind about the people I see. It's very therapeutic. Sometimes I read, mostly historical or biographical material—anything, from some ordinary person to kings and queens. There's an insatiable interest I have in how other people do this thing called life.

While I haven't used them myself, I've begun to feel more and more strongly about self-help groups: not in lieu of psychotherapy but as a support system. It's very important for us to recognize that we're not alone and to be able to compare—"Gee, did you feel like this? Is your hand shaking? Do you have blurry vision?" Things as surface as those and as deep as, "Oh, my God, do you feel afraid that your children will never trust you again?" People need to talk; otherwise we think we live in a vacuum. And it's lonely in a vacuum.

But I tend not to call friends when I'm feeling down. Mike and I have a very unusual relationship, and I'm more comfortable being quiet or moody with him than I am with anyone else.

Mike always seems to know when I'm feeling a little off. He doesn't always comment. He's just there. He's very protective of me. While I think it's fair to say he has not had to deal with the kind of agony I was able to create in the past, he has had to deal with a very strong personality—positive and negative. I have tried, in the last couple of years, to be much more aware of how my mood through the day affects other people. I realize now I didn't pay much attention to that in the past. But I have noticed that if I'm up, we're all up. If I'm gloomy, we're all gloomy. And I don't really want that responsibility.

I also know myself better now. In other people's crises, I have always become organized, strong, completely together. I could hear myself barking orders: you do this, you do that. When one of the kids was hurt or when my mom had surgery and there was speculation it might be colon cancer, it really got to me, inside my gut, but outside I was taking care of business. A lot had to do with my struggling to gain control from the demon within me. If I could control things outside myself, maybe I could control what was in me, too. Psychotherapy helped me understand that, and I've been able to give up some of that need to control and take charge.

I did have a bout with alcohol a few years ago. Mike and I were selling our house, and, of course, we had to have some wine to mark the occasion. Everything was just fine and pleasant, but I woke up with a hangover. Throughout the day and the night and the next morning I kept going to the liquor cabinet and taking sneaky drinks. Like it was a big secret, right? Finally I went to Mike and I started crying and I said, "My God, why am I doing this?"

Mike was not upset that I had been drinking, but he was upset that something was distressing me enough to make me drink. He said all the right things: "You're not a bad person. Lots of people get upset and have some drinks." He was upset, though, that I thought I couldn't have a drink in front of him. I couldn't tell him why. I didn't know. I suppose that no matter how healthy I like to think I am, there are still some residual neurotic things that need ongoing work. One of them is that I think I have to be perfect and above reproach. And a nice, noble lady doesn't drink in the daytime. She sneaks it!

That was scary for me. Very scary, because it seemed to be out of control. But the fact that we nipped it in the bud was very important. I went to Dr. Arlen for help. And as we talked about it, I realized it was a textbook case of responding to loss. We were selling the home I had lived in for twenty years, and there were lots of memories there. So I became depressed and I drank.

That's something that everyone with my illness has to be aware of. Just because you're taking medication and it is helping doesn't mean that you won't have your ups and downs. The important thing is to recognize when they're getting out of hand—when they're lasting too long or going too deep. Once we're stabilized, those of us who have been through the hell of this illness hesitate to admit that we're having a bad day. For a very long time, I was self-conscious about even using the word "depressed." I would use other words, euphemisms, because I was afraid someone would think the medicine wasn't working. Since I've been on lithium, I've made a joke of saying, "Oh, my God, I can't afford to be crazy anymore. I don't have the luxury of being loony."

But I'll tell you something else that's very naughty. I'm not sure I want all my neuroses cleared up. I'm perverse enough to think that some of them make me interesting. As long as they're not interfering with my life or somebody else's, then let me have a few. You've got to have a few to live in this world.

CHAPTER SIX

TREATMENTS THAT WORK

Anyone who has enjoyed the luxury of a mineral water bath—the kind touted by fashionable resorts such as Saratoga, New York, or Calistoga, California—recognizes the relaxed "wet noodle" feeling that persists for hours afterward. One of the reasons may be that they are bathing in water that contains lithium. And lithium has long been known as a healing substance. Patients with a variety of ailments, especially "nervous breakdowns," have been sent for mineral-water treatment. And in the nineteenth and twentieth centuries, spas in Europe and America boasted about the lithium content in their mineral waters.

◆

LITHIUM: THE WONDER MEDICINE

Lithium is a common mineral found in rocks and water and, in trace amounts, in the human body. Today it is a wonder drug, with the power to restore normalcy to 60 to 70 percent of those with manic-depressive illness.

Its effect on mania was discovered accidentally, in 1949, by an

Australian psychiatrist, John F. J. Cade, who worked in a state mental hospital in Melbourne. He was testing his suspicion that urea, a compound excreted in urine, in some way caused mania, because a person either produced it in excess or was somehow sensitive to it. When Dr. Cade tested his theory by injecting urea into guinea pigs, they had convulsions and some died. Dr. Cade then tried injecting the guinea pigs with lithium urate, the most soluble salt of uric acid. He was stunned when the pigs, instead of becoming manic, became lethargic. This suggested to Dr. Cade that lithium somehow reversed the effect of urea. So while his original hypothesis turned out to be wrong, testing it, serendipitously, revealed the miracle of lithium.

When he was satisfied that lithium was safe, he made the leap from guinea pigs to people. His results with ten manic patients, even those with psychotic symptoms, were startling. They became calm, and some were able to leave the hospital and return to homes and jobs.

His work stimulated study in other countries, and in 1954 Mogens Schou, a Danish physician, conducted the first double-blind study with manic patients. No one knew which patients were receiving lithium and which were being given a placebo, an innocuous substance not expected to bring about any change in behavior.

Dr. Schou reported dramatic improvement in the lithium patients. But doctors in this country were not listening. American psychiatrists were focused on tranquilizers and antidepressants that were synthesized in rapid succession in the 1950s. Besides, lithium was a natural substance and could not be patented, so there was no commercial interest in it by pharmaceutical companies. And doctors were wary because in 1949 lithium chloride, another lithium compound, had been removed from the market in the United States because several cardiac deaths and serious poisonings had resulted from its misuse as a popular salt substitute. It wasn't until the early 1960s that the value of lithium for manic-depressive illness was recognized here.

LITHIUM'S DRAMATIC EFFECTS

Dr. Ronald R. Fieve is an elegant, impeccably groomed psychiatrist who heads the Foundation for Depression and Manic Depression on New York's Upper East Side. His practice is crammed with Wall Street tycoons and Hollywood producers who often arrive at his office in long, black limousines. "I've had them pull up here after a huge Wall Street scandal," says Dr. Fieve, "with someone under indictment for insider trading. When they come to me for treatment, they have usually come down from a manic state and are into severe depression. Often they are desperate and suicidal." In the majority of cases, Dr. Fieve treats them successfully with lithium.

Dr. Fieve was a pioneer in the use of lithium in this country. In 1958 he conducted systematic clinical research trials of lithium in the acute ward of the New York State Psychiatric Institute and came away convinced that lithium was an effective, almost magical, treatment for manic-depressive illness.

Dr. Fieve remembers a Texas professor sent to New York for treatment whom he describes as "uncontrollably manic, writing ten books and forty research papers." His doctors in Texas had not been able to bridle his frenetic, psychotic behavior for more than a year. They were so astonished when he returned to Texas stabilized through the use of lithium that they began their own clinical trials.

The Texas results, as well as those of the New York State Psychiatric Institute's study, were presented at the annual meeting of the American Psychiatric Association in May 1965. And so lithium was introduced to the American psychiatric community.

At the time, the marketing of lithium was still illegal in this country, and it could be used only as an investigational drug with a special number from the Food and Drug Administration (FDA).

The process of approving lithium as a standard prescription drug to treat acute mania took five years. In 1970, it received the FDA endorsement; in 1971 it was sanctioned as a maintenance medication for those with manic-depressive illness.

121

HOW LITHIUM WORKS

Lithium does not "cure" manic depression in the sense that it eliminates it as surgery would do. Rather, it controls the condition the way insulin does diabetes. Lithium is absorbed freely into the bloodstream and moves into all body tissues, including the brain. It leaves the body entirely through the kidneys and is excreted in the urine.

No one knows for sure why lithium is effective. It has been speculated that it may alter the way certain brain neurotransmitters work—serotinin, noradrenaline (also known as norepinephrine), and dopamine (and perhaps others), the ones that control emotion and behavior. Or it may alter the productivity of certain nerve cell proteins whose job it is to maintain normal cell metabolism. Lithium may drive those cells back to normal, whether they are causing mania or depression.

In any case, Dr. Fieve says, "Few experiences in psychiatry are as dramatic as watching lithium carbonate in one to two weeks utterly transform a manic-depressive personality."

Lorraine: A Lithium Success Story

Lorraine was a forty-year-old wife and mother known for her volatile mood swings. No one who knew her suspected she had a mental disorder; they just knew that her behavior was entirely unpredictable. On some occasions, she would greet friends with a welcoming smile and chat easily about the events of the day. Other times, for no apparent reason, she would be irritable, unfriendly, often hostile. Even her telephone voice changed, so much so that callers would hang up when they heard "that other Lorraine."

Her children would ask their father, "What's wrong with Mom? Why does she behave that way?" Lorraine did not experience the kind of depressions that Patty Duke describes. Her "lows" were the crabby kind, the sulky kind, the "keep out of my way" kind. Several times her husband considered dissolving their marriage, but he remembered the "up times," which were so pleasant, and hoped that, eventually, there would be more of them than the "downs."

It was not until their oldest daughter, Jennifer, was taking a mental health elective in high school that anyone had an inkling that Lorraine's problem might not be her personality but a brain disorder with a name . . . and a treatment. Jennifer came home from school one day and asked for a private meeting with her father and younger brother. She told them that she thought her mother was a victim of manic-depressive illness. It didn't matter, she told them, that her depressions weren't typical. She still had them, and they came out differently than you might expect.

Looking back over the debris of her mother's lifetime—her estrangement from her parents, her limited number of friends, her inability to sustain interest in anyone or anything over time, her apologies and regrets for her inexplicable behavior—she was convinced her mother needed psychiatric help.

Lorraine resisted, protesting that she was mentally sound— this was just the way she was. But when her husband threatened to leave, with the children, if she did not go for help, she relented. Within a couple of hours, the physician diagnosed her as an atypical manic-depressive type and prescribed lithium.

"The turnaround was not to be believed," says Jennifer. "It was like we had a whole new mother. She was pleasant and predictable almost all of the time. Our only regret—hers, too— is that we did not know about all of this sooner. It could have saved her and us a lot of heartache."

HOW EFFECTIVE IS LITHIUM?

Several hundred thousand people in this country take lithium to control their bipolar illness, and it is felt that it may also be the drug of choice for the more than 20 percent of depressed patients who will eventually experience a manic episode. Patients who had their first depressive episode—especially if psychotic—in their late teens or early twenties and who have bipolar family members are at high risk. Because these clinical and familiar markers are so predictable of mania within three years, Dr. Hagop Akiskal recommends prophylactic lithium for those patients to prevent the occurrence of disruptive manic episodes during crucial developmental stages—when they are in school or in the early stages of their careers. He reassesses the need for continued lithium once they have achieved stable vocational status.

Lithium, for reasons not fully understood, both treats and prevents. When someone is manic, lithium can often stop the mania in its tracks. And when a level state has been achieved, it helps ward off future manias and depressions. "That happens," says the University of Pennsylvania's Dr. Jay Amsterdam, "because the drug is treating the same illness whether it is expressed in mania or in depression. It stabilizes the metabolism of the nerve cells involved in a person's mood swings."

Patients taking lithium for the first time often expect an instant miracle, but the drug's effects are more subtle. It usually takes from ten days to three weeks before it starts working. When it does, nothing dramatic usually happens. Mood swings generally become fewer and briefer and are not as severe. Twenty percent of those who take it regularly are relieved of all symptoms; the remaining 50 percent substantially improve. Thirty percent don't respond at all and need other kinds of treatment.

LITHIUM'S DRAWBACKS

Lithium is not a benign drug, and those using it must be monitored regularly. In fact, after Joshua Logan, in 1973, announced publicly that he wished all of his depressed friends were on lithium, there was grave concern among many mental health practitioners that there would be widespread confusion about lithium's use, that people would come to see it as a miracle drug for relieving all depressive disorders, not just manic-depressive illness.

An overdose of lithium can result in death. And for someone who is suicidal, a supply of lithium can be a handy, even provocative, invitation to end the pain. In therapeutic doses, however, the drug is considered to be extremely safe and with few side effects. The trick is to maintain patients on a dose large enough to be effective without being toxic. There is not a lot of margin for error. For most people, the therapeutic dose ranges from 600 to 1,500 milligrams a day.

The level of lithium in the blood is easy to monitor; many doctors insist that their patients come in monthly for blood work, and those on the drug often refer to their "lithium level" or their "serum lithium level." They are talking about the amount of lithium in the bloodstream, which indicates how much lithium is in body tissues. Too little will not be effective; too much can bring on troubling side effects.

Many people—as many as 25 percent—experience no adverse effects at all. Others get one or two side effects; some are troubled by a laundry list of annoying but not dangerous symptoms. Side effects most often reported are excessive thirst, frequency of urination, tremors, and memory problems. Weight gain, which happens to perhaps 20 percent of lithium takers, is especially troublesome and frequently contributes to depression. Other complaints include diarrhea, mild sleepiness, slight muscular weakness, dizziness, rash or worsening of acne or psoriasis, loss of libido, and altered taste sensation.

Often the body adjusts and these symptoms vanish. Gastrointestinal symptoms, for instance, may disappear within a couple of weeks; tremors may last longer. Approximately 20 percent of lithium users, especially women, develop a low thyroid condition that can be corrected easily with thyroid extracts or hormones.

LITHIUM, SALT, AND WATER

The most serious concern is that, over time, lithium could affect the kidneys, primarily in people with preexisting kidney disease. The danger exists because of the delicate balance of sodium chloride (salt), water, and lithium that must be maintained. If the body becomes depleted of sodium (as often happens to someone taking diuretics), the kidneys will retain lithium to compensate for the loss of sodium, making the lithium level rise. Similarly, if a person becomes dehydrated (through sweating, vomiting, or a protracted bout of diarrhea), lithium will drain from the kidneys more slowly and concentrate in the body. That's why patients who attempt to avoid the frequency of urination that may accompany lithium use by restricting fluids are headed for trouble. In fact, the increase in thirst often precipitated by lithium is the body's natural protection against the dangerous dehydration.

Travelers, too, must be conscious of the prevalence of gastrointestinal infections in certain countries, especially those with tropical climates. The resulting fever, vomiting, and diarrhea, if unchecked, can be dangerous to someone on lithium. So doctors advise their traveling patients to see a physician if they contract any undiagnosed gastrointestinal disorder while out of the country. If that is not possible and their doctor at home is not reachable, they might need to stop taking lithium temporarily. It is not harmful to stop lithium abruptly except for the possible return of mania or depression.

Anyone who has diabetes, hypertension, or congenital kidney defects or who takes analgesics (such as aspirin) chronically must be vigilant because all of those conditions affect kidney function.

Because symptoms that the kidneys are being adversely affected may not be readily apparent, and because comfortable blood levels of lithium do not guarantee that all is well, patients must be exquisitely tuned in to their bodies. If warning signs such as confusion, nausea and vomiting, upset stomach, or dizziness begin, they need to get in touch with their doctor immediately. These signs can be the forerunners of something serious, and the drug may need to be stopped or reduced to prevent escalating toxic effects—seizures, coma, and even death. Fluids such as orange juice and water, always important, may need to be increased to maintain metabolic balance.

A perk of taking lithium includes its possible boost to the immune system. Many people say that they have fewer colds and flu, and there are anecdotal reports that men taking lithium have fewer heart attacks than would be expected. No one knows for sure whether the diminishing of mood-related stress or some direct effect of the drug is responsible.

Pregnant women are advised not to take lithium, at least for the first trimester, because it can cause heart defects in the unborn child. And mothers who are breast-feeding should not take lithium because the drug is present in breast milk at about 80 to 100 percent of the level in her blood; what is therapeutic for the mother may be poison for the baby because of the vast difference in their size, weight, and body mass.

However, it is not only problems with the body's salt/water balance that can cause toxicity to lithium. Aging itself is accompanied by normal changes in the way the kidneys work. As people get older, the kidney's capacity to excrete diminishes, so the lithium level may need adjusting.

However, with all of these cautions, carefully prescribed dosages and regular monitoring of patients on lithium make it one of the safest medications, one that has revolutionized the treatment of mood disorders.

THE MEDICAL WORKUP

Doctors prescribing lithium should do a complete medical workup on their patients. The heart, blood vessels, and kidneys must be in good working order, and thyroid function has to be checked before and during lithium therapy. If the thyroid gland is found to be underactive, some doctors will prescribe small doses of thyroid medication along with the lithium.

The appropriate lithium dose is often trial-and-error until the therapeutic level is reached. It must be worked out carefully, with the patient understanding the significance of any side effects. People who are taking diuretics or are on a salt-restricted diet— or any diet where salt is likely to be lost from the body—need to inform their doctors. Indeed, doctors need to be told about *any* medication, including nonprescription drugs. Someone who is being treated for high blood pressure, for instance, must be supervised closely—careful attention to salt intake, fluid balance, and lithium levels is the only way to achieve safety for the person who is both hypertensive and manic-depressive.

Surgery on someone taking lithium is usually safe, but the surgeon should be aware of any medication the person is taking, including lithium. The doctor can then determine whether lithium should be discontinued temporarily.

WHY SOME PATIENTS SHUN LITHIUM

For every patient who extols lithium as the miracle medicine that has ended the turbulence in his or her life, there is at least one who resists taking the drug even when it has worked. It is a problem common to the treatment of patients who have chronic relapsing disorders, such as diabetes or hypertension, and whose medication must be administered on a regular basis by the patient. Noncompliance occurs frequently when a medication must be taken several times a day rather than just once.

It is a serious problem because noncompliance is the single most important reason that someone does not respond to treatment, and its consequences can be life-threatening.

Sometimes it is side effects that make patients abandon their lithium treatment. Drs. Fred Goodwin and Kay Redfield Jamison, in their book *Manic-Depressive Illness*, report that weight gain, increased thirst, a feeling of lethargy, decreased memory, difficulty concentrating, and diminished enthusiasm are the major complaints that nudge patients off their lithium regimen.

Women who put on a few pounds after starting lithium sometimes say that the cure is worse than the disease. The weight gain shoots them straight into depression.

For some, the lethargy and inability to concentrate are not worth the benefits they feel from having their moods stabilized. Marietta, a manicurist in an expensive metropolitan nail salon, says that after several months on lithium, she couldn't even be attentive enough to give the excellent manicures for which she had gained a reputation. "I'd go to the shelves to get the bottle of polish and realized that I hadn't even heard what color the customer had asked for. My mind kept wandering, and I couldn't control it. It wasn't me."

Others stop taking lithium because the idea of being dependent on daily medication for the rest of their lives is distasteful. They don't want to admit that they have a chronic medical illness that calls for lifetime treatment. They feel it will stigmatize them or someone might say something like, "Oh, she takes pills because she's crazy."

They often associate pill-taking with drug addiction. Even though she was assured that lithium was not addictive, singer Connie Francis acknowledged that she wouldn't take it for her manic-depressive illness because she was afraid of becoming "some kind of a drug addict." Eventually she relented, and admits that lithium helped change her life.

Some people protest that they want to hold on to their spectacular highs and are afraid that lithium will destroy them. Creative people especially—writers, poets, artists—are often fearful that their creativity will be siphoned away along with their illness, and that their productivity will suffer. There is some evidence that people who have experienced more mania than depression are more likely to shun lithium.

"When I took lithium, I felt so slowed down," says Morris, a Denver architect. "My work depends on a quick mind and the ability to be visionary. I was losing it on lithium. I also became less sociable, less interested in mingling with people, even less enthusiastic. There was no way I could afford to keep that up."

Sometimes a patient for whom lithium is prescribed initially to halt a manic episode will protest that the medication triggered apathy and sluggishness. But the natural history of such a patient predicts that his mania would be followed by a depression. So the lithium may actually be softening a depressive episode rather than exacerbating one. Nonetheless, once the association between lithium and lethargy has been made, many patients refuse to take the medication.

Even when there are no or minimal side effects, anywhere from

129

20 to 30 percent of people stop taking their lithium—against medical advice—when they no longer have symptoms. The first patient successfully treated with lithium by Dr. John Cade was one of those people. Dr. Cade has described him this way:

"It was with a sense of the most abject disappointment that I readmitted him to the hospital six months later as manic as ever, but took some consolation from his brother, who informed me that Bill had become overconfident about having been well for so many months, he had become lackadaisical about taking his medication, and finally ceased taking it about six weeks before."

LITHIUM COMPLIANCE: DOCTORS MUST BE SENSITIVE

Kay Redfield Jamison is a psychologist and associate professor of psychiatry at the Johns Hopkins University School of Medicine. Her clinical and research interests have focused on the relationship between the psychological and biological features of manic-depressive illness, and the combination of psycho-therapeutic and pharmacological interventions in its treatment. She has been especially interested in the psychological consider-ations of lithium treatment.

Dr. Jamison believes that doctors must be sensitive to and sophisticated about the intellectual and emotional side effects of lithium compliance. It is a delicate balance for which they must strive: the minimum amount of the drug that will work, yet enough to keep patients from tripping over the edge of either mania or depression.

"Lithium saves lives," Dr. Jamison says. "It changes people's lives around. It gives them a chance and a choice. And the em-phasis is on choice."

She explains that people have a natural resistance to taking medication on a chronic basis, especially to control a condition that has some good aspects to it. It is difficult to get people to stay on medication for what feels like a psychological problem rather than a physical illness. If the medication is effective and the person is relieved of symptoms, it seems almost incredible to them that they need to pop pills for the rest of their lives. Think about how often someone stops taking antibiotics once a sore throat has gone away, despite warnings from the doctor that the pink medicine in the bottle must be swallowed down to the last drop—or the last pill must be ingested. People stop taking lithium for the same reason they stop taking insulin or medication for high blood pressure.

"You can call it denial," Dr. Jamison says. "Or call it the 'hassle' factor. Call it whatever you want. It's there.

"We must train doctors to understand why lithium compliance is touchy for so many people. If they do not, patients will be turned off. And rightly so."

Ginny: Still Angry at the Medical System

Ginny says that she is the victim of a medical system that has been insensitive to her needs and convictions, of doctors who treated her with drugs she didn't want and electroconvulsive treatments she didn't agree to have. Today, fifteen years after her initial manic episode, she is still angry, still opposed to medication, still worried about her future.

When Ginny was in her late twenties, she began to feel like two different people. On one level, she saw herself as a gutsy, dynamic, risk-taking feminist. On the other, she saw a crumbling woman without spirit, who wanted to kill herself.

She attributed her intense mood swings to an unhappy home life, to parents who clearly favored her older brother, to the way young adults feel as they struggle to survive.

The Freudian psychoanalyst she saw every day wasn't helping her. Her mood swings became more intense, and she was fighting impulses to kill herself. She thought of all the ways she could do it: she would fill the bathtub with water and drown herself; she would stick her head in the oven; she would overdose on

131

Thorazine (prescribed by her psychiatrist) and sleeping pills. She would do it on her thirtieth birthday.

That morning—it was a brisk, sunny day in mid-October—Ginny checked into a motel and swallowed enough pills to end her life. She doesn't know how she got from the room to the motel lobby, where she was found crawling on the floor. Her next memory is the hospital, where her stomach was being pumped. "I felt as though I was being run over by a truck and I was trying to push the truck away," says Ginny. "So I guess my unconscious didn't really want to die."

Ginny was in the mental hospital for seven months, with her parents footing the bill. During that time, part of her was learning how to kill herself more successfully; the other part was wanting to get out and live a healthy life. And her anger built.

"I wasn't allowed to see my parents because I was so angry at both of them," Ginny says. "I had violent outbursts. I broke windows and slit my wrist. I put a plastic bag over my head. I was strapped down in an isolation room for twenty-four hours, screaming and crying. And I had all this rage inside me because the nature of the therapy I was getting wasn't helping me at all."

But it was through twice-a-week group therapy that Ginny was exposed to a philosophy of life that she says has embraced her and helped her survive. "A leader came to our group and asked all of us to sit in a circle and begin by chanting 'om.' It is a part of Yoga and it means God, life, infinity, faith. The first time it happened, it was so powerful for me, it was scary. I had to leave the room. It was only later that I could take in all that energy and use it as a resource to heal myself."

After Ginny left the hospital, she made another suicide attempt and ended up in a different hospital receiving electroconvulsive treatments that robbed her, for a time, of her short-term memory. When she was released to her brother's care, she went to live in a halfway house in California. By this time, the diagnoses of schizophrenia and psychotic depression had been ruled out. It was determined that she had manic-depressive illness. She was told that she would have to take lithium for the rest of her life;

if she did not, she would surely kill herself within six months.

Ginny was furious. She still attributed her problems to environmental factors. She insisted that she didn't have a chemical imbalance. And she was opposed to taking medication. However, she "played their game" for nine months because her stay in the halfway house was conditional. If she didn't take her lithium, she would be asked to leave.

"My moods leveled out," Ginny admits. "But I felt like soda without the fizz."

When Ginny returned to her home in the Midwest, she shared her history with a psychotherapist, explaining her aversion to medicines. He told her that she was a bright person with intense reactions, that she would probably live with pain all her life, and she would learn to accept it. He encouraged her to wean herself away from lithium.

That was the beginning of Ginny's spiritual exploration into herself. After reading a book about spiritual communities, she checked herself into a Yoga retreat and learned how to meditate. She began to believe that there were answers to her mood swings that were not compatible with Western psychology or psychiatry. She abandoned lithium and immersed herself in a holistic lifestyle. Her desire to end her life vanished, but her mood swings did not. She still had her euphorias—and her crashes.

Later, it was discovered that she had a thyroid condition, but no one told her that there was a connection between thyroid disease and manic-depressive illness. The unbearable gloom she felt the second week of every month was blamed on premenstrual syndrome.

In 1989 a psychiatrist, her seventh, told her sternly that there was no question about her condition. He said that she hadn't stabilized because she hadn't accepted her diagnosis—she was unequivocally bipolar. He said her life could have been very different, that it still could be different, if she agreed to take lithium.

Ginny is convinced now that she has a chemical imbalance in her brain; she is still reluctant to swallow a pill every day. She feels it is a sign of weakness, that her chanting and meditation, her daily journal entries, and her belief in the affirmation of life will eventually work for her. She has agreed to take a small daily dose of an antidepressant, which she thinks may be helping her. "I'm giving myself a year," Ginny says. "If I'm still getting these overwhelming depressions, I'll try lithium. But it scares me because it is so at odds with who I am."

LONG-TERM LITHIUM MAINTENANCE: DOES EVERYONE NEED IT?

The decision to continue lithium indefinitely is usually based on the form of manic-depressive illness and the course it takes. If episodes—either mania or depression—occur frequently (twice a year or more), if they are severe, if they precipitate hospital stays every year or two, it is clear that lithium is needed. If it is discontinued, it is almost certain that the disorder, which has been controlled but not cured, will recur in either its manic or depressive form. And untreated manic depression is likely to recur more frequently. It is much like other illnesses similarly braked by medication—high blood pressure, arthritis, and diabetes.

Whether or not someone who has had just one acute episode should be saddled with a daily medication for life is a matter of opinion. Generally, since lithium is so safe a drug when it is carefully monitored, doctors frequently opt to continue treatment rather than risk the devastation that subsequent bouts with the illness would bring.

Some people want to know: Can I take a little less lithium and keep some of my mania? This is a tricky issue that must be determined for each person in collaboration with his or her doctor. Patients should not tamper with dosage or decide how many pills to take. Often, less-than-prescribed amounts of lithium are not effective, and in this case, when mania appears, it may escalate to a full-blown, out-of-hand manic episode.

Some people, even on lithium, have breakthrough episodes of either mania or depression. It does not mean that the medication should be forsaken. Partial responses are common, and often other medications may be combined with lithium. Over time, if medication is continued, episodes may become fewer and further between.

◆

RELAPSES AND STRESS

Not all relapses come because of noncompliance with medication. Sometimes the subtle interaction between body chemistry and life stresses exacerbates mood swings in people who have been controlled by lithium for a long time. There is little information on the way medical treatment and factors in the environment work together in precipitating or eliminating mania.

But a study by two Yale University researchers tracked three such patients and found that, in each case, their relapse followed a specific kind of stressful event.

The stressors were uncannily alike, all involving situations where the person experienced failure and frustration in efforts to achieve certain goals in life. The relapses came when they felt trapped in an activity that ran counter to their hopes and dreams, but which they felt they could not avoid.

A twenty-one-year-old man relapsed his first day on a job he didn't want but felt he needed to help support his ailing father.

A twenty-six-year-old woman became manic when her mother went through a depression and took to her bed, forcing a loyalty conflict between her responsibilities to herself and those to her mother.

The patients studied were able to tolerate other kinds of stresses in their lives—death in the family, financial pressures, separations from loved ones. But the trigger for their manias was the "enforced pursuit of an activity that was at odds with their own goals and aspirations."

Other psychoanalysts, too, have noted that high-achieving manic-depressive men and women often evaluate themselves by their achievements and feel that, through their accomplishments, they are expected to rescue their families from socially inferior positions. When they are faced with a situation that highlights their failure, they feel extraordinarily inadequate—and trapped. And mania may result.

◆

SEX DRIVE AS A PREDICTOR OF MANIA

Another study showed that because an urgent sexual appetite is a hallmark of mania, it can serve as a warning that mania is about to happen—even in patients well controlled on lithium.

While psychoanalysis is generally not considered a "treatment" for manic-depressive illness, two West Coast psychoanalysts were able to help seven of their manic-depressive patients anticipate—and avoid—manic episodes. All were on maintenance doses of lithium.

The doctors found that *just before* manic episodes their patients' blood lithium level dropped and there was a dramatic increase in their sexual fantasies and impulses. After a while their sexual urges became so powerful that they spilled over into inappropriate thoughts and behavior: graphic sexual references in their conversation; the need to masturbate incessantly; obsessive, nonstop fantasies about sex with strangers. These urges appeared in the company of other manic symptoms.

When the patients were given higher doses of lithium, their mania stopped. Through psychoanalysis, or psychoanalytically oriented therapy, they were able to become consciously aware of sexual urgency that exceeded their norms. Increasing their lithium levels prevented the manias. The doctors suggest that the increased sex drive is biologically driven in manic-depressive illness and warns that mania is about to happen. Raising the lithium dose stops it in its tracks.

MOOD CHARTING

Patients can learn important information about their mood swings and the effectiveness of medication by keeping a *life chart*. They measure their feelings on paper through a series of numbers, usually from one for feeling awful to one hundred for feeling wonderful. Each day, at approximately the same time, they will mark the place on the scale that correlates to their mood. Significant life events, changes in medication, and the need for additional medication will also be noted. In this way, patients can see for themselves how their moods correlate to the seasons, to menstrual cycles, and to environmental changes. Lorraine, the woman whose daughter recognized her manic-depressive illness, says that keeping a life chart gave her a sense of mastery over her illness. As she could see the patterns of her mood swings and how they responded to medication, she felt she was an active participant in her own health care; it gave her a comforting feeling of control.

◆

OTHER DRUGS: WHEN LITHIUM DOESN'T WORK

Lithium doesn't work for everyone. But that doesn't mean that those who are lithium-resistant must continue to suffer. Sometimes another drug added to lithium will bring about effective results. And today there is a medley of other drugs and treatments to relieve symptoms in the 30 to 40 percent of people for whom lithium doesn't do the job. These often include rapid cyclers, people in psychotic mania, those with mixed states, and those whose first episode is depression.

THE ANTICONVULSANT DRUGS

Carbamazepine (Tegretol) (originally used to control temporal-lobe epilepsy or psychomotor seizures because it settles abnormal electrical impulses in the brain) is often an alternative for those who don't respond to or can't tolerate lithium or can't be managed on lithium alone. It was introduced into use for manic-depressive illness by Dr. T. Okuma in Japan and is especially effective in managing acute mania or mixed states where a patient has the overlapping symptoms of both mania and depression.

A substantial number—perhaps as many as 70 percent of people who don't respond to lithium—experience some relief with Tegretol. The drug is often well tolerated, and many patients have only minimal side effects—sleepiness, a skin rash, sensitivity to the sun, sometimes nausea or headaches. Even those symptoms will often vanish after a week or two or when the dose is lowered.

Tegretol can bring about startling improvement even in patients who are very sick. A thirty-five-year-old woman who had been hospitalized seven times in five years for severe mania came to the National Institute of Mental Health because she was totally incapacitated. She was distressed because she couldn't take care of herself or her children. Lithium hadn't helped her. But adding carbamazepine turned her behavior around quickly. She has not needed hospitalization in twelve years.

As with lithium, laboratory tests are essential because they uncover problems the patient can't see or feel. Tegretol can lower the white blood count, compromising the body's ability to fight infection, or platelet counts, affecting the ability to coagulate blood. That's why patients are urged to contact their doctor immediately if they have a sore throat, fever, or chills. Those symptoms may be, not just a cold or flu, but warning signs that their white blood count is dangerously low. Sometimes there is a benign (harmless) elevation in liver function tests.

In either case, these are usually transient conditions that reverse when the dose is reduced.

The starting dose, when the medication is used alone, is usually 200 to 400 mg and increases during the first week to the 800-to-1000 mg range. If it is not effective after two weeks and there are no unacceptable side effects, it is often increased to as much as 1,600 mg. The dose is lower when it is used in combination with other drugs, a frequent scenario.

When one of the anticonvulsant drugs doesn't work, it does not mean that another one will also fail. In fact, good responses have been seen in patients who were treated with **valproate** (Depakote, Depakene) when both lithium and carbamazepine were ineffective. Valproate has the advantage of not lowering white blood cells. **Clonazepam** (Clonopin) is becoming more popular because it is safe, is easy to use, and doesn't require blood monitoring. But because of its sedating effect, it is usually prescribed in small doses in combination with other medication. And it has not been proven conclusively to be effective by itself.

All of the anticonvulsant medications are more effective against mania than against depression.

THE NEUROLEPTICS

Neuroleptic drugs—so called because they affect the parts of the nervous system that control movement and behavior—are those traditionally used to tame the psychotic symptoms of schizophrenia; but they are frequently prescribed to halt an episode of acute mania in those with manic-depressive illness. The drugs used most often include **haloperidol** (Haldol); **thiothixene** (Navane); **chlorpromazine** (Thorazine), **thioridazine** (Mellaril); **trifluoperazine** (Stelazine). Each has its advantages. The first two are high-powered medications that can often tame an off-the-wall manic episode in a hurry and don't produce a sedative effect. The last two are more sedating, but are less likely to bring on tardive dyskinesia, involuntary movements of the face and body that can sometimes be more distressing than the mania.

Tardive dyskinesia is the most feared side effect of neuroleptic drugs because it can dramatically distort a person's face or body

139

and is often irreversible. However, this side effect usually occurs only after long-term use. Most people with manic-depressive illness will be given the medication for only a short time, usually until they have calmed down from a wildly manic episode.

In the short run, people on neuroleptic medication more often experience two troubling symptoms simultaneously: Parkinson's syndrome, a lack of or reduced movement, along with akathisia, an anguished feeling of restlessness and agitation that some doctors call a "physical frenzy." They occur because neuroleptics often block dopamine, the neurotransmitter that allows people to fine-tune their movements. Paradoxically, when dopamine has been blocked for a long time, the nerve cells in the brain become supersensitive and hyperkinetic. Their frantic search for dopamine shows itself in the jerks and flailing movements of tardive dyskinesia.

Other side effects experienced by some people are usually temporary and less dangerous: dry mouth, weight gain, constipation, vision problems, and impotence.

Clozapine (Clozaril) is a fairly new drug that has not yet been fully evaulated for treating manic-depressive patients. It is attracting attention for the treatment of schizophrenia because it doesn't produce the frightening tardive dyskinesia or akasthisia. Unfortunately, clozapine has a potentially ominous side effect; about 1 or 2 percent of those taking it experience bone-marrow toxicity, which suppresses their white blood cells and leaves them vulnerable to serious infections. Anyone taking it must be meticulously monitored.

These antipsychotic drugs are potent, and patients often cannot tolerate their side effects. The goal is to reduce the dose as soon as the psychotic symptoms of mania subside, and to add lithium slowly. By the end of three weeks, most patients are able to make the transition to lithium alone.

THE ANTIDEPRESSANTS

If the initial symptom of manic-depressive illness is depression, lithium may not be the drug of choice at the outset, particularly

140

if someone has significant eating and sleeping disturbances and is unable to function. If the depression is severe and there are thoughts of suicide, lithium by itself would not be a prudent choice. So many doctors will offer antidepressant drugs, alone or in combination with lithium, to those manic-depressives whose first episode is a depressive one. They are the same drugs used to treat unipolar depression, and most of them work by setting off a chain of chemical reactions that increases the amount of certain neurotransmitters in the brain, the substances that transmit messages between brain cells. Antidepressants include:

The MAO Inhibitors (MAOIs)

Monoamine oxidase inhibitors ushered in the antidepressant era in the 1950s, but soon fell into disfavor because they induced high blood pressure. Even after it was learned that the hypertensive reactions were caused by certain foods and drugs when they interacted with MAOIs, doctors still hesitated to prescribe them.

Today, however, interest in these drugs has been rekindled, especially for patients in the depressive phase of bipolar illness. While MAOIs are usually the second-line drug for people with unipolar depression, they are often the first for those who are bipolar because they are less likely to induce mania. It is thought that they work by blocking the activity of the enzyme monoamine oxidase, which increases concentrations of norepinephrine and serotonin in the brain.

These medicines include: **tranylcypromine** (Parnate); **phenelzine** (Nardil), **isocarboxazid** (Marplan), and **selegiline** (Eldepryl). They work for many people who have not responded to other antidepressant drugs; unfortunately, they have their drawbacks.

Uncomfortable side effects are sleeping disturbances, dizziness, dry mouth, and weight gain. But there can be extreme and potentially dangerous blood pressure elevations unless certain foods and medications are avoided. On the banned list are aged cheese; yogurt; Chianti wines or any alcohol in more than moderate amounts; canned figs; liver; concentrated yeast; meat ex-

141

tracts; any food that is pickled; fermented; smoked or aged; caffeine and large amounts of chocolate. Decongestants, sedatives, amphetamines, and hypertensive drugs must be avoided, and patients should check with their doctors before taking any prescription or over-the-counter medication.

Warnings of a rise in blood pressure usually come quickly after eating a forbidden food, and are often a severe headache, a pounding heart, a choking sensation, and sometimes a stiff neck.

The Tricyclic Drugs (TCAs)

So called because of their molecular structure, some of the better known tricyclic drugs include **imipramine** (Tofranil); **amitriptyline (Elavil), nortriptyline** (Pamelor) and **desipramine** (Norpramin). Up to 70 percent of depressed patients will have some degree of response if they can tolerate the annoying, though not serious, side effects that some of them will experience—dry mouth, constipation, blurred vision. As is the case with lithium, there may be weight gain, which often makes people more depressed.

Second-Generation Antidepressants

Sometimes a second-generation antidepressant—usually **fluoxetine** (Prozac) or **bupropion** (Wellbutrin), sometimes **amoxapine** (Asendin), **maprotiline** (Ludiomil), or **trazodone** (Desyrel)—will be prescribed. These drugs (except for Wellbutrin) block the reabsorption of the neurotransmitter serotonin (also associated with alcohol abuse) into nerve terminals in the brain.

Bupropion probably works on a different neurotransmitter—dopamine—and preliminary evidence suggests that it will probably not induce mania. This is a significant advantage, since the treatment of manic-depressive illness with antidepressants is a double-edged sword. Often they can relieve the depression, but may trigger mania—even the exhausting, often intolerable, and potentially dangerous rapid cycling between mania and

142

depression. Dr. Akiskal says this can occur in 5 to 20 percent of patientrs with recurrent mood disorders. The mechanisms involved are not fully understood, but studies have shown various risk factors, such as female gender and cyclothymic temperament.

No one knows exactly how bupropion works, but because it does not precipitate weight gain and decrease in libido (two side effects often associated with poor compliance with other antidepressants) and is less likely to cause cycling, it is an attractive medication for those who are manic-depressive. Indeed, some clinicians are using it along with lithium and thyroid hormone to treat rapid cycling.

However, doses that are higher than recommended may result in seizures or an outbreak of psychotic symptoms.

Prozac, a green and white capsule which, since its introduction in 1988, has become the most widely prescribed medication for depression, has been touted by some depression sufferers as a miracle. For many, it has worked magically where other drugs have not—and in smaller doses. Because of its effectiveness, with few or no side effects (not even the weight gain that discourages so many people taking more traditional antidepressants), Prozac has sparked an inordinate amount of public attention and has become the "celebrity" drug of choice for someone who is depressed.

It may turn out to be a valuable medication for manic-depressives as well. Results of a study of eighty-nine bipolar patients showed an impressive 86 percent response rate.

However, Prozac is still a relatively new drug and its long-term effects are unknown. Its initial success has become laced with controversy because several patients insist that Prozac sparked violent, hostile, or suicidal behavior. There is no proof, however, that Prozac was the cause, and with any "miracle" drug there are bound to be negatives before a balanced view emerges. Meawhile, many doctors, while looking at Prozac cautiously, regard it as another important addition to their arsenal of ammunition against depression.

Doctors who use antidepressants with their manic-depressive patients must manage them judiciously. When the depression is over, the drug is usually tapered and, if possible, discontinued. If it is not, it may bring on another episode, either manic or depressive.

And once the initial depression has been turned around, lithium, curious as it may seem, is able to control the sharply different symptoms of both mania and depression in most people.

◆

WHEN HOSPITALIZATION IS NEEDED

Even with the growing recognition that major mental disease, such as schizophrenia and manic-depressive illness, is caused by a chemical imbalance, not a personal weakness, hospitalization for its treatment still carries a stigma. It is difficult enough for someone to admit he is mentally ill; entering a hospital makes him feel even more ashamed. That, coupled with images of padded rooms, locked wards, and loss of freedom and dignity, makes some people with mental illness wary of hospitalization.

Yet hospitals are critical when mania or depression is out of control and incapacitating, certainly where a person threatens suicide or is so psychotically high (or low) that he is dangerous to himself or to others. It is sometimes necessary, too, when a doctor makes an initial evaluation of a patient or must monitor someone as he experiments with a variety of drugs. Fortunately, most people with manic-depressive illness, in the absence of manic psychosis, can be treated without having to be hospitalized; but those resistant to treatment may find themselves in and out of psychiatric facilities.

Today's mental hospitals are a far cry from many people's stereotypes. Even state hospitals, many of which are underfunded and understaffed, are not the nightmares people envision. They do, however, vary in quality of care from state to state, and most people, if they can afford it, prefer to be treated in private hospitals—although they, too, are not uniform in the standard of care they provide. A forty-five-year-old banking executive, who has had several hospitalizations in the past, says that even though her condition is being controlled with lithium and other drugs, she has purchased an annuity policy to cover the cost of private hospital care . . . if she should ever need it.

Laurie Flynn, executive director of the National Alliance for the Mentally Ill (NAMI), an advocacy group made up mainly of patients' relatives, advises that it is important to be an informed consumer. The patient, or a family member (if the patient is not able to do it), should make inquiries about the hospital. Is it certified and accredited? What experiences have other people had with the hospital? Members of organizations such as NAMI and the National Depressive and Manic-Depressive Association (NDMDA—another advocacy organization whose 35,000 members around the world are mainly patients) can answer such questions.

Once the patient is in the hospital, Ms. Flynn suggests that the presence of a family member goes a long way in ensuring quality care. And the questions should continue. What is the treatment plan for the patient? What medication will he be getting? What are the choices? What are the side effects? How long will he be in this restricted setting? "It's no different from what someone should do if a relative were hospitalized for a heart attack or some other physical condition," Ms. Flynn says. "Patients and families are no longer passively accepting decisions made by doctors. It is important to talk with the physicians and participate in the treatment program. Everyone has a right to be informed."

Some patients know when their symptoms are out of control and, especially if they have been in the hospital before, will voluntarily commit themselves for treatment. In other cases, relatives—often a parent or spouse—has to commit them. "It is not easy to do," says Burt, whose daughter, Sheryl, has manic-depressive illness. Sheryl is thirty-five, a rapid cycler, and has had to be hospitalized seven times since she was diagnosed at nineteen.

"When you learn your child is mentally ill, you go through so many emotions—grief, shame, guilt, and fear," says Sheryl's father. "But having to commit her to a hospital creates a situation where family trust is eroded. A parent has to sit there in front of his child and say unpleasant things about her in order to get her the care she needs. Sometimes it drives a lasting wedge because the child looks at you forever as her adversary."

The stigma of the mental hospital and the involuntary commitment of a loved one, when it is necessary, are agonizing enough. But the issue of cost adds to the already heavy burden. Medicaid and Medicare pay the bills in state hospitals, but care in a private psychiatric facility or in the psychiatric ward of a hospital is another story. Most insurance plans do not yet accept manic depression as a biologically based disease of the brain, and their coverage is much more limited than it would be for any physical condition such as heart disease, cancer, diabetes, or asthma. Many plans cover only thirty days of hospitalization a year, and up to 50 percent of the treatment costs. Usually there is a lifetime cap of $10,000 to $50,000.

"That doesn't help much when monthly hospital costs are somewhere around $597 a day for a bed, not including doctors, medications, or nursing," says Susan Dime-Meenan, executive director of NDMDA.

The nature of manic-depressive illness puts its victims at a devastating disadvantage. It often strikes in the late teen years or early adulthood, when many young people are too old to be covered by their parents' insurance policies and don't have enough longevity in the work force to have insurance of their own. Later it is difficult for them to get insurance because they have a "preexisting condition" that many insurers will not cover. And the cyclical pattern of manic-depressive illness often requires multiple hospitalizations within a year. Thirty days just won't do it.

Several of the nation's courts have recognized the injustice of health insurers' refusing to reimburse for the treatment of mental illness, and California became the first state to pass a statute that requires insurers to cover serious mental illness in the same way as other physical disorders.

ELECTROCONVULSIVE THERAPY

For some patients, drugs don't work or their side effects can't be tolerated. These patients can often make remarkable progress after receiving a series of electroconvulsive (shock) treatments (ECT).

Despite its association with pain and "mind control," ECT, while not usually the treatment of first resort, can be nothing short of miraculous in freeing someone from debilitating depression and sometimes from relentless mania. The treatment, initially called "electroshock," was introduced in 1938 to treat schizophrenia, but it was used indiscriminately and fell out of favor. Even now it has its critics, and some consider it to be a violent assault on a person.

But today's ECT is gentler than it used to be—the current is lower and the treatment takes only a few seconds. The temporary loss of memory that most people hear about and dread was common in the past but doesn't happen so much anymore because of the way that the electrodes that deliver current to the brain are placed.

It works this way: while the patient is asleep under anesthesia, an electrode, a half-dollar-sized metal plate covered with a gel, is placed against his skin—usually to his forehead and the top of his head. The press of a button sends an electrical current through part of the brain, shocking it and stimulating brief brain seizures. The body does not convulse, there is no alarming noise, and the patient feels nothing except the pinprick that, before the treatment started, delivered a muscle relaxant and anesthesia. Treatments are given two or three times a week for perhaps two or three weeks.

Not only does ECT reverse serious depression quickly, it may work for out-of-control mania, especially where medicines have failed. As many as 90 percent of people who are melancholic and couldn't recover with medication would get significant relief with ECT. It is a way to make very sick people—including those who are suicidal—well in a hurry.

◆

AFTER THE HOSPITAL: THE HALFWAY HOUSE OR INDEPENDENT LIVING

Most people with manic-depressive illness are able to live on their own once they are diagnosed and treated. But some—those who don't respond to treatment, who cycle rapidly, or who have frequent breakthrough psychotic episodes—may need to live in a transitional facility.

Residential treatment centers or halfway houses offer group living with supervising personnel who provide structure and activities and monitor the daily taking of medication. From there, some people move into independent living arrangements—often an apartment they share with one or two others, arranged for by a rehabilitation center. The kind of supervision varies: a telephone call once a day to remind about medication and the day's activities, an emergency number in case of a crisis, a visit once a day from a counselor.

Burt, whose daughter lived in an independent living program for several months, says it is difficult to get in because the demand far exceeds the supply. While some facilities are nonprofit and government-subsidized, the cost is rarely covered by insurance. Fortunately, for those with manic-depressive illness, the stay is usually a short one, providing a safety net before their return to society.

◆

THE ROLE OF PSYCHOTHERAPY

The role of psychotherapy in treating manic-depressive illness is a touchy issue, especially with psychopharmacologists like Dr.

148

Jay Amsterdam, who has little tolerance for anyone who suggests that people with manic-depressive disorder can talk themselves out of it. "Getting someone to talk himself out of manic depression is like getting someone to talk himself out of diabetes," he insists. "It's silly." He concedes, however, that psychotherapy may be helpful in cases of double depression, where someone is depressed about *being* depressed.

Other psychiatrists believe that psychotherapy is an effective and necessary addition to treatment, to help people cope with stress and recognize the danger signs, and especially to help family members understand a condition that baffles and angers them.

Many patients agree. They frequently testify that they could not imagine dealing with their illness without psychotherapy in addition to their medication. Their unpredictable mood swings have left a trail of debris and devastation behind them and have taken an incredible toll on their relationships, their families, their careers, and their self-esteem. Talk therapy helps them figure out how to "mop up," as Patty Duke expressed it.

PSYCHOTHERAPY AND FAMILY RELATIONSHIPS

Margie, a forty-two-year-old woman who has been stable on lithium for two years, says that family therapy made a significant difference for her, her husband, and her children.

"After a few months of seeing a psychiatrist on my own and gaining some insight into what I was like to live with, I didn't know where to start making amends—or how. How could I apologize to my children for the ball games I never went to, for the school nights I missed, for shutting them out of my room and my life when they needed me the most? How could I tell my husband that I couldn't help the affairs I had, the scenes I caused, the embarrassment I brought him? I was so ashamed, it felt overwhelming.

"I also needed to know what they were feeling. How angry were they? Could I make it up to them or was too much chipped away? And I wanted them to know what I was still going through, the terror I still have about going out of control again.

Other people wake up full of energy, they feel great. Me, I wonder if it isn't the beginning of a manic episode. When I'm feeling blue, I start sweating and clench my teeth, hoping that I won't sink into the bottomless depressions I used to have. I needed my family to understand so I could stay well."

THE PATIENT'S ISSUES

Patients also need to wrestle with their own resistance to taking a pill every day, and to make peace with their need to preserve their essence while swallowing medication that keeps them healthy by altering their behavior patterns.

Jimmy, thirty-seven, a musician who has been taking lithium for ten years, says that he needed psychotherapy to help him work through feelings of loss. "When I swallowed my first dose of lithium, I had mixed emotions," Jimmy remembers. "I knew I couldn't go on living with the manias that kept interrupting my life. But I liked my personality when I felt high. I was fun and outrageous, and that's what people expected of me. What's more, it's what I expected from myself. I wasn't sure I wanted to let it go. I was afraid I would become a stranger to myself. Psychotherapy helped me grieve for the part of me I had to give up to stay healthy."

Mollie, a thirty-nine-year-old interior decorator who is what she calls "even" for the first time in her life, experienced similar feelings. "Everyone likes me better now that I'm on lithium and stable," she says. "But I'm not sure I like myself. I feel flat, not exuberant, not interesting. I'm still creative, but less willing to be daring, to take risks in the way I decorate. All in all, I think the trade-off is worth it, but it makes me edgy, and I need my weekly visit to my shrink to keep my sanity."

There are other issues, too: anger for having the illness in the first place; the stress of having to live with a chronic, uncertain condition that may erupt at any time; concerns about genetics and resentment about the attention that must be paid to even minor changes in mood.

"I can feel it when my motor starts to race," says Sharon, a thirty-two-year-old journalist. "I'll be busy on a story, smack up against a deadline, and my motor's going. With most people, they would think it's natural. Under those circumstances, with an editor standing over you for your copy, anyone would feel a little frantic. But me, I wonder if I'm getting sick again. I hate having to monitor myself so carefully, and it's the main thing I'm dealing with in therapy."

Sharon is participating in **cognitive therapy,** which she says works for her. It is based on the principle that your moods (in the absence of a chemical imbalance) are created by your "cognitions," or thoughts, that the way you feel depends on the way you think. This treatment teaches people how to alter their thinking processes.

Other therapy techniques, some of which overlap, include:

- **Interpersonal psychotherapy,** which presumes that past and ongoing personal relationships are related to depression, and that conflicts about these relationships must be resolved to relieve the condition.
- **Behavioral therapy,** which maintains that emotions and behavior are learned, rooted in one's upbringing. To unlearn what has been learned, behavioral therapists suggest that people focus on how they act, not on how they think or feel. Usually, specific goals will be set and a program shaped to institute new behaviors.
- **Psychoanalysis,** which digs deep into one's childhood to unearth reasons for current feelings and behavior. While most other therapies are short-term, psychoanalysis may take years and usually involves sessions several days a week in the analyst's office.

◆

GETTING ON WITH LIFE:
THE ROLE OF SUPPORT GROUPS

Many people with depression or manic-depressive illness say that their most effective therapy—the kind that helps them move past their illness and on with their lives—comes from attending a support group. At meetings, they share stories, hear lectures, and exchange information that makes them feel less alone. Often friends and relatives come, too, and gain better understanding of the way the disease works and the devastation it brings to those who have it.

Because individual psychotherapy is expensive, support groups are more accessible to large numbers of people. NDMDA has grown from a single chapter in Chicago in 1978 to 250 chapters today. And NAMI, based in Arlington, Virginia, has 1,046 affiliate chapters and 140,000 members.

Janet, who has been a member of NDMDA for three years, says that when she was diagnosed in 1979 after eight years of unexplained mood swings, she was so ashamed she told no one about her condition. But at a wedding dinner in 1988, the woman sitting next to her—a total stranger—confided to her that she suffered from manic-depressive illness. Janet says it was "in the stars that we should happen to meet and have instant rapport." She told Janet that a support group was being formed and invited her to join.

"I didn't want to," Janet recalls. "I didn't want to sit around with a bunch of crazy people. And I didn't know what good it could possibly do me. But this woman insisted, so reluctantly I went to a meeting.

"I was stunned. I had my own stereotypes, and this was not what I expected. The people didn't look crazy and they didn't act crazy. They were, for the most part, well educated, well dressed, and very articulate. There was a woman who was pregnant, concerned about passing the illness to her child. And a man whose wife had just left him because she couldn't tolerate his mood swings. He was in tears. It was a revelation to me."

Since that time, Janet has missed only two meetings and says she derives enormous comfort from each one she attends. "Going through a manic or depressive episode is scary," she says. "You worry that it is going to happen again, and that you could be sent to a hospital and put away for life. There is a fear you always have—please God, don't let it happen.

"I thought I was the only one who felt that way, who spent my life tripping on eggshells, but I found that this is universal. So is shame. I was so ashamed of having these moods, of behaving in weird ways, then having to face people the next day. I believed that people were afraid of me."

The support groups have given Janet more confidence in herself. Even though she is a rapid cycler and has had difficulty finding effective medication, she gains strength from talking to people with similar troubles. From the lecture series initiated by her chapter, she has learned about the significance of postpartum depression, new drugs, manic depression and pregnancy, and, perhaps most important, how to monitor herself.

"I have learned to recognize the signs of incipient mania," Janet says. "If I don't sleep for two nights or I get irritable or if people start looking at me funny, I know something is going on. It's time to call my doctor. An episode caught in the second day is different from one caught in the second month. Each of us has a pattern, and now I know what to look for. I'm not ashamed anymore, and I've encouraged friends to tell me if they think I'm acting strangely.

"Before I came here, I thought constantly about this terrible thing that had happened to me, this thing that I couldn't even talk to my best friends about. It dominated my life and paralyzed me. It kept me from living. Here I have found the freedom to go on with my life. I can discuss my condition with others and know that I'm not being judged. If you have aching feet, you like to hear that someone else has aching feet, too. That's the way we human beings are."

CHAPTER SEVEN

ACTING IT OUT

Did you ever think, "I wish I could be at my own funeral so I could hear what they'd say about me?" Well, making the television movie "Call Me Anna" in 1990 about my manic-depressive illness was a little bit like that. There were many, many times once we began to cast and shoot the film that I wondered, "What in God's name made me do this? What will the neighbors think? What will the children think?"

In the very first scene, where I played myself, you could hear my screams in the dark, those weird-sounding screams I used to make, and then you got a glimpse of me crouched in a corner banging my head against the wall. When I read the script, I thought it would be a tough scene for me; it didn't occur to me that when the time came I was going to have any sort of little monitor going off in my brain saying, "Why are you doing this, Anna?"

We rehearsed that scene once at a quarter of the tempo at which it was going to go eventually so the crew could see where their lights needed to go and where they needed to place the camera. And then we had to rehearse up to speed so they would know how quickly they needed to react to things. It was at that point that I did this wild, wrenching screaming which I have not, thank God, done for a very long time. And as I was preparing to do that, the way I would do it if I were acting someone else, I got scared, embarrassed. The shame of behaving that way in front of strangers really got to me. I remember in real life feeling really ashamed, too. I started to tighten up, to freeze. I didn't know how I was going to do it. I took a few deep breaths and told my-self that if I really wanted the impact of what manic depression is like to be seen by those who need to see it, then I had to do this as fully and freely as I could.

As I reminded myself of my goal—using the power of televi-sion to get information to people about depressive illness—I resolved to let fly. I took another deep breath, and then I did it. And the people who had to watch me—the crew, the director—because that's their jobs, didn't quite know where to look after-ward. If they looked at me, would it be an invasion of my pri-vacy? I was told by a number of them later that although they hadn't necessarily witnessed the kind of behavior they had just seen, each one had had contact with someone like that, someone who was mentally ill. Our director, Gil Cates, and crew were so caring and so supportive—anything but judgmental. And so, al-though I felt very bruised and battered when the scene was over, I also felt safe doing it.

But I knew that this might be a discomforting scene for people to see, even for strangers, because it's Patty Duke playing herself. I also knew that people might be more interested for that very reason—it was so real because it *was me*. And as long as they watched and got the information about this illness—that, yes, it is awful, but it is controllable, it is fixable—that was the whole point. The tendency to want to look away is something that we've been doing for too long when it comes to manic depression.

Under usual circumstances, when I see myself on the screen, there is a strange kind of objectivity that comes over me. I can praise my work and I can damn it, and everything in between. But this scene that I did had an extra little spin on it. I've had to admit that my objectivity about this experience will always be skewed.

In some ways, doing that scene made me think back to *The Miracle Worker*—the physicality of it and the intelligence trying to get out. That's what I see when I look at my version of Helen Keller. I see that brilliant soul trying to fight the shackles.

It's impossible for me to describe now what was going on in

155

the mind and spirit of the twelve-year-old Patty Duke when I did *The Miracle Worker*. At best, it's guesswork because, at twelve, I didn't know what I was doing. I didn't dissect it. I just did it. I think it was my lack of self-consciousness that made the way I played the role so believable.

My emotional identification with Helen Keller was strong. In retrospect, I believe that I could identify with Helen, this blind, deaf child, who was trapped physically while I was trapped emotionally. Without knowing what I was doing, I used Helen as a vehicle to temporarily break out of my prison eight times a week. She was a life jacket for me. The character of Helen allowed me to beat the bejezus out of an adult (Annie Sullivan, Helen's teacher) every night. Today we might call that some form of therapy.

In the last scene of *The Miracle Worker*, the moment of impact for me—even to this day, when I see it—is the moment when the teacher screams, "She knows." I will never be able to explain why the impact of those words was so enormous for me every single time. I didn't know why for me, as a child, it stirred up all it did and evoked the ecstasy I felt.

It was a scene where Helen—after she says her first word, "wawa" for water—takes from her mother the keys to the dining room, the scene of so many struggles between Helen and the teacher, walks across the stage, and hands them to Annie Sullivan. There was an incredible melancholy for me in taking this symbol away from my mother (in the play) and giving them to this relative stranger (the teacher) whom I somehow loved. As a child, my feelings were simple and pure. In retrospect, I can see the analogy of being taken from my mother and given to the Rosses. Of course, in the play, I was going to a healthy place. In real life, I was not.

But the docudrama of *Call Me Anna* that I did for television was different—totally different—for me because, in addition to its being about my life, it was the first time I was part producer, part writer, part actress.

I had worked with Gil Cates on a television movie after my

book *Call Me Anna* was published in 1987. Besides loving how he directs—he puts a lot of fine-tuning into acting—I liked him as a person. I liked his grace, his style, his dignity, and his caring about people. I began to think that if we were ever going to turn *Call Me Anna* into a docudrama, this was the man I wanted to do it with.

However, so much time had gone by—it was now 1989—that nobody was making any more offers. But Gil read the book, mulled it over, and then took the idea to ABC. That was as far as we had to go. They wanted to do it with the caveat that I play myself, as much as possible.

So Gil and I made a list of writers, and the name of John McGreavey came up on top. I had met him years earlier, and he had done some wonderful television movies. He understood how I felt, and gave me the freedom to make script changes I thought were necessary.

Still, I had a lot of trepidation. We had to kick around how you telescope forty-two years into ninety minutes or less. What was going to be left out? What had to stay in?

For me, it was simple. I wanted the movie to track my illness. Certainly, some of the show-business aspects would have to be there; they would be obvious by their absence. But mostly it was to be the story of a little girl from a dysfunctional family, transferred to yet another dysfunctional family. And the goal was to explain a very complicated medical condition to people while they were still being entertained.

It was important to me that the docudrama be a story of my illness, not of other people's weaknesses. I didn't want it to be an exposé of other people's foibles, and I didn't want people who are still living to have their lives intruded upon.

When the script was finished, I read it to my mother, very carefully. There were some parts where she cried. But she said, "That's the way it was. You know I couldn't do anything else. I just couldn't." I answered, "I know that. I just want to make sure *you* know that: that your illness rendered you incapable of doing anything else."

157

Even though I knew a little about writing and producing and directing, you're not really fully aware until you put those boots on. So all of this was very educational for me. Once I heard myself saying to the associate producer, Peggy Griffin, with whom I shared an office, "Oh, my God, I'm liking this producer stuff."

What I liked about it is that the producing is the decision making, that I was able to use my creativity but also be organized enough to size up a situation and make a decision about it. How much creative license was I willing to take with the way my life was portrayed, for instance? Questions came up about all kinds of things, such as: What color was a certain lamp? Or was there a flag on your father's coffin?

This was a milestone for me because, all of my life, making decisions simply wasn't within my realm of possibility. When I was growing up, the Rosses made them for me, even to the basic act of taking away my name. As my illness progressed, my mind was rarely organized enough to make rational, thoughtful choices of any kind. I just sort of drifted along, and what happened happened. Now I was really functioning as a full, whole human being.

I didn't have that other-worldly sensation of mania that I used to have, but I didn't miss it because I never really accomplished anything that I could call my own during those times. I could never complete anything. I could certainly never have co-produced a movie. I was all so fragmented and crazy. Even my conversation is more creative now than it ever was when I was out of control. I may have been more colorful then. I may have been able to make more puns. My alliteration may have been fascinating. But I certainly wasn't capable of really communicating with anybody because I never really heard what they said.

One of the hardest things for me was staying away while most of that movie was being made. Other actresses were playing me at different stages of my life, and I wanted to be sensitive to their needs. It is difficult enough to play someone who is still alive. I've done it. You feel enormous responsibility. And sometimes there are things that are out of your control and you can't live up to the responsibility the way you want to. Having been through those kinds of wars, I understood what those young women, the ones who were going to be me at different ages, were about to embark on. I also understood that, to a person, there was tremendous love and respect for me. But that can also be a burden when you're trying to do your work.

I remember the first reading of the script. We were all there, sixty-some of us, and we were reading aloud. A first reading takes place in a pretty rarefied atmosphere, and here it was the only time we would all be together. In some ways, first-reading performances are just raw and kind of exciting. In other ways, we're "fumfering" all over the place, trying to figure out who plays who, and so on. There was a strangeness for me . . . I could not take my eyes off the script, even though I certainly knew all the words. My brother, Raymond, who played my father in the movie, was sitting just to my left and slightly behind me, and to hear those echoes of the past when everyone read their lines was just too weird. Also, there was a little bit of the competitive actor that came out. I wanted to "play my part good." And I knew from the reading that the other people were good, too. Some of them were younger actors who were getting all this information about me for the first time. It was fascinating to peek down this long table and to see the looks on these faces of kids whose knowledge of me had been gained from watching reruns of *The Patty Duke Show* on *Nick at Night*.

When it was over, there was much hugging and kissing and wishing good luck. Then we had rehearsals for a couple of days with smaller groups of people, and it was during those rehearsals that the director and I realized it was probably going to be a lot easier and more efficient if the other actors didn't feel that I was lurking around, reliving every second and judging every twitch they made. So, having made that decision, I felt very generous and very trusting.

And then they started to work. And I felt very left out. I would be home in Encino playing out in front of the house with Kevin on his fire engine, and there were people, elsewhere in the city, doing my life. Gil Cates called me at least once every day, which is a big deal for a director. He's on location and he has to leave the set. He has to find a phone that works, get through—all that stuff. He would tell me how it was going, and then he'd say, "Are you okay?" And I would always say, "Yeah, I'm fine. Just fine. Fine." Then I'd hang up the phone and cry. Finally one day he called in the afternoon—I had just been wondering what they all might be doing at that moment—and he said, "How're you doing?" There was this little catch in my throat and I said, "Gil, it's really hard. The only analogy I can give you is did you ever take your kid to the emergency room and somebody said, 'Would you just stand outside, please?' You know that you've done the right thing and you know that the experts are doing all that you cannot do. But you feel so empty. And impotent. And lost. That's how I feel."

My poor husband entertained me the way he would entertain Kevin. One day when the three of us—Mike, Kevin, and I—were having a particularly good time, suddenly my mind jumped over to "Gee, I wonder what they're shooting now." Then I laughed, and Mike, of course, didn't know what was so funny. So he asked me what I was laughing about. And I said, "I just thought of something. Here we are. I'm having the best time with my husband and my baby, we're eating food we like and having fun together—and there are about sixty people on the other side of town doing the shit of my life." So, once again, humor allowed me to see it in a perspective that made it okay.

That movie was a turning point for me. It enabled me to review that time of my life and to be finished with it. When Sean saw it, he said, "Mom, how do we even discuss this? As a filmmaker, I can come at you from five thousand different angles. And none of them are in the 'I hated it, I loved it' category. What can I say about the scene showing your freak-outs, when you were flying around the room? When I looked away from the television and just listened, it was like old times. But there's no point in doing something like this if you don't take risks. You took the ultimate risk, Mom. And I admire you."

Actors take risks all the time. So do painters and writers and sculptors and poets. We put ourselves on the line. But I have always thought of myself more as a re-creative artist than as a creative one because what I do is re-create someone else's work. After all, somebody else put the words there for me to say. A novelist or a poet has to get an original idea. So I thought I was just a sort of puppet. It is only recently that I've come to believe that it *is* creative to be able to interpret someone's words and breathe life into them. And certainly I have wondered, mostly when queried about it, if my manic-depressive illness in some way fueled my creativity.

I know my son Mack thinks so. He thinks the illness gave me the capacity to be what he calls "an extraordinary actress." And even though I don't have the manias anymore, he thinks the residuals are there. You don't forget. Those memories, those contrasts between the highs and lows, stay with you: the access to something deep inside you, the ability to feel intensely, to have a heightened sense of awareness.

I chose for many years to call whatever it was I had a gift. A gift that I came with. Maybe—and I don't think I'll ever know this—maybe the gift was mania. Who knows? I do think there was a connection—on the manic side, not the depression side. I think it is possible that the mania—though it had not really reared its ugly head when I was a child—may have been at work in a positive way for me. The question is: Could I have been a successful actress without the disease? The gift and the curse. If I had been diagnosed at twelve and began the medication, could I have played Helen Keller the way I did? I think so. Lithium doesn't take away the ability to be creative. It's not like having a lobotomy. Who knows? I have to accept the givens. That's how I look at it philosophically. The givens are that I have the disease, so it may have been a component.

And the ability to feel intensely the highs and the lows, to have the capacity to be at one with the human condition, is something

161

I wouldn't have traded for anything. I would not have liked to go through life dulled, even though there was a time when I did envy people who were dull. Oh, God, for a long time I wanted to be like them. They weren't afraid of life, they weren't afraid of death, they weren't afraid of anything. It took me a long time to recognize that they also didn't experience one one-millionth of what I did on this planet. So I stopped envying them.

This topic—the creativity/manic-depression connection—is one that I have shied away from for a lot of reasons. One is a kind of false humility—the very thrill of being on a list with some of the most remarkable people who have ever lived is very real to me. And it made easier to accept that I may have had a fine madness that Abraham Lincoln and Robert Lowell and Ernest Hemingway and so many other luminaries probably had, too. On the other hand, I don't want people to believe that manic-depressive illness and creativity necessarily go hand in hand. And I don't want people who are manic-depressive, but who are not creative, to be ignored. I continue to be surprised at how many of us there are, whether we're in the arts or not.

But I can look at my work now, and I think that whatever it is that makes up me—and that chemical imbalance is surely part of it—gave me a certain amount of energy and insight at a very young age that allowed me to do things that most little kids don't. I can look at The Miracle Worker now, thirty years later, and say, "How did she do that? How did she know how to play that the way she did?"

Well, I don't know how I knew. There were moments when I played Helen Keller when I felt literally transported in time and space and reality. I didn't have the ability to express that except in retrospect, but I still know what it felt like, so I can describe it very graphically. I was transported. And occasionally it happens now. Every once in a while, there's one little moment when you're just not there. Whoever it is you're inventing is there. And the older I get, the more the skill is molecular. The sense of safety I have now that I'm controlled with lithium lets me focus my energy on my performance. I'm not derailed by the mania or the depression.

I don't take it lightly when I say there are moments in the theater that are to me a religious experience. The ability to feel what other people feel is almost mystical. It is a mental, spiritual, and physical, indeed chemical, communion of people. I have the sensation that I've sent something out there into the audience and I feel this wave come back. It really *is* an energy. It's an actual thing. If you had special cameras, you could probably take a picture of it. An X ray of the soul. Someone baring her soul and a whole bunch of people embracing it and sending a piece of theirs back. It's a thrill when I send it out there and they get it. And we share this one infinitesimal moment of unity.

Of course, I have just as many nerves as anyone else when I'm going out "naked" in front of the public. But I have a comfort with people that comes through. I'm not afraid of them—except the ones taking notes for the morning paper. Part of that comes with confidence, I think. And then there's that unknown quantity I've never been able to define. I don't know what it is, but I'm able to take myself and, I hope, the audience to another reality, to another time and space.

When I cry onstage now, usually it's quite organic. It comes right out of the moment. I don't often use the classic Stanislavsky method of going to something in my own past—at least, not on a conscious level. It is very rarely necessary for me to do that. But I think that's because there is this swell of commonality with other people—and my imagination. The same imagination I had when I was that little twelve-year-old girl still exists for me. I may be a little more restricted now, either by my physical insecurities or by my emotional ones, but the imagination is still there. And the ability to drop myself into that other life form is very real. I keep it sharply tuned.

When I'm onstage, I can be obsessed. I know, for instance, that every time the camera rolls, you don't have to be perfect the first time. You can do take two and take three and take four and take five and on into the double digits until you get it right. But unlike other people I have worked with, for me every take is the last one. There was a time when if I was ever so slightly off—some-

163

thing that nobody else would ever have noticed—I was bereft, and the second chance didn't matter. Even though I took the second chance and fixed it, I didn't like anyone out there seeing that I wasn't perfect the first time.

For instance, I might have been in a scene where I had to walk across a driveway and stop just before I passed a basketball on the grass. If I was talking in the scene and I didn't notice and passed the basketball, I just wanted to scream inside. If somebody else missed his mark, I wouldn't have a problem about it, but I couldn't allow myself that kind of mistake.

It's hard for me to pick apart, of course, precisely how much of my obsession about what I do onstage has to do with my illness and how much has to do with the training I got from the Rosses. We get into an area that is very gray for me. Did this come from my life with the Rosses and that training and that fear that they would say I hadn't done it right? Or is it my own demands that I make of myself? But there is *something* . . . something is going on inside me, in my eyes, in the cells of my face that is, in a strange way, so alive and yet so mysterious. Is that mystery the gift? Is it the illness? Is it a certain intelligence? Or fear? In my opinion, it has to be a combination of all of those things.

In any case, this profession I'm in is almost a manic-depressive's dream society: it's full of ups and downs, and that's how people describe it. You always hear someone say, "I'm in down time." My up and down times in the business didn't always coincide with the highs and lows of my manic-depressive cycles, but I think that was probably one of the pluses. In some ways I was like Lazarus—I'd be depressed in bed, but then I'd get up, go do a Movie of the Week. And everybody was happy. I even joke now about how the kids would say things like, "Oh, God, Mom, it's been two weeks now. You better get a job." And maybe it was just a smart-alec thing that kids say, but maybe behind it was the recognition "If there are many more weeks of this without a job, you know where we're going with this woman."

And when I was manic, I was able to put some of that energy

somewhere, be applauded sometimes, even given awards for playing roles where the characters exhibited really antisocial behavior. I've played a hooker in *Rattle of a Simple Man*, a drug addict in *Police Story*, a terrorist in *The Streets of San Francisco*, and a child abuser in an after-school special, *Please Don't Hit Me, Mom*. My son Sean played the abused child.

In another business, I guess I would not have been able to get away with it for as long. In a way, directors and producers who let actors get away with any kind of weird, even maniacal behavior are "enablers," just like the people who go along with or make excuses for the behavior of those who drink or take drugs.

And for all kinds of reasons, society has excused and cultivated eccentric behavior in artists and actors. It's colorful, it makes for good newsprint. What is it about us that we need, that we're titillated by, excited by celebrity gossip? And the way we've evolved in the last twenty years, the stranger the gossip the better. It used to be we were satisfied with who was sleeping with whom, but that no longer does it for us. Maybe it's just a case of misery loving company. This is not to suggest that I think people maliciously want someone to stay sick. I think they just see celebrity gossip as a form of entertainment and don't take it as seriously as they would bizarre behavior in other walks of life.

If you're a stockbroker or a surgeon or a bank teller or a supermarket checker and your behavior gets crazy and destructive, I think questions are asked and people are fired more quickly. In show business, there is more tolerance. It's dismissed as eccentric actress behavior—unless you are costing a production money: not showing up on time or not knowing your lines. Even that is tolerated sometimes. But when it boils down to dollars and cents, it isn't cute for too long.

And isn't it interesting that both show business and manic-depressive illness are so totally unpredictable? There is such vagary about what it takes either to get the next job or to do the job that you've got. Talk about an inexact science! When teenagers or kids in their early twenties who want to be in the theater or television ask me *what it takes*, I am absolutely at a loss for

165

words. There is no plan, there is no right way, and I don't think you ever get used to that. In the rest of the world it seems that if you go from A to B to C to D, you're going to wind up at E, and that ain't necessarily so here. Now, none of this means, of course, that you have to be manic-depressive to be an actor. But there are elements of craziness to this business that seem somehow to match the illness.

And it never stops, this roller coaster. You never stop having to prove yourself. Maybe that's the penalty of being in creative work, or maybe it's the challenge. But it makes me mad. It never feels good. Those of us who have been around for a few years have come up with some platitudes that work for a little while—things like "You won't appreciate the successes unless you've got the down times, too." But even when you very seriously think about finding an alternative career that may be as creatively satisfying, as ego-gratifying, but maybe more predictable, you don't do it. There is this terrible, terrible, almost tidal pull that nudges at you and whispers, "Just one more time. Let me try it one more time." And, of course, the ability to perform doesn't go away. I suspect that as an old lady, I'll be trying it one more time.

But who knows? I've never planned a thing in my whole life. I never planned to be an actress. I never planned to get married. I never planned to have a baby. It was just all sort of thrust upon me. And I always felt like the other shoe was going to drop. I didn't know what the shoe looked like or what size it was. Some days the other shoe might be: I'm going to kill myself. Or just this strange foreboding that didn't have a name. I always felt that.

Another thing I've felt that has given me strength is the messianic message I felt or heard back in 1977, the time I ended up in Dr. Arlen's home at two in the morning. Dr. Arlen insisted I had had a psychotic episode. I said—and still say—it wasn't. It is a dicey issue between us, and we haven't talked about it in a long time. It's one of those things that will probably never get resolved.

That night when I was so manicky, John and I were making love. Suddenly I experienced a sensation of other-worldliness—

not necessarily being out of my body, but just an awareness. I said aloud, "Oh, my God, John, there *is* life after death."

I felt I had left my body. Not in the classical sense you've read about, where you look down at a scene that is happening. It was just that I wasn't "locked" into me at that point. That sensation continued for a little bit, and I felt an attraction to whatever this pull was—this promise.

Then John got nervous and frightened. When I perceived his fright, I started to feel my own. So I began yelling, "I'm dying. I'm leaving. Call me back. Call me back." And then I said to him, "Hit me on the back," and I almost kept chanting, "Hit me on the back, hit me on the back." Why I thought his hitting me on the back would solve the problem, I don't know.

So what else is he supposed to do? He's trapped. He hit me on the back. And I said, "Harder. Hit me harder." And he hit me harder, and then I felt "back."

I can't describe any feeling of reentry. But I just felt safe. I spent a little time frightened, but the basic thing that I came away with was a sense of comfort, that I had been given an answer which finally worked for the fear of death I have.

I remember being very protective about that one moment. True, it was only a sensation. There was no vision. I didn't see anything. But I had the feeling, "Oh, my God, I will see you again." Finally, after all the years of panic attacks about death, the continuing torture, something answered me and it satisfied.

I was very angry with Dr. Arlen that night when he wanted me to agree that what I had experienced was a psychotic episode, part of my manic depression, and that in order to get well I had to give it up. When Dr. Arlen talks about it, it is in this very down-to-earth, logical, borderline-analytic way. He says when people feel this way it's because there is still something unresolved in them, something they still carry guilt for.

Well, I have every reason in the world to believe everything that man says, but I can't imagine what the hell could be left that I haven't resolved, that I feel guilty about, that I think I did wrong. Did I drive my father to drink? No, I don't think I caused that. Have I reconciled my situation with my mother? I think as well as anyone on the face of the earth could. So there's this missing link. It's very missing. And to this day—you can hear it in my voice when I talk about it—it makes me mad.

I have been clinging to the memory of that night even in the face of wanting to be well today and taking my medication. I have been holding on to it privately since 1977. But I haven't said it aloud because if I do, I'm not cured, right?

I've tried to fit that vision into a healthy life and still be able to believe it. I've listened to church bells and said to myself, "I think so-and-so who lives next door is normal and she goes to church several times a day. So why can't I have my little shrine—this experience that seemed so real and so true?"

Maybe it *was* part and parcel of a psychotic episode. But maybe it wasn't. Maybe it is part of the *gift* of my illness, the capacity of my mind to wander to far-off places. Maybe it is, in some way, connected to creativity. In any case, if I give it up completely, I give it up at a price. And as long as it doesn't take me down a manic road, I think it's okay to still get some comfort from it.

I often think that those of us who have this illness find our own "creative" ways of surviving. One of them is certainly an extraordinary ability to manipulate people and situations. Even as a child, I was constantly jockeying in order to survive—figuring out which was the safest thing I could do or the safest place I could be. Like all the stories I made up about having bad dreams or staying in bed for weekends just to blot out the reality.

You think you're so clever, not unlike an addict or a drunk. You are funny. You can spin great tales. Part of the reason we're so good at spinning them is that we believe them while we're spinning them. There are times we are very devious, creatively devious. To carry out the kind of bizarre behavior we do takes a certain amount of guile. None of this is premeditated or purposeful. It isn't like Haldeman and Erlichman in some back room contriving some scheme. It is just a facility to arrange things the way we like. An instinct. We don't even know we're doing it. It's as much a symptom of the illness as going on outlandish spanding sprees.

Sometimes we get away with it for a long time. Some people never catch on. I think others can see through it, but during our manic phases we are usually very well-liked: belle-of-the-ball, man-about-town types, charming, attractive to people. There is something magnetic about us. Over time, I don't think it wears well because all the other negative facets start to click in. And certainly the charm, creative though it may be, wears thin for someone who's living in the same house with the manic-depressive. We're the kind of people you like to hear stories about, but not people you'd want to live with for very long. Now that I'm controlled by medication, I haven't lost that ability to manipulate. I just use it better. And sometimes I'm very naughty with it, but not destructive.

But I can also identify easily with all of the manic-depressives who are not in the least creative. For so many years of my life, whatever my public persona, I saw myself as a drone, a compulsive drone. The elaborate dinners I used to make, for instance — some people called them creative, but I never saw them that way at all. I never got any satisfaction from having made them. I felt a strange sense that someone had directed me to prepare those meals; therefore, I didn't even experience a sense of accomplishment or joy from having cooked interesting dishes or set a beautiful table.

Everyone in my family ate the dinners, they liked them, and they'd say, "Good dinner, Mom." A nice little round of applause for Mom. But I felt nothing. Still, when I'd have potluck dinners and someone would bring a salad, say, I would be, honest to God, sad with envy. Look how nicely she cut the carrots with the little curlicues. Or look at the way she shaped the little circles of butter. Why didn't I think of that? I was never right enough, never good enough, never healthy enough, never pretty enough. Even when I wasn't in bed, when I was "functioning," the insistence on failure was always there. I couldn't take a compliment. Of course, in social settings, I knew how. I had been taught. Someone com-

169

pliments you—you plug into number 43B and say the right words, the right thank-yous. But when I didn't need the social smoke screen, I couldn't hear anything nice anyone said about me. It wasn't that I thought John was lying or the kids didn't mean it. I didn't think about *them* at all, or their sincerity; being praised just felt false to me.

Only after I was diagnosed did I become aware that I expressed myself creatively. I noticed that I *was* funny, that I could tell stories in a colorful way that made people laugh. I began to respect my command of language and my ability to communicate. And I really enjoyed it. It didn't matter what the topic was, it was a thrill to be talking to someone and see in their eyes that I had made a connection, that we had a communion of spirit. I still get high from that. When I talk to groups of people about manic depression I get so thrilled about using the right words, the words that make people able to come up to me later in restaurants or public bathrooms or in the supermarket and talk to me about themselves or someone in their family.

Since I was diagnosed and treated, I have never been more creative. Now, some people might look at my career and say, "She's more creative? She hasn't won an Emmy in years." What matters is: Do *I* think I'm more creative? Is my work satisfying to me?

I'm able to be inspired now, when I read a script, about how to interpret a role . . . or when I sit down with a blank piece of paper to write a speech. My God, I've never been able to write in my life. And now I see a blank piece of paper and all of a sudden thoughts flow onto it, and they make sense, and there are moments when I think they are pretty profound or moving or at least able to touch somebody in some way. I know I couldn't have done that ten years ago. I simply couldn't have. I have looked at some of the writing I did in the seventies, diary-like things, and they are ravings. And they're not even interesting ravings. They're just rambling.

I know that without treatment I would have never been able to harness my creativity in such a successful way. I like the word "harness" rather than "balance" because the word "balance" scares people who are manic. They think if they are "balanced" they are boring or nonproductive. That's why I don't even read too much in the literature that speaks to the alliance of creativity and mental illness.

Maybe there *is* a concern within me that I haven't dealt with yet, that I could be seduced by something that says you will be far more creative if you are out of control. And I know that some people are afraid to take medication because they are afraid they will lose their creativity and genius. But I don't want to tamper with the way I am now. I feel great. And I'm from the old school. If it ain't broke, don't fix it. There *have been* days when I was rehearsing some movie or play that I felt like the dullest, most uninspired lump of a so-called actress. Everyone feels that way sometimes. But I didn't think my well had dried up. Once you've experienced what I have, you know it's there, and you'll find a way back to it again.

I'm often asked by people whether I would ever stop taking my medication. I can't imagine that. Even if I did and went into a manic episode, I don't believe I would be more creative. I can't imagine needing any kind of creativity so much that I would give up the balance I've found—the balance that I ached for, that I longed for, that I screamed for, that I cried for, for so many years of my life.

CHAPTER EIGHT

THE CREATIVITY CONNECTION

The audience in the concert hall of the John F. Kennedy Center for the Performing Arts in Washington, D.C., was gathered for a unique and gripping event. The National Symphony Orchestra was ready. Dr. Kay Redfield Jamison came to the microphone.

Dr. Jamison is well known for her interest in the link between creativity and mood disorders; she has written a major study on mood disorders among British writers and artists and is author of the book *Touched with Fire: Manic-Depressive Illness and the Artistic Temperament*. She is president of the Manic-Depressive Illness Foundation, to increase public awareness and understanding about the nature and treatment of manic-depressive and depressive diseases.

"Welcome," said Dr. Jamison, "to 'Moods and Music.' Tonight's concert revolves around the lives and music of five composers: George Frideric Handel, Robert Schumann, Hugo Wolf, Hector Berlioz, and Gustav Mahler. These men were extremely different in personality and background, but all of them share in common a powerfully destructive disease.

"By presenting the lives and music of these manic-depressive composers, we hope to convey a sense of the emotional chaos and destructiveness of this disease. We have chosen music because nothing can so induce—or capture—moods. Their music deeply expresses the range of human emotions: from joy to sorrow, and from exultation to despair . . . "

From the opening selection—the triumphant and exultant music of Handel's Coronation Anthem, "Zadok the Priest," to the last ecstatic note of "O Glorious Prince" from his oratorio *Belshazzar*—the audience was mesmerized, both by the music and by the eloquent explanations of how that music reflected the agonies and ecstasies of those who wrote it.

◆

MUSICIANS AND MOOD DISORDERS

While the men whose music was featured did not have a name to describe their moods and behavior, the way they lived, their letters, their journal writings, and the writing of their biographers—graphically quoted in the concert program—portray what we now know to be depressive or manic-depressive illness. The words used to express the intensity of joy and misery the composers felt are words of their time—different from those we might use today but poignantly conveying the depths of their emotions.

In 1785 Charles Burney, George Frideric Handel's biographer, wrote: "Handel's general look was somewhat heavy and sour; but when he *did* smile, it was his sire the sun, bursting out of a black cloud."

Robert Schumann, in 1849, wrote: " . . . And if we musicians live so often, as you know we do, on sunny heights, the sadness of reality cuts all the deeper when it lies naked before our eyes."

Handel, unlike the other composers whose work was presented that evening, left little written record of his psychological and emotional world. But in light of his recurrent mood cycles, modern psychiatric opinion agrees that he was a victim of cyclothymia, one of the milder forms of manic-depressive illness. Handel had long periods of high energy and extraordinary productivity, interrupted by episodes of depression that blunted his

173

ability to work. His major depressions were called "nervous breakdowns," and during those times he was pessimistic and despondent, had a poor appetite and difficulty sleeping—the hallmarks of depression.

Typical of those with manic-depressive illness, Handel's mood swings cycled with the seasons: depressed times came in the late spring and early summer; late summer and early autumn brought bursts of productivity. In the early 1740s, his librettist Charles Jennens described Handel as having a head "more full of maggots than ever." His biographer Percy Young wrote: "The maggots came from mental derangement on the one hand and flooding inspiration on the other."

The Kennedy Center audience gasped when Robert Winter, professor of music at the University of California at Los Angeles, related Robert Schumann's family history. His father, an author, translator, and publisher, was an unstable, ambitious, and brooding man who reportedly suffered a nervous breakdown from which he never fully recovered. Like his son, he worked in phenomenal bursts of energy. During one eighteen-month period, he wrote seven novels. Robert's mother suffered from recurrent depressions. His sister committed suicide. One of his sons went insane in his early twenties and was confined to an asylum for thirty-one years. Another son became a morphine addict.

In intense letters and passionate confessions in his diaries, Schumann described his own struggles with mania and melancholy. He wrote to Clara Wieck, the woman he eventually married: "In the night between the 17th and 18th of October [1833], I was seized with the worst fear a man can have, the worst punishment Heaven can inflict—the fear of losing one's reason . . . Terror drove me from place to place. My breath failed me as I pictured my brain paralyzed. Ah, Clara, no one knows the suffering, the sickness, the despair, except those so crushed."

Eight years later, in 1841, Clara wrote in her own diary: "On Tuesday Robert finished his symphony; so begun and ended in four days." Schumann himself said that he sketched out the Spring Symphony in a single "fiery hour."

In 1849, another year of extraordinary productivity, Schumann wrote: "I have been extremely busy this whole year. One has to work as long as the daylight is there."

The daylight did not last long for Schumann. In 1854, after a period of wildly fluctuating moods, he rushed out of his house sobbing and threw himself in the Rhine. He was rescued and placed in an insane asylum, where he died of self-starvation in 1856. He was forty-six.

Another of the featured composers, Hector Berlioz, described his affliction as a "moral sickness, a disease of isolation. There are . . . two kinds of spleen," he wrote in his memoirs, "one mocking, active, passionate, malignant; the other morose and wholly passive, when one's only wish is for silence and solitude and the oblivion of sleep. For anyone possessed by this latter kind, nothing has meaning, the destruction of a world would hardly move him. At such times I could wish the earth were a shell filled with gunpowder, to which I would put a match for my diversion."

Gustav Mahler lamented that he was a prisoner of his mood swings. When he was nineteen, he wrote to a childhood friend: "The fires of a supreme zest for living and the most gnawing desire for death alternate in my heart, sometimes in the course of a single hour. I know only one thing: I cannot go on like this . . . "

Dr. Jamison produced this highly unusual concert as a way of cultivating interest in severe mental illness. She wanted to lessen the stigma of such illness by showing the enormous contributions of "these full human beings, who suffered enormously, but gave enormously, too. They are not just people off on a back ward somewhere," she said. "Mental illness is just not that simple."

While many of manic depression's victims have lived tempestuous lives that ended in suicide or confinement in mental institutions, they may also have made brilliant contributions to society: Lord Byron and Edgar Allan Poe, Anne Sexton and Virginia Woolf, Vincent van Gogh, who completed more than three hundred paintings in the year and a half before he killed himself.

175

Their names form an impressive honor roll of creativity and accomplishment.

MOOD DISORDERS AND LEADERSHIP

While there have been studies on the relationship between excellence in the arts and mood disorders, there has not been a rigorous investigation of the link between leadership and depressive and manic-depressive illness. But it is known that many great leaders have demonstrated excesses in rage and energy and also suffered from despairing depressions. It is not possible to go back in time and say with certainty that they were depressive or manic-depressive, but their biographies show that their characteristics closely match those of people with mood disorders.

Dr. Jamison says that "an early sense of destiny, often having a grandiose quality to it, is not uncommon in great leaders. Inspiration is as important to powerful leadership as it is to creativity in the arts," she says. "Hypomanic states share many characteristics with certain types of impassioned authority: high energy level, enthusiasm, intensity of emotion, persuasion by mood, charisma and contagion of spirit, gregariousness, increased belief in oneself and one's ideas, optimism, heightened alertness, unpredictable mood changes, mercurial temperament. The ability to inspire—through words, actions, or traditions—is especially important in leadership."

Oliver Cromwell, the seventeenth-century commander-in-chief and Lord Protector of England, has been described by his biographers as manic-depressive or cyclothymic.

Abraham Lincoln's depressions, some of which were suicidal, are legendary. New York's Dr. Ronald Fieve has called him a "mild bipolar manic-depressive," but his depressions were more obvious than his highs.

Menachem Begin, the controversial former Prime Minister of Israel, was subject to sweeping mood swings throughout his public career. Periods of abject depression rotated with times of frenetic activity. Often he worked with a vengeance, then retreated into bleak seclusion, avoiding all but the most important public appearances.

Winston Churchill's biographer Anthony Storr describes him as cyclothymic, with alternating periods of severe depression and high energy that sometimes affected his judgment. In *Churchill: The Man*, Storr wrote: " . . . had he been a stable and equable man, he could never have inspired the nation. In 1940, when all the odds were against Britain, a leader of sober judgment might well have concluded we were finished."

He also wrote: "All those who worked with Churchill paid tribute to the enormous fertility of his new ideas, the inexhaustible stream of invention which poured from him . . . [they] also agreed that he needed the most severe restraint put upon him, and that many of his ideas, if they had been put into practice, would have been utterly disastrous."

◆

BUSINESS TYCOONS AND MOOD SWINGS

"You don't want to label people," says Dr. Ronald Fieve, who heads the Foundation for Depression and Manic Depression in New York City. "But the roller-coaster existence of many tycoons that we read about in *The New York Times* and *Fortune* magazine are not dissimilar to what you see in manic-depressive patients. They, too, are enhanced by their manic-depressive temperaments."

Dr. Fieve describes what he calls the "manic-depressive entrepreneur." Long, hectic days, marked by no sleep, nonstop talk, risky deals, and boundless energy—abruptly truncated by plunges into bleak depression—characterize some of the country's highest profile business leaders.

"Personnel departments of many offices look for this type of person—the kind that has an upbeat approach to things, who is a workaholic, who is overactive, overproductive, and who is full of ideas," says Dr. Fieve. "And if they don't go crazy over the top or retreat into the pits of depression, as long as their judgment is not impaired or they are surrounded by people who can keep them from going over the edge with disastrous business decisions, these would be the ideal people to staff a very productive office with. They are envied by their colleagues . . . until their mania goes too high or a depression washes over them. Then they accomplish nothing—or they get into trouble."

Robert Campeau, the Canadian entrepreneur and former owner of Bloomingdale's, Jordan Marsh, and Burdine's, has apparently never been called manic-depressive, but he does seem to have the temperament noted by Dr. Fieve. As *Fortune* magazine, in a 1988 story, said of Campeau, "eccentric may be too tame a word [for him]."

The magazine story said: "Having suffered several nervous breakdowns, Campeau brought a psychiatrist, reportedly his own, onto his board for two years. He divorced his wife to marry his mistress, with whom he already had sired two children his first family didn't know about."

Known for his love of glitz and dazzle, Mr. Campeau is a man who craves the spotlight and seems to thrive on erratic behavior. Those who have worked for him say he is charming and has an intriguing boyish demeanor about him. But there is another side they call "volatile." One of his former employees said he had an "Ivan the Terrible" management style. Another said he doesn't mind calling employees at three in the morning. And still another noted that he "can go from high to low in about two seconds." Mr. Campeau has said of himself, "I'm full of the spice of life." In January 1990 he lost control of his retail stores and his company filed for bankruptcy protection.

John Mulheren, Jr., described by writer Connie Bruck in a *New Yorker* article as a "legendary Wall Street trader," broke the code of silence about manic-depressive illness when he protested in court that his manic-depressive illness, while it often enhanced his abilities on Wall Street, also distorted his reasoning and judgment. Mr. Mulheren was a former fellow-arbitrageur with Ivan Boesky, an admitted felon whose cooperation with the government precipitated a rush of Wall Street prosecutions. Mr. Mulheren was convicted of manipulating Gulf + Western stock by driving up the price as a favor to Boesky. His conviction was overturned on appeal.

According to the *New Yorker* article, Mr. Mulheren said that "the depressive part of his cycle, which rendered him so profoundly anergic that he would take to his bed, unable to process even simple information, robbed him of perhaps thirty days a year . . . In his excited, hypomanic state, he did his most inspired trading.

" 'When I would finally get high enough that it impaired my judgment, I'd lose—and I'd get so bummed out by losing that I would just leave. I'd say, Let's all go to Atlantic City. Or I'd go out on my boat. Or I'd go shopping. I love to buy stuff when I'm high. I say, Gee, I really like this shirt—I'll buy nine of them, in every color.' "

A psychiatric report by Dr. Ross J. Baldessarini, a psychiatry professor at Harvard Medical School, prepared for Mr. Mulheren's trial, stated that he experienced mood shifts "about twice yearly" (despite being treated with lithium) and that "on at least one occasion, in November 1987, he spent 'twenty-one hours walking the streets of New York' in a state of possibly altered consciousness, 'dressed only in pants and an undershirt.' "

Mr. Mulheren was also known to be enormously generous, not only to philanthropic causes, but to anyone in trouble. Frequently, said the *New Yorker* article, including every Christmas Eve, he would put about twenty thousand dollars in envelopes—several hundred-dollar bills in each—and hand them out on the Bowery. He may have chosen that part of New York because his uncle, who also had manic-depressive illness, had lived on the Bowery in his later years.

On the other hand, Mr. Mulheren was known for raging at his employees, firing some of them without their ever understanding why. But, as Dr. Fieve has said and the article points out, "On Wall Street, especially, varying forms of behavioral

179

pathology tend to accompany talent, and Mulheren was far more conspicuous for his benevolence than for his temper . . . His willingness to maintain a close business relationship with [Ivan] Boesky showed a pronounced, and perhaps characteristic, lack of judgment."

According to the *New Yorker* article, Mr. Mulheren who said he felt "a drive to be different from the moment I dropped," would go to work on Wall Street in jeans, or camouflage clothes, or leather pants and Hawaiian shirts, or, on at least one occasion, a gorilla suit; for black-tie functions, he wore black silk pajamas.

Like many high-powered people, Mr. Mulheren did not take his lithium regularly. He was afraid it would dull him, he said, and he believes that when he is not medicated, he is livelier, more creative, more focused—what he calls "one hundred and fifty percent of normal."

Dr. Fieve tries to prevent his business tycoon patients from getting into trouble by forming a "committee" around them. The committee may include the executive's lawyer, accountant, medical doctor, and Dr. Fieve. Having four advisers at his beck and call feeds the executive's narcissism, Dr. Fieve says. But this committee has a strategic role: it protects him from making outrageously dangerous decisions, such as buying a worthless piece of land in the middle of the desert, or just from extending himself into financial disaster. "I like to have this committee," Dr. Fieve says. "One committee member could never, alone, talk the executive out of a foolhardy scheme. But a committee frequently can figure out a way to handle it. You are often dealing with someone brilliant and conniving, so you have to outmanipulate him."

Kay Jamison cautions that not everyone who is unusually creative or productive is a suspect for manic-depressive illness. Making that claim, she says, "mocks the notion of individuality." Highly creative people may be slightly to one side of the mean in terms of emotions and sensitivity. But that's not the same as having a crippling, disabling condition such as manic-depressive illness.

It is equally wrong to confuse "workaholism" with manic depression. Many people are compulsively driven, can get along on just a few hours' sleep, and can function at a very high energy level, but are not mood-disordered and do not come from a family that is. "No one would think, for instance, that former British Prime Minister Margaret Thatcher has many dark nights of the soul," says Dr. Jamison. "But she is very disciplined, manages on three or four hours of sleep, and is enormously driven."

And to label people who are just a bit moody or tense or have sustained high energy as having manic-depressive illness trivializes a serious disease. Only when a person's family and personal history have been considered, when mood swings have a cyclical, perhaps seasonal, pattern, when they have interfered with a job or family relationships, or when they have stimulated thoughts of suicide, would you be inclined to call a person manic-depressive.

◆

INSPIRATION AND INSANITY: A LONG HISTORY

Human beings have speculated about the relationship between inspiration and insanity for centuries. Even pre-Grecian myths drew a connection between being mad and being singled out by the gods. The notion was already a cliché when Shakespeare wrote, in *A Midsummer Night's Dream*, "The lunatic, the lover, and the poet, are of imagination all compact."

The Romantic-period fascination with the link between genius and insanity has been studied anecdotally since the mid-1860s, when Cesare Lombroso, an Italian psychiatrist who explored genius and insanity, concluded in his book *The Man of Genius* that "genius, whether in the study of philosophy, in affairs of state, in poetical composition, or in the exercise of the arts, has been inclined to insanity . . . It seems as though nature had intended to teach us respect for the supreme misfortunes of insanity; and also to preserve us from being dazzled by the brilliancy of those men of genius who might well be compared, not to the planets which keep their appointed orbits, but to falling stars, lost and dispersed over the crust of the earth." Lombroso suggested, too, that both creativity and mental illness seemed to run in families and referred to a "hereditary taint."

In 1921 Emil Kraepelin, the pioneer in identifying manic-depressive illness, also commented on its connection with creativity. But it is only since the mid-1970s that several scientific studies have taken a hard look at such questions as: Is there really more psychiatric illness among creative people than in the general population? If so, how common is it? Does it occur among people who have specific kinds of talent, such as writing or painting or composing? Is creativity different from intelligence?

No matter whether the study includes painters or poets, architects or actors, the conclusions are remarkably the same. Creative people tend to have a mix of characteristics—intelligence, independence, and sensitivity, combined with strong egos. They are often nonconforming, introspective, and socially detached; they enjoy being challenged and are self-assertive. Their personality style allows them to be more adventurous and more willing to take risks.

Most important, they have the capacity to tap into a rich and mysterious resource deep inside themselves. It is a resource which opens a window into a world only they can see, and which gives them a unique ability to translate that world into music or poetry or paintings—or theater. The "flight of ideas," speed of thought, and exquisite heightening of the senses—the most common symptoms of mania—allow the artist to conceive, without restraint and inhibition, his most original, imaginative, and often awesome creations. This liberation from conventional taboos frees him to challenge society's norms and to be persistent in the face of rejection.

Dr. Kay Jamison says, "Their associations are genuinely unusual. And having extremes of emotion is a gift—the capacity to be passionately involved in life, to care deeply about things, to feel hurt: a lot of people don't have that. And it is the transition in and out of the highs and lows, the constant contrast, that can foster creativity."

A much quoted 1987 study of thirty writers—twenty-seven

men and three women—who had served on the faculty of the University of Iowa Writers' Workshop, was conducted by Nancy J. C. Andreasen, of the department of psychiatry at the University of Iowa College of Medicine. The Iowa workshop is the oldest creative writing program in the country; its students and faculty have included such distinguished writers as John Cheever, Robert Lowell, John Irving, Philip Roth, and Kurt Vonnegut.

During her fifteen-year study, Dr. Andreasen found that 80 percent of the writers had had an episode of mania or depression at some time in their lives. Four had suffered from severe manic disorder that required prolonged and repeated hospital stays.

In contrast, only 30 percent of a control group not in the creative arts had mood disorders. The control group was matched for age, education, and sex with the creative artists, but their occupations were such as hospital administrators, lawyers, or social workers.

The writers also had a significantly higher rate of alcoholism, which, as we have seen, is frequently associated with manic-depression—30 percent, compared with 7 percent in the control group. During her study, two of the writers committed suicide.

Schizophrenia was conspicuous by its absence among the creative artists. Dr. Andreasen speculates that the perceptions of schizophrenics tend to be more bizarre than original, and are accompanied by impairments in thinking that inhibit rather than enhance creativity. And because schizophrenia is a chronic illness, those that suffer from it do not have the periods of normalcy enjoyed by manic-depressives, during which they often do their best work.

The families of the manic-depressive writers studied by Dr. Andreasen, including brothers, sisters, and parents, were also strikingly more creative—and had more psychiatric disorders. Forty-one percent of the writers' brothers and sisters showed creativity, as did 20 percent of their parents. Relatives included several highly successful journalists, an accomplished pianist, and an award-winning choreographer.

Dr. Andreasen suggests that a trait or traits fostering creativ-

183

ity—curiosity, a tolerance for ambiguity, a dislike for the conventional—are transmitted through families. Coupled with high energy, those traits in a person whose brain is "wired" for math may produce an engineer; someone better wired verbally may become a writer; a person with organizational acumen may become an outstanding business leader. A single faulty gene or genes added to that combination could result in bipolar illness.

Another leading study—this one of forty-seven top British artists and writers was conducted at Oxford University and St. George's Hospital in London by Kay Jamison. It revealed, too, a startlingly high number who said they had been treated for depression or manic depression. Ninety percent of her subjects were men and were chosen to be part of her research because they had won at least one of several top prizes or awards in their field.

All painters and sculptors were either Royal Academicians or Associates of the Royal Academy, an honor established by King George III in 1768. Nine of the eighteen poets were represented in *The Oxford Book of Twentieth-Century English Verse*, and six of the eight playwrights had won the New York Drama Critics Award or the *Evening Standard* Drama Award (the London critics' award). Three of the five biographers had won the James Tait Black Memorial Prize, one of Britain's most prestigious literary honors.

The playwrights topped the list of those who had suffered from mood disorders with 63 percent having sought treatment for depression or manic depression. However, more than half had been treated only with psychotherapy.

More than half the poets had been treated with drugs or been hospitalized. This high figure is especially significant because men are less likely than women to seek treatment.

Interestingly, the biographers, while outstanding in their field, were the least likely to be associated with "creative fire"; they also reported no history of mood swings or elated periods.

Overall, about one third of the writers and artists reported histories of severe mood swings and one fourth said they had had intense, elated mood states. All of the poets, novelists, and artists,

88 percent of the playwrights, and 20 percent of the biographers had a past peppered with intense, creative episodes, which lasted from one hour to more than a month at a time. During these periods, they were enthusiastic, euphoric, full of energy and self-confidence, and felt that their mental associations and thoughts were faster and more fluid. Just before these creative spurts came, they needed less sleep, often awakening abruptly at three or four in the morning. Half said they felt a sharp change in mood just before the beginning of an intensely creative period. They said things such as "I have a fever to write . . . "

◆

WRITERS AND ALCOHOLISM

One of Dr. Donald Goodwin's favorite stories, which he recounts in his book *Alcohol and the Writer*, involves writers and their passion for alcohol.

"Dorothy Parker and a friend went to a funeral home in New York to pay their last respects to a famous writer who had just died an untimely death. The friend sighed as they gazed down into the coffin. 'Doesn't he look just wonderful?' Replied Parker: 'And why shouldn't he? He hasn't had a drink in three days.'"

No one knows for sure why so many writers suffer from alcoholism and also from manic-depressive illness. It is uncertain whether the two are related or whether they are independent disorders surfacing in the same person. Which comes first: the alcoholism or the manic-depressive illness? How many people with the illness are using alcohol to obliterate the unbearable symptoms of the disease? Does the excessive drinking in itself brings on symptoms of depression or mania?

In the preface to his book, Dr. Goodwin writes: "As a researcher, my first discovery was that writers drank a lot—maybe more than anyone else. Six Americans had won the Nobel Prize in literature and four were alcoholic . . . Through the years I have become more and more convinced that alcoholism among American writers constitutes an epidemic."

F. Scott Fitzgerald wrote: "I was drunk for many years, and then I died." Ernest Hemingway, who suffered from a mood disorder, reportedly drank sixteen double frozen daiquiris in one night at a Havana bar.

It may be that alcoholism, like the moods of manic-depressive illness, gives writers access to feelings they need to write uncensored by their own psyches. It may liberate their spirit, critical to their ability to create.

Manic-depressives who also abuse alcohol often do so more when they are in a hypomanic or manic stage than in a depressed one. The sense of abandon that is a hallmark of mania may permit the excessive use of alcohol without guilt or remorse. And alcohol does offer some relief from the agitation and frenzied activity associated with mania.

Nonetheless, many alcoholic creators acknowledge that their best work was not done while they were under the influence of alcohol, just as manic-depressive artists achieve little when going through the tortures of depression or the wastefulness of mania. The late Raymond Carver, one of the most noted modern writers, said that he lost several years to alcoholism in the mid-1970s. He described it as a "completely destructive activity," out of which nothing good ever came. He said, "Any artist who is alcoholic is an artist despite the alcohol, not because of it. I never wrote so much as a line that was worth a nickel when I was under the influence of alcohol. When I was in the height of my drinking— the all-night sessions, the blackouts, the hangovers—I did no writing. I could have . . . easily gone down the toilet, if I'd turned right instead of turning left."

◆

TEMPERAMENT, BLUES MUSIC, AND ARTISTIC CREATIVITY

Given that Memphis is the "home of the blues," it seems natural that Dr. Hagop Akiskal and his wife, Kareen, a psychologist, would have been interested in the temperaments of blues musicians. They suggest that the song "Born with the Blues," by Memphis Slim, a prominent blues musician who died recently, shows an insight into the nature of mood disorders "deeper than that of many professionals." The haunting lyrics are in part:

My mama had them, her mama had them
Now I've got them too . . .
I've got something, something you just don't learn in
school
You'll never find them in no books . . .
You just got to inherit the blues.
When I'm sad and lonely, even when I am happy too
All of a sudden, I find myself singing the blues
That's why I know I was born with them.

Furthermore, when the Akiskals studied 750 psychiatric patients at the University of Tennessee's mood clinic in Memphis, they discovered that those with mild manic depression or mood swings, rather than other mental illneses, were more likely to be creative artists. They found such mood swings, too, among people who were successful in business and leadership positions.

Over the past eight years the Akiskals have been working on a sample of Parisian artists—including writers, painters, sculptors, and musicians—to further explore these provocative leads from the Memphis study. Their main finding, not yet published, supports the high rate of cyclothymia rather than major mood disorders among them.

◆

ROMANTICIZING MANIC DEPRESSION: A DANGER

Because of this prevalence of manic depression in highly creative people, many mental health practitioners worry about the tendency to romanticize the illness. Dr. Nancy Andreasen warns that manic depression is not a disease to be taken lightly. Nor is it one that should be wished for, even by creative people. Fiction writing, for instance, takes more than a creative spurt and a vivid imagination. It requires a lot of knowledge and thinking about people because so much information must go into a novel or short story. And writing is hard work: it takes organization and discipline as well as insight. "Sensitivity is not the same as eccentricity," she says.

"This is an illness that torments," declares Dr. Kay Jamison. "And no one who is confined in a psychiatric hospital is being creative. No one who is spending six or seven months a year sleeping fourteen hours a day is producing anything. No one is achieving when he is dead."

In his book *Movie Stars, Real People and Me*, Joshua Logan, the theatrical director and producer, once said that over a period of twenty years he experienced manic elations during which he "would be going great guns, putting out a thousand ideas a minute, acting flamboyant—until I went over the bounds of reality" and then got to a point where "I had a profound wish to be dead without having to go through the shaming defeat of suicide."

A manic-depressive artist in Boston said that when he was hypomanic he felt "juiced up" and knew he could paint brilliantly. And for a while he could. But as his manic symptoms speeded up, he became scattered and totally disorganized. Once his studio was littered with a hundred paintings, none of them finished. His mind was racing so fast that ideas toppled over one another. He would begin a painting, get an inspiration for a new one, abandon the old, and move on. Finally he collapsed in exhaustion, realizing the disaster he had created.

It is a common scenario because someone in the grip of mania is so distractible that he moves from project to project, expending a lot of energy but accomplishing little.

Of course, not all people with manic-depressive illness are creative. Many resent the focus on the creativity connection because it doesn't reflect their experience—one characterized by lost jobs, broken marriages, and fractured relationships because their moods seesawed out of control. As Dr. Anthony Rothschild of Boston reminds us, "For every Hemingway, there are thousands of manic-depressives whose lives are ruined."

◆

RELATIVES OF MANIC-DEPRESSIVES MAY HAVE AN EDGE

A tantalizing research project at McLean Hospital and Harvard Medical School suggests that it may be not the manic-depressives who are the most creative but their normal and cyclothymic relatives, those with milder mood swings. Psychiatrist Ruth Richards and psychologist Dennis Kinney looked at seventeen manic-depressives—not eminent creative people, just those living ordinary lives—sixteen cyclothymes, and eleven of their close relatives who were psychiatrically normal.

While the seriously ill manic-depressives were neither more nor less creative than a control group of people without the illness, it was those with a milder form of the illness and those who had no symptoms at all who were the most creative. Creativity, as they measured it, was not limited to the creative arts. They counted imaginative thinking in carrying out the tasks of everyday life at work or at leisure—housekeeping, hobbies, even caring for a disabled child.

The study suggests that it is characteristics associated with manic depression—a richer kind of thinking, greater emotional sensitivity, and a high energy level—that may be conducive to creativity. The link may not be limited to a handful of prominent people, or to a few fields such as the fine arts, but may extend to literally millions of people in a wide variety of occupations and hobbies.

The researchers believe that moods that are mildly elated, the kind that give people fuller access to unusual ideas and allow them to take risks and challenge the status quo, may facilitate creativity without producing full-blown mania. A person may be more imaginative during mild manias, then be able to evaluate his ideas and thoughts when he has moved on to a less elated state—a combination thought to result in creativity.

◆

CREATIVITY AND LITHIUM

Given that manic-depressive illness may offer creative people some advantage, they often balk at taking lithium or another drug that may ease the pain but, they fear, may also shut down their creative juices.

Patty Duke offers a strong argument for creativity being enhanced by lithium. Others do not agree. They try lithium, then stop abruptly because they miss the energy and imagination that accompanied their manias. Or they need a spurt of euphoria to meet a crisis or to make a difficult decision. And it is easy to forget the inner torment of depression once it has passed.

Many people, including those who are not extraordinarily creative, are reluctant to try medication in the first place because they don't want to let go of the highs that feel so spectacular.

The big question is: Does lithium or carbamazepine or other medication really reduce creativity?

Two studies of thirty artists, writers, and businessmen taking lithium revealed that three quarters of them did not feel less creative on lithium. Some even reported an increase in productivity.

On the other hand, 25 percent said they felt less productive, and 17 percent stopped taking lithium because they felt it reduced their creativity at work and in their personal lives. It may be the frequency, severity, and type of manic-depressive illness that make the difference.

Before starting to take lithium in the spring of 1967, poet Robert Lowell spent much of his life fighting the demons of his manic-depressive illness. He was in and out of the hospital many times, having had fourteen or fifteen breakdowns in eighteen years. Once on lithium, he noticed a dramatic drop in his mood swings accompanied by an equally astonishing surge in his creativity. Between June and December of 1967, he wrote seventy-four poems. Ian Hamilton, Lowell's literary biographer, claims that the poems Lowell wrote after starting lithium show a "low-key agreeableness," perhaps a loss in poetic power. But Lowell himself seemed to be pleased about his new stability and improved productivity, and felt that he had improved rather than declined as a poet.

Dr. Mogens Schou is emeritus professor of biological psychiatry at Aarhus University in Denmark, and a world authority on the implications of lithium therapy, especially in creative people. In 1979 he conducted a study of twenty-four manic-depressive artists for whom lithium had been effective in lessening or preventing mania or depression. He wanted to know how their creative powers were affected by the treatment.

Among the creative artists he studied were a forty-nine-year-old journalist, a forty-two-year-old composer, and a sixty-three-year-old author. Each responded differently to lithium.

The journalist had developed manic-depressive illness when he was in his late twenties, and suffered from manias so violent and depressions so debilitating that he could no longer write. After starting lithium treatment when he was thirty-six, he was able to return to work writing both books and film scenarios. He admitted that he missed the manic highs, but recognized how fruitless those highs had been, and said he was much more productive as a result of taking lithium.

The composer, who had been manic-depressive since he was twenty-five, complained that during his depressions he had no initiative, felt slowed down, and thought about suicide. He was manic only occasionally; however, his creative juices flowed at the beginning of either mania or depression. Once the episode was fully developed, his creativity vanished. While treatment with lithium did not prevent his mood swings, they became shorter and less frequent, and his thoughts about suicide disappeared. He believes that his productivity has not been affected one way or another by taking lithium.

On the other hand, the author stopped his lithium treatment

because he felt it reined in his creative energy. While he wrote a successful book while he was taking the drug and another book while he was partly on and off lithium, he felt the writing done after he had stopped lithium was of higher quality.

Others who were unhappy about what they perceived as the bridling of their creativity were a forty-two-year-old female composer who discontinued lithium because she did not have sufficient drive to put her ideas on paper; a forty-two-year-old female author who felt that during treatment she lacked inspiration and ideas; and a sixty-three-year-old male author who felt that lithium blocked his creative energy.

So doctors must be sensitive to reservations that some people, especially creative ones, have about tampering with their talent. And they must be willing to work with their patients, juggle their medications, and understand the delicate balance between preserving their creativity and productivity, and blotting out the twelve-weeks-in-bed stints or the off-the-wall manias that leave a trail of chaos and destruction.

Dr. Kay Jamison, who has worked with many highly creative manic-depressives, tries to make ingenious use of all she knows about manic-depressive illness when treating her patients. She encourages physicians to consider the seasonal patterns of their illness, perhaps altering medication and its dose to match their seasonal highs and lows; to experiment with drugs other than lithium when that approach seems appropriate; to adopt a less rigid attitude about treatment, one that will not throttle her patients' creative bent.

"You have no credibility with somebody in the arts if you start saying, 'Well, just take your medication. Be grateful it's available.' They would say, 'Fine. Buzz off,' and appropriately so. You have to be able to say, 'There are lots of possibilities here. It's not an all-or-nothing sort of thing.' You have to make a good case for why somebody should be on medication."

Responsible physicians believe that they must help patients sort out the possibilities for treatment and let them know what might reasonably be expected. The concerns of patients—often that their world will become flat and colorless, that they will lose their uniqueness—cannot be cavalierly ignored. The unique way in which each person is "wired" must be considered. And the person with manic-depressive illness cannot be allowed to leave the doctor's office believing, blithely, that all will be well if he takes the medication for a month or two or three.

Dr. Jamison thinks that the ideal treatment would be one that preserved the good aspects of the illness while getting rid of the painful ones. But this, of course, is not easy. "Certainly, depth and intensity of human feeling must be a part of great artistic achievement," she concedes. "Maybe it always takes a certain amount of suffering to do something marvelous in the arts," she suggests. "Who knows?"

While Dr. Jamison is as eager as others in the field to isolate the gene or genes that cause manic-depressive illness, she worries about the long-term implications of genetic research. If a gene is identified, will we be tempted to tamper with it in an attempt to eradicate manic-depressive illness? "If we find the gene or genes," she speculates, "will doctors recommend amniocentesis and will some people want to do it? Then do you abort someone who carries the manic-depressive gene? Do you try to change the gene pool around?"

As president of the Manic-Depressive Illness Foundation, an organization that wrestles with the ethical and societal issues of manic-depressive illness, Dr. Jamison hopes that won't happen. She works toward public acceptance of severe mood disorders, emphasizes their positive aspects, and encourages understanding, and financial support so that the devastation brought about by the illness can be eliminated.

She cites a study done forty years ago on the incidence of manic-depressive psychosis in socially prominent American families. In their description of one family, the authors said, "If sterilization had been done . . . two psychotic individuals would have been eliminated from the American scene, patients with manic-depressive psychosis, but there would have gone with them a man internationally known, whose writings still remain as a source of inspiration and life orientation for many people, whose school of thought is still to be reckoned with and who is frequently cited as a figure unique in America and uniquely American. The group who clustered around this man left their influence on the whole of America. His descendants are still extremely eminent and also still send patients to hospitals for mental disease."

"I'm real concerned about that sort of thing," Dr. Jamison says. "Do you want to get rid of that kind of color and liveliness and impulsivity, that high-energy, risk-taking group? At the same time, these are lethal and destructive illnesses. They kill people. They ruin families. They ruin individual lives. I don't think you have to have van Gogh dead in his thirties."

CHAPTER NINE

MY FAMILY AND FRIENDS

I believe that all of the important people in my life prior to 1982 were victimized by my illness. Because I was married to John Astin the longest, because the setting of that marriage was seemingly the most sound, and because my cycles of mania and depression became more intense during those years, he and the children were the ones who were most affected.

With Harry Falk, I was no picnic either. There were the suicide attempts, and they were certainly high drama. But the marriage was briefer and there were no children, and that makes a big difference.

From the time Sean was born, until I was diagnosed, I was murder to live with. I don't think I was marriage material until six or seven years ago. By that I mean being a whole person who chooses to be with another whole person and who has a plan for life, a plan that is flexible but at least with some goals. I didn't have any. I just kept wandering—or racing—into the next momentous event in my life.

John Astin had not been privy to any of my manias prior to our living together, except for having seen my strange appearance on *The Dick Cavett Show*. There had been a long separation during which I had Sean and wasn't behaving strangely at all. I had gained a good deal of weight, oddly enough, after the pregnancy; since I didn't have anybody to talk to, I ate. So now I was this kind of nice, round, placid lady who was very much in control of herself. How could John—or I—have predicted the next ten years?

He and I began to live together, and I don't think we had been together six months when his eldest son, David, came to live with us. So we had David, who was twelve, and Sean, who was a baby.

Around that time, I was also doing a movie in Minnesota and I recall some small manias, actually some manicky agitation going on in me, and yet I wasn't acting it out. I was just feeling it. I felt irritable and on edge. Part of it was not knowing what to do with David. After all, what did I know about a twelve-year-old boy?

So it was very unpleasant a good deal of the time for David— for all of us, but mainly for David. He lived with us for six months and then went back to his mother. For another six months or so, things were quite normal and pleasant. It was John and Sean and me and his three kids on the weekends.

And that was when we decided to get married. This time I decided to do it according to tradition. A month after we were married, I found out I was pregnant. I was okay for a while, but after Mack was born, our household turned into real crisis. All three of John's boys—David, Allen, and Tom—came to live with us. So we had five boys between the ages of infancy and thirteen, plus two dogs and two cats and three fish. No money. I was twenty-four and didn't know the first thing about how to raise children.

Everything went downhill from there. God knows we tried. But David and I didn't get along at all. And I didn't do all that well with Allen or Tom either. I was always screaming at the top of my lungs, and John and I were up all night arguing.

We were dead broke, there was a screenwriters' strike going on, and as a member of that union, the Writers Guild of America, John could not work as a writer, nor would he cross a picket line to work as a director or actor. We could, however, work as actors in the straw-hat circuit. So, off and on for almost five years, we took our show on the road. It provided us with a healthy income and we had the opportunity to work onstage together.

For most of those years we traveled cross-country in a van, schlepping from city to city with my mother, five kids, and a baby-sitter while John and I were performing. What a setup for insanity! The van was not exactly what you'd call luxurious, and I remember bologna sandwiches thrown all over the place and the kids peeing in paper cups. Mackie was an infant, so we were dragging diapers, and toys for the other kids, and tons of games and luggage and pieces of the scenery. Invariably we would leave something behind.

Once, in Chicago, when John and I were doing *Rattle of a Simple Man*, the critics said mean things—not about my performance but about the way I had lived my life—and they offended my dignity. So those were grounds for an agitated depression. No matter what I did, it seemed I couldn't stop them from writing that garbage. It had a terrible effect on me, and I became obnoxious. I kept picking fights with John and doing a lot of that blood-curdling screaming.

Most of the time we lived in rented houses, and my mom had a ton of shopping bags that she insisted on dragging from place to place. For six weeks in Milwaukee, all of us lived in a hotel. Can you imagine? It was freezing and snowing, and these kids were cooped up in a hotel room. They were throwing things out of the windows, tossing furniture around, and yelling all over the place.

There was mayhem going on, but it seemed as if John never noticed. He went someplace in his mind that was quiet and bucolic. I sure envied it.

Mild depression became my way of life for a long time. Getting out of bed, but not until two in the afternoon. Or getting out of bed only if someone was there to notice that this mother was slovenly and not taking care of her kids. Because of the stress in our house, there was a justification for this depression. But I know now there would have been a depression with or without a crisis.

197

From then on, it was all repetitious—cycles of a kind of agitated mania alternating with depression. The only variation would be that in some depressions I would go to bed for six, eight, ten weeks at a time.

When I was in one of those deep depressions, I was shut down, everything shut down. Of course there was no sex, and of course guilt for not having sex. But that didn't last very long before the other feelings—the agitation and the anger—became overwhelming.

There were times during depression that I would somehow summon something to perform sexually. But my guess is that John didn't really feel loved at those times.

Those periods when I stayed in bed, behind closed doors for all those weeks, I felt dirty, smelly. Part of me thought I should get up and wash myself, and then I would dismiss that because I just couldn't get up. My thoughts would vary from blaming others to wishing for the absolutely unattainable peace of mind. And also thoughts of: Why is this happening to me? Why am I like this? I'm a terrible person.

I guess the word to describe it is self-pity. I remember thinking, "If I can be here and I can cry all the time, why can't I get up and do something? It doesn't take that much more energy to do that." But like the old joke—I lay there long enough and the thought went away—that's what it was like. You just lie there and you can't transform those thoughts into any action that will change anything. And I could never tell anyone else what I wanted them to do for me. The kids, John, they would have done anything. But I didn't know what I wanted: just not to feel like this anymore.

I would hear all those speeches that loved ones make to their loved ones who are ill. "You have everything. Look at your beautiful home, your husband, look at your beautiful car." It was meaningless. And then the guilt on top, the guilt for feeling that it was meaningless. There are people starving to death on the streets, and I have all this nice stuff and I can't stop crying. So each things just compounds the felony.

Coming out of that kind of deep, deep coma-like depression was like coming up from *Twenty Thousand Leagues Under the Sea*. I would feel totally hung-over.

As the boys grew up, my manias took the form of irritability and unpredictable flashes of rage. I can't even say "angry." It was as intense as rage. For instance, let's say it would be a typical afternoon and evening when I had all five boys at home. Throughout the day, there would be the sadness, the borderline depression. But I'd function—clean the house, go to the market, start dinner. Then the kids would start coming home from school, and the noise would build and they wouldn't do what I asked. I'd say "Clean your room, hang up your clothes." They'd say, "No, I don't want to." Or they would simply ignore me.

I mean, these are the everyday things that go on in a family. But for me it would start the motor running, a grating on my nerves. Still, I would go ahead and make a full-course dinner every night. I'm not exaggerating—I'd make a very large roast turkey or chicken or meat course, six or seven fresh vegetables because some of the kids were vegetarians. An enormous salad. Dessert. And this was every night. With each item I made, I would get angrier and angrier and feel put upon.

Yet there wasn't anyone there saying, "Would you make seven vegetables and three loaves of bread and salad for twenty, please?" These were things that I insisted on and demanded of myself. And as I would clean the carrots or whatever, I could just physically feel the tension building.

Yes, the kids' noise *was* getting louder. They *were* hitting each other. They *were* throwing things. They *were* running in and out. They *were* roller-skating in the house. They *were* bouncing the basketball. Yet my agitation—I know because I've lived for a few years another way—was far beyond any of the aggravating stimuli.

Now I'd wait for John to come home for dinner. And, of course, if he wasn't there the absolute second he said he'd be there, that was grounds for a tantrum. Or if when he came in he wasn't ready either to visit with me or to sit down to eat—if he had something he wanted to do first—that, too, was grounds for a tantrum. And the tantrum would start by emotionally removing myself from the group. I got very cold, very icy. I would slam things down on the table and be very brusque. If the kids asked me a question, I gave them a snappy answer if I gave them any answer at all.

Then, invariably, one of the kids or John would say something that I felt, at the time, was provocative. In retrospect, I can see that it was not at all. I would start screaming ugly foul epithets, either at a particular kid or at John or at the group in general, or at the world. And if the words weren't enough and I would feel physically on fire, I would start throwing things—the food, the plates, the glasses.

Then there would be some point where something would click in my mind, where I would sense that I was out of control, that I was crazy. Then the embarrassment and the guilt would kick me even further into crazy behavior. Now I had to run to the bathroom and try to kill myself because that was the only way to save face.

There's a certain logic in the way I'm describing it, and there was very little logic in what was happening. So the kids really didn't know what to expect. There was almost a kind of predictability that there was going to be some kind of mayhem, but when it was coming, and in what form, they didn't know.

During my manic and depressive outbursts, John was always amazingly calm, very fatherly. I would hear such phrases as, "No, Anna, I think that you'd better not do this because if you do you're going to be very unhappy and you're going to feel terrible . . . " There was this almost hypnotic tone that he would use, which, of course, would send me further into spasms. He was very analytical, classical psychoanalytical, strenuously suggesting that I go to a psychiatrist, but always, it seemed to me, in terms of what had happened to me in the crib. And instinctively I knew that wasn't right, that it wasn't going to work. So I just did more raving and ranting.

John did not chastise me, but his very tolerance and all-forgiving behavior was agitating. Once in a while he'd say, "I know you're just testing me to see how far you can push me before I tell you I don't love you." I didn't think I was doing that though I could see how he could have gotten that impression. I would provoke and provoke and provoke, and I can't tell you how many times I screamed at him, "I don't want to be married to Jesus Christ. Come down off the cross . . . " So maybe it *was* a test. Maybe it was just me thinking, "I want to see if you're really perfect of if I can get something out of you that makes you human. If I'm so *out of control*, how can you be so *in control* all the time?" And every once in a while—not too often—I would go too far and he *would* start yelling. But it would take three, four hours of arguing before he'd lose it. The first time it happened, it surprised the hell out of me. And he can yell real loud. It had a very salutory effect.

I never felt adequate to express myself to John or in front of John. This very loquacious woman that I am now didn't exist then. I could not explain to him what I was feeling. And I felt intimidated by his facility with the world of analysis, a world that was foreign to me.

But John *was* the buffer with the kids. He was the buffer on the phone all the many times when I was unavailable, when I wouldn't speak to anyone. He made excuses when we were to be at a social event, and suddenly we were not going. And he tried to bolster my self-confidence and feelings of self-worth all the time. I think that was sincere and pure. He believed that I was a worthwhile person and he wanted me to believe it.

Our lives weren't always chaos. After an episode, I would apologize to John and to the kids and try to explain myself. And then there would be a restorative time that was kind of nice. Everyone was taking a deep breath and went out of the way to make things pleasant. But you just never knew when the good time would be over.

As the years wore on there were strains in the marriage and I began to look elsewhere for companionship. Only now do I recognize that that was the beginning of some mania. And John was devastated, outraged—and forgiving. Had he not been forgiving in 1977 when I had the major manic episode that took us to Dr. Arlen's office in the middle of the night, the marriage would have been over then. I pledged to try harder—almost a feeling of falling in love all over again. But John got involved in a new business venture and became more isolated from me. And I began to notice that I was not devastated by his absence. In the old sense of growing apart, we grew apart. There was more depression from me, more anger and acting out. Arguments came more often and they were louder, more intense, uglier. I didn't know if I wanted to be married anymore. I didn't want to live from crisis to crisis.

I can't even remember now what triggered the incident that ended our marriage. But I remember being so enraged that I felt capable of violence against John. I didn't think there was any other way to convince him I didn't want this marriage anymore. One day I stood in the hallway screeching at him, "Don't you see, we're going to make headlines?" For the first time, instinctively, I knew that these tantrums could result in serious, violent behavior. I was afraid my anger would get so out of control, something dangerous would happen. Up until then there had always been a bit of a governor on my behavior. The abuse I dished out was mainly verbal, but that time I became aware of something different. I didn't know I was manic, but I knew I was out of control. Maybe, that day, he got the feeling that enough is enough. And he agreed to separate.

People have often asked me whether I think my marriage would have held together if I hadn't been manic-depressive. It is possible that the debilitating effects of my illness had me remaining, in a lot of ways, very childlike, wanting the kind of stability that John represented. I don't think John was looking for a daughter, but I do think he was the kind of man who felt he could fix anything with enough love and enough caring. That may be true in many instances, but when you're dealing with a chemical imbalance in the brain, all the love in the world won't fix it.

One of my biggest regrets is how little contact I had with my brother and sister for so much of my life. I envied my sister because, somehow, in the face of the Rosses, she had the strength to maintain her integrity. She wanted nothing to do with show business and she *had* nothing to do with show business. She was the one who said, "No, you're not going to change Anna Marie's name. No, she's not going to another school, she's going to a Catholic school. Yes, I will see my father whenever I please." Now, she lost all of those battles. But she did win—and this is the thing I always longed for—the war of independence.

Today I'm thrilled that we have a close relationship even though my sister and her husband live in Florida. We seek each other out, and I call her for companionship. My brother lives in California, and I don't see him or his family nearly enough. On the holidays. And some birthdays. But I always had fantasies of living in the same neighborhood and going down the block to drink coffee and see my nieces and nephews. That just didn't work out.

But my greatest pain comes from knowing I shortchanged my kids. The fact that I have credibility with them today is a happy surprise for me. Maybe they lucked out and have this same capacity that I have to forgive and accept what's going on in the here and now. But they certainly had a lot to forgive.

The suicide attempts—little boys banging on the bathroom door, saying, "Mommy, please. What are you taking?" And not knowing what I was going to do next. The fear they must have felt. And the guilt. The kids would often hide in their rooms when I was going through a manic outburst. Sometimes they'd try to intervene, the older boys as well as Sean and Mack. They would plead and plead—"Stop it." The little ones had the gift of ignorance. Then they would disappear. Or the older ones would leave the house and take a little one with them. It makes me ache that I missed a lot of their childhood. While it is fun with Kevin, it is not a substitute. It is painful to try to remember. When you reminisce and a kid asks you, "When was the first time I walked by myself?" and you don't remember, it really hurts. I missed a lot of their milestones, even the ones where I was physically there.

The other dynamic—my illness—was so great that those milestones were diminished.

I resented John for that, too. You can feel only so much guilt
before you start blaming someone else. I resented John for being
closer to the children than I was. I missed a lot of their baseball
games. The times I did go I assumed all the other mothers there
had it together. Everyone but me. Their nails were done and they
cooked spectacular dinners. I bet if you talked to some of those
people who sat in the bleachers like I did, they would be shocked
that I felt that way. I was always pleasant and responsive. After
all, that's the way I was trained.

The tension of holidays—you could have cut it with a knife.
I had expectations that everything would be perfect, expectations
that could never be realized. And then, when someone screwed
up in any way, I would fulfill the prophecy. Since the occasion
couldn't be what I had hoped, it would be shit. So I made it shit.
I did things like tearing down decorations, throwing silverware
around, and just screaming. It had nothing to do with thinking,
just with feelings and reactions to feelings. I would be tearing
around in the kitchen and John would be standing there saying
calmly, "Now, Anna . . . " I had the feeling I couldn't get
through to him no matter what filthy, disgusting thing I said. I
remember standing there with a stack of plates and smashing one
after the other, asking some rhetorical question, then destroying
another plate until I had shattered every one. We had a new coun-
tertop in the kitchen, and I took a butcher knife and slashed into
the counter until I chipped the whole edge away. Then I had to
look at it every day and be reminded of what I had done. At one
point we ran out of things I could break, and we got unbreakable
dishes. But it didn't stop me from throwing them. And I know
my kids will probably always have a lump in their throats around
holiday time, remembering that their mom always screwed up
holidays.

I did hit the kids—not often, but it was there. I have the worst
aim under normal conditions, but in a state of frenzy, I had the
best aim in the world. I would send something whizzing by your

head so you heard the whizzing, but it would not hit you. It was a conscious choice I made.

I was the door slammer of all time. After I was treated, I had to teach myself to go slowly through doors.

I still have a lot of pain about my deficiencies, especially where Sean is concerned. Sean went from being an only child, the literally fair-haired boy, king of the mountain, to the middle man of five in a centrifuge. He had to be strong for Mack, so therefore he wasn't going to cry. And when I hit him, Sean would just stare at me. There came a time when he did fight back, when he would swing at me, but that was later. I never told him this, but he was so much stronger than I that he scared me. And he was only fighting back in self-defense. Mack fought for Sean, and Mack stood up to me—toe to toe—whereas Sean felt if he submitted, it would be over faster. A couple of years ago, I had a long talk with Sean and I made him cry because I thought he really needed to do it, to express himself. He held me tight and he cried for a long time.

Mack and I have talked, too. We've done it frequently when some memory comes up and prompts a conversation that turns into real exploration. I think the psychiatric community, in an effort to move us along with our lives, sometimes gives us the impression that you can set a date to sit down, discuss something, resolve it, and have that business all done and over with. That would be nice and neat, wouldn't it? But it's not the way it happens. We can learn the tools from our therapy. We can learn how to be tuned in to other people. So when a memory or an issue comes up that needs resolution, you can work on it. And we need to keep working on it. We can't do it all at once.

So often I think about Mack and Sean and try to imagine what it must have been like for them to grow up in our house. I know there were lots of positives.

We were an interesting family. We lived comfortably and we traveled a lot, and my children were exposed to a lot of exciting things not usually available to kids that age.

In the early days of our marriage, when the kids were young—

maybe six and eight—we gave lots of big parties with tents outside and noisy celebrating. In the later years, when I became president of the Screen Actors Guild, we had meetings at our house, and it was always jammed with verbal and fascinating people.

And our house was one of tremendous energy. There were always people going in and out and so many different interests being expressed. David and Allen were electronics freaks and loved taking apart and reconnecting televisions or guitars, and Tom slaved away writing computer programs. Sean and Mack had Little League teammates popping in. I think my kids' lives were enriched because of that kind of variety and from having been presented with so many options.

And even though we all tend to dwell on the negatives, there was so much that I tried to give my children, sometimes small things, ordinary things. Picking them up at school and really being glad to see them. Wondering what kind of day they had. Having an appreciation for each child and his individuality and creativity. Feeling the wonder of each of them. Praising them for the play they put on in the living room. None of my kids ever heard anything from me except, "You can do it." No matter how abysmal the world may have seemed to me, it was with absolute faith that I told them, "Yes, if you want to be a major league baseball star, you can. If you want to be a sportswriter, you can." They never had to worry about my reaction if they brought home a report card with grades less than we had hoped for. There was an exploration of why they had taken a dive in such-and-such a subject, but recrimination was never a part of it.

None of these things are the kind you can mark on a calendar. But they make up healthy and loving memories.

On the other hand, I can only surmise how frightening it must have been for them to live with the kind of unpredictability that characterized our way of life. They referred to what used to happen to me as "Mom's freak-outs." And I have heard them say how scary it felt because they didn't know when I was going to lose it, when I would send something flying through the air or take to my bed or lock myself in the bathroom threatening that "this time I am really going to end it."

Mack and Sean, both in show business now, saw the way other people lived, and they had to know that in our house things were very different. Mack once told a friend that before I was diagnosed he thought I was just a "hot-tempered lady," and that while he could sometimes blame my past, he often blamed himself. He had the feeling that no matter what he did, he couldn't do anything right. And that makes me feel really sad.

It makes me feel sad, too—real physical pain—when I think about some of the especially nice times we had that I spoiled because something would trigger me into a manic or depressive episode. Those wonderful New Year's Eve parties, for instance. We'd have hundreds of people over and celebrate in a big away. But inevitably, after the party was over and the guests had gone home, John and I would get into an argument. Dishes would crash, glasses would shatter, and there was nothing I could do to stop it. It was a kind of unspoken law: first the party, then the craziness.

It seemed that when we were having the most fun there had to be a breaking point. Sometimes, at the end of a lovely dinner when all of us were laughing and probably looking like the Brady Bunch, I would get manicky for what reason I don't know. But there would go the dishes again flying through the windows and Oscar sailing across the room. Or I might destroy something that was important to the kids. Once it was a model airplane that Sean had just made. Or it might be a picture one of them had drawn.

You can imagine how devastated I was when Sean once revealed that he never valued any possessions he had, from computers to Christmas presents to heirlooms. It was a survival technique, I guess. He learned that the more he cared about something, the more likely it was that it would be destroyed. So he got skilled at not becoming attached to any one thing.

Of course, after I did all this devastation, I felt remorseful and would try to make it up to the children any way I could. I would clean and reorganize their rooms, make them perfect and beautiful. And I probably overindulged the kids with gifts and toys. It is hard to orchestrate how a person makes up. If a husband and wife have an argument and one buys the other flowers afterward, is that insincere? It is a way of demonstrating what is going on in our hearts and minds. But there is, of course, a matter of degree.

When I have spoken to groups of people who are concerned about the effect of their illness on their children, they often ask me which I think are worse for the kids: the manias or the depressions. I tell them that neither, of course, is easy, but at least with the manias, my children knew there would be an end within a reasonable period of time. They knew that the mania would stop.

But once I was in bed, behind closed doors, they didn't know what I was thinking or maybe what I had taken. Nobody ever went into Mommy's room; I was just sort of in there like Mrs. Bates at the motel. No matter that I had attempted or threatened suicide in the past and never succeeded, I don't think the kids ever get used to it. In the back of their heads they have to wonder if maybe this time it'll really happen.

I'm ashamed of what I did and what I missed. It brings back my own lost childhood, and I can't fix it. That's the debris I can't sweep away. I can't put it in this book and make it better. It makes me think about my mother and it is like walking for a while in her shoes. I know and understand how her shoes were pinching her. It is history repeating itself. But I've gotten past that kind of thing with my mother. I can have fun with her now. If I can do it, I hope my kids can do it, too.

My best friend, Mary Lou, keeps assuring me that I was a good mother. She's become this very popular decorator and she's working all the time. But she's the kind of friend that you can pick up the phone right where you left off, whether it's been a week or a year. She used to live right across the street from me in Westwood. When she and her family moved, about five years before I did—and they only moved a few blocks away—it changed things. It didn't change what's in my heart; it just changed the practice. It's just not the same as running across the street in your bathrobe.

Although I liked to blame our not seeing each other on Mary Lou's flourishing career and the geographical distance between us, I know there was something else going on, too. I wasn't in the practice of having friends over and making dinner plans. I would think to myself, "I've got to call Mary Lou and we'll go out Saturday." But before Saturday, fifty other things would get in the way. And, for some reason, I didn't make seeing her a priority.

But when we lived on the same street, we'd go shopping together, we would wrap Christmas gifts together, we'd decorate our houses together. Mary Lou was shocked when I told her that that was the first time I'd ever had a girlfriend next door, and how much fun it was. She couldn't believe that I had grown up without a best friend to play with and do things with. But Mary Lou was there for me through the difficult years, and I don't think that my behavior affected our friendship. But Mary Lou seldom saw the worst side of me. I saved that for the family.

So I empathize with family members of anyone who is manic-depressive. They are the innocent bystanders who are being ravaged by this thing, and they don't have the benefit of the insight of the person who is feeling the extreme mood changes. They can't begin to understand how someone can cry for three months in a row or fly off the handle at the flip of a switch. I see family members desperate to help and showing loyalty and love and stamina—and they're in the dark. Until someone gives them the proper diagnosis, they are suffering just as much as the person in depression or in mania. But *they're* not lying in bed. They have to go about their lives, and no one is paying a whole lot of attention to them. The person in depression, whether aware of it or not, is getting a great deal of attention. Not that it helps. But who's giving attention to the attention-giver? Who's replenishing that well?

And the guilt that these people feel—unfounded, completely unfounded guilt—brings them exquisite agony. There is a

209

documentary about manic-depressive illness where a young girl talks about her father tapping on the window of the mental hospital where she leaves him for treatment. That girl's face is exquisite agony. There is no way I could direct a person to act that scene and have it come out that way. I'm not so sure I could even act it. It was so organic and so deeply rooted in pain born of guilt because she was leaving her father there. And she wasn't feeling sorry for herself. She was feeling for him. And God knows what he had done to mortify and embarrass her. But she still was saying, "Oh, my God, look what we did to him."

Mothers and fathers, sons and daughters, husbands and wives, sisters and brothers—they feel impotent. The simplest analogy I can use is to my memories of being a surgical patient and seeing the looks on the faces of my family members who were standing next to the bed while I was in pain. And then remembering times when *I* was the impotent family member standing over a loved one in pain. The position I liked least was watching and being able to do nothing.

After diagnosis, family members have to do a lot of healing. And I am amazed at how well so many recover from the emotional beatings they've taken. It is one of the things that is so reassuring to me about humans: the capacity to forgive once they understand. But I also could never condemn anyone who reached the point where they said they'd had enough. I find that tragically sad, but I can understand that person's need to survive in another way.

I'm thankful my children and I have gotten past that. They don't always follow my advice, but that was something I'm not sure I ever really expected them to do because of my instability for so much of their lives, especially during their formative years. But they have said straight out that they are proud of me. And the most valuable thing they may have absorbed from me is the ability to say I was wrong and I'm sorry. I did a very bad thing, I'm really sorry, and I'll do the best I can to fix it.

Still, I know that all of this doesn't get resolved in five months or even five years and that work on the relationships has to continue. I know that there will be surprises that jump out as the years go by, and that everything is not tied up with a neat little bow. Feelings will probably surface at all those trigger times in our lives—at someone's death or someone's graduation or someone's marriage. But the good news for anyone who is manic-depressive and is being successfully treated is that the work with relationships can continue and you do not have to fall apart under the pressure of difficult times.

Recalling the past will never stop hurting, and I keep wishing there were some way I could make it all up to my children. I have tremendous pride in them, and I think that now they understand that for much of my life I was ill and not in control of my behavior. I think they know how much I love them, and I feel certain they learned from both John and me a strong sense of family loyalty. They have a passion about family bonds, much as I have.

I've encouraged Mack and Sean to talk to me about anything, and I feel as though I have a special, though certainly not perfect, relationship with them. Mack and I have a friendship that is very personal. He's my best audience and I'm his best audience. Sean has said he wouldn't trade his life for any other. When a friend told me that he had described me as the "best mother," one who had given him direction and opportunities for growth, I wept.

I still weep. If only I were able to creep into their heads and their psyches and vacuum out the unhappy memories. But even the most caring mother doesn't have that power. I do what all of us do. I hope and I pray. And I trust that our family bonds are strong enough to dim the past and allow us to enjoy today . . . and tomorrow.

On March 15, 1986, Patty married Michael Ray Pearce, whom she met at Fort Benning in Columbus, Georgia. Patty was working on a television movie, A Time to Triumph, *and Michael, an eleven-year army man, had just graduated from drill sergeant's school. He had two children—Raelene, ten, and Charlene, seven—from a previous marriage. Michael was sent to teach Patty a couple of drills for her role as a woman who joined the*

Army to get medical benefits for her sick husband. This is how Michael describes Patty (whom he calls Anna) and their relationship together.

When I hear about the symptoms Anna tells me she had for all of those years, I can't even imagine them. It's as though I'm hearing about a totally different person.

I remember how I felt when she first told me she had manic depression. It was as though she had said, "I'm wearing a green dress." I had never heard of manic depression, much less known anyone who had it. I only knew that Anna had a certain sweetness about her—I don't like to sound corny—but she had no edge to her. She was so approachable—people just walked up to her and talked to her. They weren't awed by who she is because it's just a human being she presented to them in such a sweet way.

I met Anna in September 1985. My company heard that this television movie was looking for a drill sergeant to audition for a part. And they sent me. I had never done anything like that before. I had never even seen a movie camera. They didn't choose me to be the drill sergeant in the movie, but they wanted me to be an adviser. So that became my role.

When I met Anna, it wasn't an instant "I love you" or "I'm infatuated by you" or "I lust for you" kind of thing. She was kind and friendly and she respected what I had to say. I liked her right away and I asked her how she wanted to be addressed. "Do I call you Miss Duke? Do I call you Patty?" She said "Well, you can call me Patty or Miss Duke, whatever you like. But my name is Anna and I would prefer that." I like that because she wasn't trying to be this actress showing off in front of a bunch of army guys. She was just Anna, this really nice lady.

I worked with her for about two weeks, every day on the set, giving her whatever help I could. The last night, there was a party for her and the other actors. When it was over, she began walking to her dressing room where she was staying during the shoot. I ran over to say good-bye and suddenly we both started crying.

I'm a drill sergeant—I never cried before in my life. I didn't know what the hell was going on. Nothing had happened between us. We had only worked together.

Anna said, "What is happening here?" I said, "I don't know. But I don't want to lose contact with you. I feel like you're part of my life. Can I adopt you as my little sister? Something?"

We were still crying as we said our good-byes, and I left. I thought that was the end of it. But Anna had to come back for another weekend shoot, and I got word that she was in town. Without telling her that I was coming, I went to see her at the hotel. I knocked on her door; she opened it and said, "I'm not going to deny fate. Are you?" And that was the beginning of our relationship.

About a month later, she told me, "I take pills because I have manic depression." She explained that she had been diagnosed in 1982 and that she takes a pill in the morning and a pill at night. She told me a little bit about her past, what manic episodes are, what depressive episodes are. I have to admit that it didn't scare me or bother me then. I was a little intrigued because I wasn't familiar with any of this. And in working with her and getting to know her, I had never seen any of the behavior she was describing.

It has been six years now, and I've still never seen those bizarre, off-the-wall episodes. I know the Anna she is now, not the Anna she says she was. What I've heard and what I've read doesn't even seem possible. There's a small percentage of me that says, "I don't know what this is all about. I don't necessarily buy it. I know it's there. I know it's real . . . but I've never seen it."

This family we have is a very open one. I thought I really worked hard to have an open relationship with my children, Charlie and Raelene. But I didn't know what an open relationship was until I came into this family. Anna and the boys—they can have these very open discussions and express their views and question each other. And they can all be so quick and snappy—not in a mean way, but they'll certainly call a spade a spade.

And the honesty! One of the boys might say to Anna, "You're

just being a bitch to me today." If I had said that to my mother, my dad would have knocked me down the stairs. So it was a little startling. I felt embarrassed—horrified at times—at the openness of their relationship. But it is so much better. You speak your piece, and that's it.

Anna gets whatever is bothering her off her chest. She doesn't harp on it, she doesn't come back to it, and she doesn't use it as a weapon like so many people do. She doesn't do it with a vengeance. She'll say, "This is the way I feel. This is what's wrong, and I think this is the way we can work it out."

Getting to this point hasn't been easy for her. Manic depression or not, habits of a lifetime are not easy to break. And everything wasn't perfect—especially early in our marriage. I saw a few glasses fly or a telephone smashed against a wall or a crying jag.

In those early months, when Anna got angry, she could be so quick, so witty, so very vicious when she wanted to be. She knew all the right buttons to push. And, oh, it hurt. When that happened, I began to lose confidence in myself and wondered if I was the one who caused it, or what I could do to make it stop.

There were a couple of times when we had a fight about something, and Anna would just leave. Luckily, we had a car phone, and I would call her or she would call me, and we would talk.

Or she would have a down time, crying and not wanting to face the day. I have to admit I did get scared. Was this the manic depression breaking through?

Sometimes I'd ask Mack and Sean, "What did I do? What do I do now?" They would comfort me and say, "It's all right. It'll work out." But, of course, they were upset, too. They were hurting.

A couple of times I talked to Dr. Arlen about it. He told me to be patient, to understand that it takes time to break old patterns. Part of this illness, I have learned is getting over the illness. And someone, even on lithium, can have ups and downs. Anna herself knows when she's feeling a little manicky, and she'll go in to have her lithium level checked.

I can't tell. I have never heard the rapid speech and I have never witnessed the "flight of ideas" that she says used to mark the beginnings of her manias. I have seen her angry, sad, happy, nervous, exhilarated, on cloud nine, and everywhere in between. You lose a job, you're sad. Your son gets into college, you're happy. But to me they just seem like normal mood shifts, the kind all of us have. Anna, however, monitors herself well.

I do know her weaknesses. She absolutely has to eat on time and she has to get enough sleep. I try to see that she is not shortchanged on either. When she is, she does get irritable, and neither of us wants to run the risk of that kind of thing triggering an episode.

Sean and Mack had a tough time making the transition between a manic Anna and an angry Anna. When they got into an argument or she became worked up about something, they would immediately think, "Oops, Mom's manic again." It was something they had lived with so long they couldn't easily let go of it. They couldn't accept her anger or frustration as her way of dealing with differences. And they couldn't let her be normal.

I tried to explain to them that there was a difference between being upset and being manic, that she was not going to take off and not come back or stay in bed for weeks. But it took them a while to really believe that. They would ask me, "Does Mom take her medicine all the time?" I assured them that she never misses a day.

It helps that Sean and Mack truly love their mother and that they sensed, even with all the craziness they lived through, that she was there for them. They knew that when an episode was over, it was over, and that she was their mother, she stood by them, and she wouldn't let anything tear them apart.

When we adopted Kevin, I think it made all of us more of a family. Anna and I wanted something between us. We had his, hers, mine, theirs, but not Ours. And we didn't adopt him so we could say, "We have a child." We wanted to give him what we experience together, the love we share, the affection. Both Anna and I gave up a lot for each other. I was a kid from Idaho coming

215

out of the Army who's still learning not to use double negatives. She had to deal with all that. And me, I gave up drinking, partying, being the macho guy I was. But we wanted something special between us, and we wanted this little guy. Mack, Sean, Charlene and Raelene are crazy about him, and we're one very happy family.

CHAPTER TEN

FAMILIES SUFFER AND LEARN

Not everyone who is manic-depressive is as out of control as Patty Duke was. Not everyone shatters china and trashes computers. Not everyone swallows pills and leaps out of cars. But no matter what the form or severity of the symptoms, the families of those who are manic-depressive suffer emotions as intense and racking as those experienced by the victims of the disease. They leapfrog from empathy to exasperation, from anxiety to anger, from fear to frustration. They try to be patient, and fail. They try to understand, then feel guilty because they can't. Sometimes they make it—the marriage stays intact; the children stay connected; the parents offer support. Sometimes they don't. Friends wear out. Spouses lose patience. Children feel overwhelmed and back off. And the victim of manic depression ends up isolated and alone. Whatever the scenario, for every person who is manic-depressive, there are multiple others in agony.

◆

WHEN YOUR CHILD IS MANIC-DEPRESSIVE

"Until I was forty-five, I lived a charmed life," says Miriam, the mother of a thirty-five-year-old daughter with manic-depressive illness. "I had a devoted, prosperous husband, four beautiful children, a lovely home with a swimming pool, and many good friends. Then it all came apart."

When Ellen was in high school, a high-achieving student bringing home all-A report cards, it was difficult for her parents to take her mood swings seriously. If she became especially agitated when exam time was nearing, it didn't seem so unusual. If she locked herself in her room for a weekend because she had no friends, she was just having what her mother calls "social problems." It happens to a lot of sixteen-year-olds. When she went on shopping sprees, spending a lot of money on fancy dresses and floppy hats and chocolate candy, her parents looked the other way. Maybe it was her way of compensating for her loneliness. Besides, Ellen had always been moody, even as a child. Her older sisters would say, "What's wrong with Ellen? Why is she so miserable?"

"In retrospect, there were plenty of signs that something serious was wrong," says Miriam. "I just wasn't tuned in. It was like seeing someone with a fever and a rash and a sore throat, but you don't know what it means. Only when the doctor says it's chicken pox, do you say, 'Oh, yes, I should have known.'"

By her senior year in high school, Ellen's behavior became more peculiar. There were days she couldn't get out of bed and nights when she couldn't sleep. Then her pattern would reverse: she would be up for days at a time, full of energy, cleaning her room, scouring silverware until four or five in the morning. Her sisters, two in college and one in graduate school at the time, urged their parents to take her to a shrink.

"I was beginning to recognize that her behavior wasn't normal," says Miriam. "But my husband didn't want to hear about it. He said I was crazy. This was his beautiful daughter, his perfect family. He couldn't accept that anything could be wrong with her."

So Miriam took her daughter to a psychiatrist without her husband's support. That's when their marriage became shaky. "We were not a team," says Miriam. "We were pulling apart. It became me against him. And it was very upsetting for me to have to go through this essentially on my own."

The psychiatrist said Ellen was depressed. Her father didn't even want to hear the word. "Stop worrying about her," he told his wife. "When she goes to college, she'll settle down. She'll be fine, just fine."

"My other kids agreed with me," says Miriam, "that Ellen needed continued psychiatric care—and it was four against one—but my husband carried more weight."

Ellen started college in September of 1975. A month later, she had her first serious manic episode. She couldn't sleep, and partied all night, a dramatic switch from the withdrawn loner she had been in high school. She began to call home in the middle of the night just because she was up and wanted to chat. She tracked her mother down at work, at her friend's home, at the theater. The minute Miriam walked into her house, she was greeted by the insistent, relentless ring of the telephone, and she would break into a clammy sweat.

Even with Ellen's obvious symptoms of mania, doctors at the college health service could not tell her what was wrong with her. By the time she came home for Christmas, she had escalated into a frenzied manic episode.

But Ellen, you might say, was lucky. The psychiatrist at home recognized instantly that she suffered from manic-depressive illness. He called her mood hypomanic, meaning that her high was short of manic and certainly had not reached psychotic proportions. He prescribed lithium and sent her back to college, confident she would "even out."

"Unfortunately, Ellen was not one of the people who took lithium and lived happily ever after," says her mother. "We never knew whether she was allergic to the drug or whether she just took more than the doctor had prescribed. But she began to have tremors and diarrhea. Her whole body shook. She blew up like a balloon and she couldn't creep out of bed. Her kidneys became affected, she became dehydrated, and she ended up in the intensive care unit of a hospital. I had a Who's Who in the medical field in to save her life."

Three months after her release from the hospital, Ellen switched into depression. And from that point on, she progressed to become a rapid cycler with mood swings that switched every few weeks. Other medications—antidepressants, anticonvulsants—were tried, and failed.

Today she is being carefully monitored on Prozac, with other medications introduced on a trial-and-error basis.

Miriam says her daughter's illness has changed her own life. She had hoped she could return to school herself and complete her degree in accounting. She had to abandon that plan to care for her daughter. Ellen was able to complete college only if she lived at home and commuted. In that way, she could harness her energy to get through the days while her mother took care of her daily needs—shopping, laundry, meals, personal chores such as taking shoes to the shoemaker's and buying a birthday gift for her sister. Most important, her mother monitored her medication because Ellen tended to overmedicate herself.

Today, seventeen years later, Miriam is still her daughter's caretaker. Ellen eventually graduated from college and became an interior decorator. "The only way she can work," says her mother, "is if I do everything else. I'm afraid to leave her alone because there is always another crisis. It's the kind of thing an outsider could never pick up. That's why she can hold a job. But, living with her, I see the signs right away. Talking a little too fast. Sleeping only two or three hours a night. Buying twenty-seven boxes of chocolate-covered cherries.

"She can't be responsible for her own medication. And sometimes when she comes home from work, she gets into bed to energize herself for the next day. She can't wash her own clothes or clean her own room. When she's switching into mania, she doesn't usually pick up the subtle behavior changes that tell me her motor's starting to run, so I have to be vigilant and get her to the doctor before she gets out of control."

Miriam worries about what will happen to Ellen when she may

be too old to care for her or when she is no longer here. She says her daughters worry about Ellen, too. They keep hoping she'll improve enough to live on her own and, perhaps, marry someday. They have visions of "being stuck with her," and they don't like the idea.

Miriam is resentful because her daughter has robbed her of her future. It was a time in life when she had hoped to travel and to become "reacquainted" with her husband, who is close to retirement. Instead, she feels as though she is a prisoner. And her relationship with her husband has suffered. He thinks she babies Ellen too much, and Miriam admits that he may be correct. Even people in Miriam's support group have told her that she may be impeding her daughter's journey into health because she is too available, enabling her daughter to remain dependent. "I may be wrong, but I can't help it," Miriam says. "She's my child, and this is what I have to do."

Parents of children with manic-depressive illness are likely to share problems similar to those experienced by Miriam and her family.

- Fathers are frequently reluctant to acknowledge that their child is in trouble. It is too personal, too close; they feel as though their role as protector of the family has somehow been usurped. It makes them feel guilty, and angry, and often they have no one with whom they feel comfortable discussing those feelings.

  While Miriam was able to join a parents' support group and gain strength from other people's experiences, her husband refused to accompany her. He still finds it easier to deny that his daughter has an illness.

- Conflict between husband and wife about how to handle their ill child is not uncommon. Miriam's husband calls her an "enabler," insisting that Ellen could manage just as well or better on her own. He wants her to get her own apartment so he and his wife can enjoy what's left of their lives. This kind of fundamental disagreement, in addition to the

221

daily strain of living with a manic-depressive child, often results in ruptured marriages.

- Even though parents recognize that the condition is biochemical, it is impossible for them to ignore the influence of environment. They are overwhelmed with guilt and can't resist poking around in the past for clues about what went wrong. They often blame themselves. They were too strict or too permissive. They spent too much time working and not enough with the children. They set a poor example. And they produced "damaged goods."

- Families frequently become socially isolated. In Miriam's case, she and her husband have stopped entertaining because they are tired of answering questions about "why Ellen shakes." And it is difficult for them to explain to friends why they can't accept a dinner invitation or join them for an evening at the theater. Except for Miriam's sister, who lives nearby and holds her hand during the difficult times, she feels very much alone. Her other children are supportive, but they live in different cities and can visit only once a month.

Parenting responsibilities that accelerate rather than diminish as children reach adulthood stimulate resentment and anger. Parents say it throws their lives "out of sync" because they are not prepared to be caregivers again. Husbands and wives vacillate between fulfilling their responsibilities to their child, to each other, and to each of them as individuals.

"I don't think there is anything worse than mental illness in a family," says Miriam. "It affects me every minute of every day."

WHEN A PARENT TRANSMITS
THE ILLNESS TO A CHILD

A parent whose child has manic-depressive illness feels uniquely guilty, especially when she has the illness, too, and feels responsible for having passed it on. Many such parents say it rekindles memories of their own troubled past, and they feel exquisitely the pain and torment of their children.

However, as Patty Duke has said, the manic-depressive parent has an advantage, too. She knows more about the illness, is quicker to spot telltale signs—even subtle ones—and can initiate early treatment.

That's the way it was for Marjorie, who noticed disturbing behavior in her married son, Danny. She got what she calls "vibes" when he began flying from Minneapolis to Las Vegas every weekend, and her daughter-in-law grumbled that he was irritable all the time.

Athough Danny was aware of his family history, he denied that he had a "real" problem. He refused to see a doctor. But more than eight months after these subtle symptoms, he had a manic attack so frightening that his wife rushed him to the emergency room of a hospital. It was three in the morning and she was awakened suddenly by the sound of shattering glass. Her husband was not in bed. Startled, she saw the figure of a man silhouetted outside her bedroom window, his hand pushing against the broken windowpane. As she fled from the room, she heard a familiar voice whispering, "Honey, it's me. Don't be scared."

Later, Danny remembered that he had been lying in bed and seized with a sudden urge to wash the windows of his house. He and his wife had been talking about hiring a window washer, so he had been dreaming about it. The next thing he knew, he was on a short stepladder scrubbing down the windows in his ranch-style home. Inadvertantly, he leaned too heavily against the glass, and it broke.

At the hospital, he admitted that he had had several attacks of what he called "small manias." The pattern was not unusual: racing thoughts, delusions of grandeur, a lifting of inhibitions. Because of his mother's experience, he recognized the symptoms, but tried to conceal them. Admitting that he, too, had fallen prey to the illness represented a sign of weakness. Even though he believed that manic depression is caused by a chemical imbalance, he was certain that it wouldn't happen to him, that he would have the power to wish it away.

Danny's mother says that, knowledgeable as she is about the condition, her son's diagnosis brought her a lot of pain. She sought help through a support group in the Midwest, where, for the first time, she talked with other parents who had children with depressive or manic-depressive illness. Marjorie was not a newcomer to support groups. She had belonged to one for seven years, but it was a group that included mainly victims of the disease, not their offspring or other family members.

"I had forgotten how nurturing it can be to let your hair down and communicate with someone in the exact same position you are. I could feel my guilt draining from me drop by drop. I began to think of all of the conditions we unintentionally hand down to our children—that's what genetics is all about. So should we feel guilty if our daughter is not pretty or our son is born with one leg shorter than the other? But mental illness is different—it still has that stigma all its own and, maybe because you can't see it or touch it, you have the feeling that you should be able to keep it from being transmitted."

Dr. Jan Fawcett, the Stanley Harris Senior Professor and chairman of the department of psychiatry at Rush Presbyterian–St. Luke's Medical Center in Chicago, is well known for his compassion for the victims and families of those with mental illness. He was instrumental in working with Marilyn Weiss and Rose Kurland, the two Chicago women who founded the Depressive and Manic-Depressive Association in 1978, to get the organization started. This organization evolved into the National Depressive and Manic-Depressive Association. Susan Dime-Meenan, NDMDA's executive director, says that without Dr. Fawcett the organization would not have happened.

"When a parent feels she has transmitted manic-depressive illness to her child, the guilt is incredible," Dr. Fawcett says. "I tell such parents that passing on genes is one of the hazards of living. I tell them to blame Adam and Eve.

"If a child gets cancer or heart disease, parents don't feel the same kind of guilt. They don't walk around saying, 'See, I've passed on this cancer gene.' With a mental disorder, it is different because there is still such a stigma attached to it. But it is so unproductive for parents to keep beating themselves up."

◆

WHEN A SPOUSE HAS MANIC-DEPRESSIVE ILLNESS

Tracey and Adam: A Marriage That Survived

Even before Tracey and Adam were married, she noticed that he had mood swings. But she thought that he was just a moody person; once they married and settled down, he would become more even.

That didn't happen. In fact, Tracey began to notice worrisome behaviors that were sometimes so subtle no one else would have picked them up. A sudden tightening of the jaw. A slumping of the shoulders. Long quiet times. Then, suddenly, nonstop talk, talk that often made little sense. Grandiose ideas. Speeding on the highway. At first Tracey thought it was her fault. She thought the mood shifts were caused by something she said or didn't say, something she did or didn't do. But she had no idea then that Adam's behavior would become so erratic that she would consider ending their marriage.

Within a year, Adam's symptoms worsened. He swung rapidly from high to low with no provocation. During the highs, he felt powerful and concocted schemes that Tracey knew couldn't materialize. Her husband's attitude became hostile: "If you won't go along with my ideas, I'll find someone who will."

When he was down, he was frightened that Tracey would leave him, and said, sobbing, that he couldn't live without her. She kept getting mixed messages and admits that she felt as though she were losing her mind. The fear and disgust came later.

Adam is a big man—large-boned and husky—with a booming voice. Tracey is five feet tall and weighs ninety-five pounds. When Adam became more manic more often, he slammed doors, pounded on furniture, and ripped every towel in the linen closet to shreds. When Tracey tried to calm him, he frightened her. She sensed he was out of control and might do something violent. She remembered the movie *The Three Faces of Eve* and thought her husband was perhaps one of those people with multiple personalities. The two Adams she saw were so different from each other.

When he went through depressions, which extended from a couple of days to a couple of weeks, he would lie in bed, crying and sighing. He wouldn't shower or change his clothes or brush his teeth. He grew a scruffy beard because he wouldn't shave. Tracey says she had to change the linens with him still in bed, a formidable task for someone her size. She began to loathe this man she once loved.

Adam refused to see a doctor. He said there was nothing wrong with him, that Tracey was the one who needed help. It was only after his wife said she was consulting an attorney about a divorce that he agreed to see a psychiatrist.

"The period before Adam's diagnosis was the worst time for me," said Tracey. "Not knowing what is wrong with someone is terrifying. You begin to question yourself, and sometimes you feel as though you are being gaslighted. When the doctor diagnosed Adam as having manic-depressive illness, I felt this wonderful sense of relief. It wasn't me. It was Adam, and he did have a disease."

Tracey had begun to see a psychiatrist even before her husband was diagnosed, to help her think through the idea of divorce. Now she continued because she needed to talk with someone about her anger and resentment and her fear of the future. Through the psychiatrist, she was referred to a support group for families of patients with mood disorders.

"That psychiatrist and the support group were my lifelines

during a very difficult time," says Tracey. "Everyone can identify with how hard it is to live with a person who is just moody. But you can't imagine what it's like to wake up every morning wondering what the day will bring. Will your husband be pleasant or sullen? Will he be tearing around the house in a frenzy, or will he spend the day crying in bed? I felt as though I had to walk on eggshells, and my stomach was in a constant knot."

Because Adam became a rapid cycler and was resistant to treatment, it took five years for him to find the combination of medication that worked. There were many times during that period that Tracey thought she would lose her own mind. But the support group and the presence of friends and family helped.

"Normally, I'm a private person, and it makes me uncomfortable to share my most personal feelings with others," Tracey says. "But therapy helped me understand that if I allowed myself to be more open, to share my secret, I could get the strength to wade through the grimmest time of my life."

Tracey has a strong faith and believes in the power of prayer. She prayed every day. She learned to take one day at a time. Now, eight years later, she feels rewarded for having stayed with her marriage. She and Adam have two sons, and Adam has become, once again, the man she married—warm and sensitive, deep-thinking and creative, someone who is genuinely concerned about his family and about the community.

Many family members agree with Tracey that the period before diagnosis is the most troubling. Without knowing that a spouse suffers from an illness, it is almost impossible to tolerate the sharp behavioral changes, the inexplicable, often abrupt shifts from the heights to the depths. When mood swings are more subtle, a spouse often doubts her own sanity. She wonders why other people don't see what she does.

But even after diagnosis, even with the knowledge that this is an illness, the strongest, most loving marriage is severely tested when symptoms are frequent and disruptive. Often those marriages do not survive.

227

Christel and Larry:
A Marriage That Shattered

During their three-year courtship, Christel saw no signs that her husband-to-be, Larry, was mentally ill. He was quiet, gentle, and soft-spoken. But eleven months to the day from their wedding, she saw a stranger on her porch, screaming and banging on the door. Larry was talking nonstop about a scam at work, but nothing he said made sense. He paced the floors and insisted he was God. Abruptly, he left the house and drove to his boss's home, where he beat on the windows until they broke. It was obvious that Larry was very ill.

He was admitted to a mental hospital immediately. But the next morning, Christel was notified that Larry had vanished during the night. Two days later he was found wandering around the railroad tracks, carrying a Bible and giving communion to passersby. Although Larry had never been a churchgoer or even a devout man, his form of mania—believing that he was God and could "save" people—is common. It demonstrates the grandiose feelings that often engulf those in extreme mania.

A month later, when insurance coverage had expired, Larry was released from the hospital. He was still soaring in mania, and Christel was terrified.

At home, Larry, an outspoken abstainer, began to chain-smoke cigarettes and pipes. He put on a hat, perched on a chair, surrounded by pillows, and announced that he was God. His magic number was five. He had to eat five cookies, buy five lawn mowers, make five telephone calls. He tore through magazines, yanking out anything showing the number five, and pasted them helter-skelter on the bedroom walls and ceiling. He threw flour and water together in a pot and shoved it into the oven to make what he called "stone cakes"—five of them. He began a dozen projects, but finished nothing. He was driven to wash clothes . . . but he never dried them. So drawers were stuffed with water-logged sweaters and pajamas and towels.

A week later, he was back in the hospital. Neither Larry nor

Christel had slept in three days—he because he was manic, she because she was petrified.

This time, he was hospitalized for three weeks, and at the end of that time he was diagnosed as having manic-depressive illness. For the next six years, Larry took his lithium every day, and Christel felt revived. Her husband was stable and held a job, and they were able to entertain family and friends without worrying about Larry's doing something embarrassing. Christel relaxed in her marriage and finally felt reassured enough to have a baby.

The night she went into labor, Larry's mania burst through again. "I woke him at two in the morning to say I was having labor pains, and I could see he was manic," Christel says. "His eyes were glassy and he talked a mile a minute. I couldn't understand anything he said, but somehow he managed to get me to the hospital.

"After I delivered the baby, his mania became full-blown. He went home from the hospital every day and sold almost all of our furniture. He gave my car to a church. He invited six hundred people to a welcome-home party for me and the baby—crates of liquor, sixteen hundred dollars' worth, arrived at the house. He bought five of everything the baby needed—five bibs, five bottles of baby oil, five infant seats. Then he bought flags, dozens of American flags, and stuck them in our lawn. When the baby and I came home from the hospital, he was God again, this time a Jewish God. He was wearing a prayer shawl and a yarmulke."

That's when the relationship between Christel and her parents became strained. They urged her to leave Larry, insisting that he was going to ruin her life and that of their child. "It got so bad, my mom and I argued every time we talked or saw each other. I couldn't confide in her about the bizarre things he would do because I knew what she would say: 'Get rid of him.'"

Another hospital stay followed, his longest, three months and four days. Money had long since run out and the bills were piling up. Christel was afraid they would lose their only possession— their house.

By the time Larry was discharged from the hospital, he had

moved into his first depression. He wrecked his car and tried to kill himself with pills. He was taking lithium and antidepressants and sleeping pills because the doctors warned that loss of sleep could precipitate mania.

The next time Larry became manic—two months later—he was violent. He hit Christel, pushed the baby down the stairs, and claimed he was receiving messages from a higher being.

"That did it," Christel says. "I couldn't take any more. I called my mother, who by this time hated Larry for what he was doing to me. I bundled up the baby and took a cab to my parents' house.

"Later that week, a friend told me, 'You marry for better or for worse. If you love him, you should stand by him.' I told my friend not to judge. 'Until you walk in my shoes, don't tell me how I should feel.' There is no way anyone can imagine what I had been through. Sometimes I don't believe it myself. I really loved Larry. But love wears out. And that's another person in his skin, not the one I married."

Christel's worries are far from over. Larry's family history is rife with mental illness. His twenty-six-year-old sister, also a manic-depressive, killed herself by taking an overdose of sleeping pills. A brother, happily married, with two beautiful children, also committed suicide. Larry's grandmother on his father's side had been institutionalized for severe depression, and his grandfather on his mother's side, while never having been in the hospital, is described by family members as "crazy."

Christel is concerned about her son, Chris, now five. Will he inherit the gene? Can she do something to prevent mental illness in him? If he does have the condition, will lithium work?

"I try not to think about it," she says, "and the further I get from the nightmare I lived through, the easier it gets. But no matter what happens to me as I grow older, I'll never forget. Those days and nights are carved into my memory forever."

Like many spouses who are left to raise children alone, Christel is resentful and angry. She wants her son to know his father, but she is afraid to allow them to be alone together. A court order states that because Larry's illness cannot be controlled successfully with medication and his behavior remains unpredictable, all visits with his son must be monitored. Chris has asked his mother why he can't go to the zoo alone with his father or why she won't let him take a trip to Disney World with his dad.

"Chris is not only a child of divorce, which is tough enough, but the child of a manic-depressive parent and maybe the child of an alcoholic, because in the last year Larry has started drinking excessively," says Christel. "I am furious. I know I shouldn't be angry at Larry for being sick, but I can't help it. It is just too hard for me to separate out how much is him and how much is the illness. But at this point, the difference for me is a semantic one. My child does not have a father. I do not have a husband. And I have a long, tough road ahead of me."

"This illness is tremendously destructive," says Dr. Fawcett. "The divorce rate when a spouse is manic-depressive is very high. The husband or wife who must endure a day-to-day relationship with someone from whom they can't get a positive response and whom they can't help is demoralizing.

"People like to think that they contribute to a person's getting better. They feel that if they provide the right support, if they cheer him up, if they tell her to count her blessings, they can change the course of the illness. It has to do with the way we separate mind and body. But it doesn't work, and the spouse feels rejected and gets enormously frustrated.

"Spouses blame themselves for not being able to turn the illness around, and often there is ambivalence about who is the failure: the one who is ill or the one who can't make him better. When someone whose spouse is in a manic episode asks me what he or she can do, I tell them to close the bank account and wait it out. Understanding the limitations of a person with manic-depressive illness often brings some peace. But the longer it goes on, the more it corrodes a marriage."

When a relationship is poor to start with, the ill person is usually blamed right away, and is not supported, and the marriage can deteriorate quickly. In a healthy family, the spouse will usually do his or her best to help. But if a person is not treated, or if he refuses to take his medication or is not responsive to medication, a spouse gets exasperated and discouraged. "Over time, it can extinguish even the strongest relationship," Dr. Fawcett says.

WHEN A SIBLING HAS MANIC-DEPRESSIVE ILLNESS

"I wish I didn't hate my sister, but I do," says Judd, who laments that his sister's illness robbed him of his childhood. Judd, now thirty, has been in psychotherapy for two years to help him feel less guilty and find a way to have a comfortable relationship with his sister.

From the time Judd was three, he remembers his older sister, Arlene, as being willful and moody. She threw tantrums, spoiled family vacations, sulked in her room for days, and picked fights with him several times a week. Until he was six or seven, he accepted that "that's just the way my sister was." It never occurred to him or his parents that she had a mental illness.

"As we got older, Arlene became bossy and domineering and no one could tell her anything," Judd says. "The word that describes her best is 'disagreeable.' She thought her way was the only way—the only way to make a bed, the only way to wash dishes, the only way to cook an egg.

"But then she went off the deep end. She would make telephone calls all over the country to people she had met on some trip or at camp. Some of them didn't even remember her. Usually she called them in the middle of the night.

"When my father got the telephone bill, he would explode. So my house was always crackling with tension. It was an unpleasant place to grow up. All of us—my mom, my dad and I—kept waiting for her next outburst.

"Sometimes she would go to the cemetery in the middle of the night; she said she heard voices that told her to do it. Then when she was about eighteen and I was seventeen, she went through what I thought then was a promiscuous period; she became flirtatious and wanted to seduce every male she saw. It didn't matter whether it was a waiter in the restaurant, the paperhanger who was doing our kitchen, or my friend Barry, who wasn't the least bit interested in her. Once, when Barry came over, she jumped on his lap and started to unbutton his pants.

"That did it. I couldn't even bring a friend home without being humiliated. I screamed at my parents to get her out of the house, that she was a nut case, that she belonged in an institution. Nobody normal behaved that way. In retrospect, I probably overreacted, but I carried on so badly that my parents sought medical help for her.

"I went with them and helped describe my sister's behavior. The doctor kept nodding his head as though he knew what I was going to say next. We spent three hours there while this doctor asked us all kinds of questions: Did she get moody when the seasons changed? Did my mom have postpartum depression? When did the family first notice her mood swings?

That day, the doctor diagnosed Arlene as having manic-depressive illness. He explained that she could not control the way she behaved. Judd remembers feeling guilt and shame. His sister had a disease and he had been hating her for it. Still, he kept thinking of the toll her illness had taken on him, how it had "spoiled" his growing-up years, and he couldn't stop being resentful.

Unfortunately, his sister did not respond well to medication. In the next five years, she was in the hospital seven times.

Judd remembers the first time with anguish. "Arlene looked after me and my parents as we walked down the hall to the elevator, and she was crying. She kept saying, 'Please, don't leave me. I'll be good. I promise.' That picture of her when she was twenty-one and pleading still haunts me.

"Today I say to myself, 'How cruel can you be? You know your sister is so fragile. When will you stop hating her?'"

Judd hopes that his therapy will help him find a way. "I don't want to carry this bitterness with me for the rest of my life. And I also want to get rid of the guilt that tags along with me every place I go. I feel as though I just can't win."

Brothers and sisters often are the strongest supports for their manic-depressive sibling. But if the illness has gone on for a long time, as in Arlene's case, resentment builds toward the sibling who has received all the attention. "The longer a brother or sister has been in crisis, sucking up all the feelings and resources in the family—a frequent occurrence—the more bitterness there will be," says Dr. Fawcett. "And often they fear that they will be next. They may cope by disassociating themselves totally from their manic-depressive sibling because it is the only way they can survive."

PATTY DUKE'S SIBLINGS: THEY WOULD HAVE HELPED

Patty Duke's brother, Raymond, and sister, Carol, had a different experience because they did not live with their sister during her most turbulent times. Most of what they knew about her they read in magazines or newspaper articles.

But like Judd, they did not recognize that Patty could be suffering from a mental illness. Raymond thought she was just "flaky"—a little "wired," maybe a victim of too much alcohol. Carol attributed her sister's behavior to being a celebrity, being caught up in the eccentricities of show business.

But in the early 1970s when Raymond visited her in California, he saw a side of her that stunned him. "She had some kind of argument with Desi Arnaz, Jr.," Raymond remembers, "and then there was this sudden explosion. I've seen people have arguments before, but not like this. She went tearing around, throwing things, taking it out on everybody in the room. Everybody paid the price. It didn't make sense. It scared the hell out of me. Still, it never occurred to me it was a sickness."

Carol and Raymond both say that had they known Patty was mentally ill, they would have been supportive. They would have been there when she needed them. "No matter how little we saw each other, no matter anything, she's my sister," says Raymond, "and if someone would have let me know she was in trouble, I'd have been around for her."

"The years we missed together were a loss for both of us, and I still feel sad about that," Carol says. "But it is what is happening in our lives right now that is important, and today my sister and I are very close." Carol's advice to the loved ones of people suffering from mood disorders is "Continue to love them however they may hurt you because they don't mean to do it. Try to be supportive and hang in."

◆

WHEN A PARENT HAS MANIC-DEPRESSIVE ILLNESS

Children who have a parent with manic-depressive illness often carry the scars for a lifetime. Even when they are old enough to understand that their parent's behavior was not intentional, it doesn't always make up for the deprivation or the abuse they suffered as children. As thirty-three-year-old Annie says, "I forgive my mother. But I will never forget."

What Annie can't forget is the feeling of being alone, of having no one to give her direction and care what happened to her. Although she had a father and an older brother, her mother, she says, was never there for her. She was either hiding her head under the pink-flowered sheets on her king-size bed or giddy with bursts of energy that were meaningless because they were so unproductive. The highs meant vacation plans that never materialized and parties that never happened. The lows meant suicide threats.

"I didn't know what was wrong with my mother," Annie says. "The times my mom stayed in bed for days, I felt as though she had died. I used to go into my bedroom and pray. I would ask God to make her come out of the room, to be the mommy she was last week."

When Annie was as young as four, she remembers screaming out at night and awakening stiff as a board. When she got older, she thought about running away. But she was too scared. By the time she was thirteen, she was anorexic, although she didn't

235

know then that there was a word for being five feet four and weighing sixty pounds. She was afraid to eat because she always felt as if she were going to throw up. It didn't help that friends would say to her, "Your mother is crazy."

When Annie was fifteen, she began to smoke pot and drink because there were no limits set for her. Her mother was always sick and in her own world, her father was weak and ineffectual, and her brother was in college. The first time she had sex, she became pregnant and had an abortion.

All the while, no one in the family knew that Annie's mother had a bona fide illness, although she had had symptoms for fifteen years. It had begun with postpartum depression right after Annie was born.

Annie's brother, Joe, remembers his mother walking around the house with dark glasses, never smiling. He said she had "this otherworldly look about her" and just stared into space a lot. "She was uncommunicative, sad, in great despair, and unreachable," Joe recalls. "I would sit with her for hours and try to talk to her, thinking I could help. I learned how to cook and do the laundry and clean the house because I thought by doing these things I would lighten her load and she would feel better."

It was the evening of their parents' twenty-fifth wedding anniversary that changed their lives. Annie and Joe had planned a surprise party, something really special at the best restaurant they could afford. But that day their mother became despondent and wouldn't even get dressed. They had to reveal the surprise so she could be "dragged to the party." The next morning, Joe made an appointment with a leading Boston psychiatrist. Two days later his mother was diagnosed as having manic-depressive illness and was placed on lithium.

Today, Joe is gay and his sister is having a relationship with a woman. She doesn't call herself a lesbian because she has been attracted to men in the past and said she probably could be in the future. But both of them believe that their current sexual preferences are not a coincidence.

"My mother never talked with me or showed me by her behavior how to relate to men," Annie says. "And I've spent my whole life searching for the mother I never had. Right now I think I've found her in a nurturing, caring, and strong woman who fills my emotional needs. But it isn't easy, and it certainly isn't the way I had envisioned my life."

Joe agrees. He believes he was the product of a dysfunctional household with distorted role models, and that it propelled him toward homosexuality. He moved to England when he was twenty-nine because "it is just too painful to be near my parents."

Children of manic-depressive parents do not have an easy road, says Dr. Fawcett. The parent is at best unpredictable and at worst abusive. A child has no capability of understanding that kind of behavior.

While Dr. Fawcett has not seen children turn to homosexuality because of a parent's manic-depressive illness, he says it isn't hard to imagine. "A lot of people seek out what they missed. If what they missed was a nurturing mother or a strong father, they may very well look for that as adults. They are angry about what they didn't get, and that anger lives on."

Children often move away, as Joe did. They may refuse to see their parent and bar any association with grandchildren, even after the parent has been medicated and is under control—because the memories are too painful. Disassociating—shutting them out—is the only way they can go on with their lives.

Psychiatrist Steven Secunda, formerly with the National Institute of Mental Health, has a busy practice in Springfield, Pennsylvania. In his experience, most family members have more trouble before a patient is diagnosed, before they know that his bizarre behavior is not willful and deliberate. Once they know that their relative suffers from an illness, their anger and resentment usually soften.

It is during manic episodes, says Dr. Secunda, that the patience of a family is most severely tested. While the manic-depressive patient is energized by his highs, those he lives with dread them.

"It is much more difficult," says Dr. Secunda, "for most people to endure mania than it is depression because it is unthinkable that a person isn't somehow responsible for what he is doing, that he isn't able to control his behavior. It is easier for others to have sympathy for someone who is hurting."

One of Dr. Secunda's patients, currently in a manic phase, is "driving his family crazy." They can handle his depressions but not his manias. Dr. Secunda is trying to sensitize them to the total illness that is manic depression so that they understand both phases of it. If they can, not only will their frustrations and anger ease, but they can become invaluable members of his treatment team. They can give Dr. Secunda critical feedback by observing the effects of medication and describing symptoms that the patient cannot recognize.

Patients are poor at discerning and reporting the details of their manias, Dr. Secunda says. Unless they are experiencing psychotic or near-psychotic symptoms, they may notice only that they sleep a little less, that they feel a little better. Family members can see even minor behavioral changes—spending sprees, speaking at high speed, agitation, the inability to sleep—that could signal the start of a manic episode. That kind of feedback from the family to the doctor can make a critical difference in the success of treatment.

However, as Patty Duke has said, even effective treatment doesn't solve all the problems of the past. In addition to the always present concern about recurrence of episodes, there is a lot of unfinished business for all family members. Discussing them in family or individual therapy is often helpful. So is attending support group meetings for families. These groups, with their newsletters and hot lines, their information and referral services, their educational programs, and their easy access to other people who have been through the same wars, can often be a lifeline to the future. They can keep people anchored and help families get on with their lives.

CHAPTER ELEVEN

LIFE AFTER MANIC DEPRESSION

I'd be less than honest if I said that manic depression is not part of my life today. For one thing, it is my genetic heritage, and that never goes away. Second, I am who I am, with behavior patterns that have been going on for years. Just taking a pill doesn't mean I'm going to become a different person. The whole world doesn't immediately turn rosy. So I keep working really hard to break behaviors I don't like in my myself. I practice. It's like playing the piano. I practice. I screw up. I practice again. But it keeps getting easier. The worst fear anyone with manic depression has is that someone will call her crazy. Well, now someone has. So I can relax and try to fix it.

I work at not flying off the handle, at not having outbursts that will put me and my family through days or weeks of torture. And I'm much, much better at it. Each of us develops our own way. Some of us learn to count to ten or just walk out of the room. I've used both of those methods. Or sometimes I'll just recognize that I'm crabby, but in a kind of curmudgeony way now, not in a manicky way. I'll admit it—I'll just say, "I'm crabby now. Leave me alone." And I'll go off by myself for an hour to chill out. To me, that's an unbelievable freedom. It's a freedom I never felt before because I had to be something or some way that someone else wanted me to be. Or because my illness was pushing me to be a certain way. Now I'm in control. If I don't feel like talking, I don't talk, and I don't have a problem about it. I don't have to go around saying, "Are you mad at me because I didn't talk?"

It is a question of relearning—or maybe learning for the first time—how to behave the way you want to behave. I may have had the same desire before I took lithium, but there was no way I could have done it. I'm light-years away from that now.

I'm conscious of how much more stable I am and also of how far I still want to go. But because I made the decision, five years ago, to use my celebrity status to spread the word, the world of manic-depressive illness is never too far away from me.

When *Call Me Anna* was written, I suddenly found myself "out of the closet." I had been very up front in the workplace and with everyone I knew because for me my diagnosis was something to rejoice about. But writing it down, making the words permanent, was a nerve-racking experience. When I read the first draft of that book, it was a cathartic experience for me. And when I went on tour with it, I became aware that I was into the twelfth step of Alcoholics Anonymous's famous twelve-step program: spreading the word, shining light on someone else's life.

Then came the invitations to speak. I had never thought of myself as a public speaker and it terrified me—not so much that I was going to be talking about my illness, just that I was going to stand up there by myself and "speechify," as I call it. But it was another opportunity to perform that twelfth step.

In the beginning, I tried to write a speech, something I had never done before. And there was a lot of running around my bedroom, babbling, "Why did I do this? I can't do this. Tell them I'm sick! Oh, my God, what have I done? Now I'm obligated to stay sane. Me and my big mouth." But the mania never kicked in because I wasn't manic anymore.

And I never did write a speech. I'd write a few words and then I'd be constipated—I couldn't go on. So I just made some jottings about points I wanted to get across. For someone who has spent a lifetime being very disciplined and prepared in the workplace and in public, this felt very odd. Talk about living on the edge.

But, during the first speech I made, I realized what was going on. I wasn't preaching to an audience. I was having an exchange with them. As I was being introduced, I thought, "This is really show-and-tell. So I'll show them some of mine and then they'll show me some of theirs." I got up there and I began to talk. I don't know where they came from—the words or the structure—but they were there. The speech had a beginning, a middle, and an end, and it even had some jokes in it.

It lasted about twenty minutes, which surprised the hell out of me. If anyone had told me I could speak off the top of my head for twenty minutes, I would have had them committed. It was exhilarating, especially when I had finished and we moved into an open forum. I can only liken it to a revival meeting. People were standing up, saying things they had never said to themselves or to another soul—like talking to a stranger in an airplane. "I think this is what is the matter with me, or with my sister or my son." They cried, they laughed, they searched themselves, and some of them made decisions—there on the spot—either to get help or to stop fighting the help they were getting.

At the end of the two hours, I was spent . . . and inspired to do it again. Once I had made the decision to reveal my big, ugly secret, it was like eating peanuts. I had to keep going. If I could help just one person, I would be happy.

It wasn't easy. It never got easy to stand up before a big group of people and say, "I have a mental illness." But each time, as the numbers accumulated, as more people came, it made more sense. What I was doing had a purpose. I was confident enough myself to make others feel safe in revealing their secrets. I tried hard to say the right words, to hit a nerve, to give them hope. I'd try eighty-seven different approaches because it mattered to me that they got what I was saying.

Sometimes, as people told their stories, their pain was so rampant I thought I would die just listening to their agony. Afterward I would go home with a big-time migraine headache. It took me

241

a long while to figure it out, but I understood, finally, that I didn't have enough training to put a buffer between myself and those people in pain. If I did, it probably wouldn't have worked as well. But I was absorbing everyone's experiences, and feeling them so deeply that I was oatmeal for three to five days afterward.

After some exploration, I began to learn how to monitor what I expected of myself and to accept that my responsibility was limited. I'm not a doctor and I couldn't stand up there, diagnose everyone, prescribe their medications and their form of follow-up therapy. I started to perceive my role more realistically, as that of a facilitator, and to recognize that my batting average would be right up there with Henry Aaron's. I wasn't going to make a hit every time with every person. These were people out there with real-life crises going on, and I could never take any of that lightly. What I said to them was very important to me. But some of the folks I talked to were *not* going to go for help, and that had nothing to do with me. My job as a communicator was to let them know they had options and to show them, through my own experience, that they could become healthy, functioning human beings.

For a year I toured the country, meeting with small groups of patients and talking to audiences who were interested in manic-depressive or depressive illness.

Many people in those groups were family members who were struggling to figure out whether their husband or wife or son or daughter was mentally ill. That's a tough one. Not everyone with mood swings has manic-depressive illness. Sometimes a cigar is just a cigar. With information, they could learn the difference. I would encourage them to see a doctor, preferably someone they knew and trusted—at least for a referral. Then they could make a choice: about their loved one and about themselves, about their willingness to stay in the situation they described.

Rarely did someone stand up and admit, "I'm ill." They would say, "Oh, my God, I do what you describe." I don't know what brought them to that meeting, but they did not know that what was wrong with them was a mental illness. Or at least they wouldn't acknowledge it to themselves.

Typical questions were:

Did lithium make you gain weight?

What kind of side effects did you have?

There seemed to be a lot of trepidation about taking medication. And I could understand that. My response was "Okay, suppose you get diagnosed. And you take the medicine for three or four weeks and you don't like it—for whatever reason. You're getting too fat. It's giving you blurry vision. You prefer to be manic. Whatever it is, no one will be standing there with a gun insisting you take the next pill. I don't recommend *not* taking it, but it's *your* choice. How will you know unless you try it?"

That sounds so simple, but sometimes it is the simplest, seemingly most inane, most practical stuff that matters the most to someone. We can explore all the esoteric concepts and philosophize all we want to, but sometimes somebody just wants to know, "Is it a yellow pill or a green pill? Do you take it with water or milk? Is it going to make you throw up?"

When I went to Washington to testify at congressional hearings, I kept harping on the cost-effectiveness of treatment for depression. It is all there in those lovely black-and-white numbers they love so much. In my own case, my general medical bills have dropped by fifty thousand dollars a year since my diagnosis. Up until then I was always in the hospital for some phantom illness, running up bills that the insurance company was paying. I'd be in there ten days at a stretch and nobody could find anything wrong with me. But there I was with symptoms, real symptoms born of depression. I haven't been in the hospital since I was diagnosed.

On a few occasions, I talked to legislators at special breakfasts in California. They thought they were coming to hear this actress stand up and make a pitch for funding for mental health. They were not expecting to hear a personal account of my illness. But I would look around, and as I was saying things such as, "Depression was something that ran in my family . . . " you could just see jaws drop. And as I continued I could see little nods of recognition. The people didn't necessarily know that I noticed, but they were revealing that they had personal knowledge of what I was talking about.

There are some points I always try to make. You can have manic-depressive illness without having an ounce of creativity. If you are creative, don't be afraid of medication. I don't think it makes the well dry up. It certainly didn't for me. Once you have experienced creativity, you'll find a way back to it.

I tell people to monitor their self-pity. Self-pity is very unattractive. A sense of humor is wonderful, and I've noticed that it's something those of us who have been diagnosed and treated have in common. You can say we're crazy in front of us and we don't wither and die. I think the humor comes out of the relief.

There are enough people out there who still equate mental illness with damaged goods that can't be fixed. We make jokes about being crazy—it's part of our lexicon. Someone acts strangely—they're crazy. They have the scarlet letter on them and that's that. I emphasize that people should not be ashamed of mental illness, that they don't need to talk about it in hushed, conspiratorial tones. That's why I think it's important for people who are well known to speak out and reinforce for those who don't have famous names that they are part of a club that is a healthy one . . . or can be.

And I keep harping on making amends to those you have hurt—using your diagnosis as an explanation, not an excuse, for bad behavior.

I continue to be startled at how pervasive mental illness is— how many people are affected. One night about nine o'clock, I was in the supermarket checkout line. The second person behind me leaned forward and said, "I just want you to know I have the same illness you have. I'm taking my medicine and you make me feel good every time I see you on TV." Then the woman in the middle spoke up and said, "I have it, too."

Now, what are the chances of three of us stacked up in the

supermarket line, all of us with manic-depressive illness? I've learned that the chances are pretty good. At one time, these women would have whispered to me privately. Now they just blurted it out. That's progress.

I often think of how lucky I am that I live in a society and work in an art form that is more liberal, more accepting, more understanding than the rigid business world. I remember embracing women after a seminar and having them say softly in my ear that they can't go out, as I do, and talk about it yet. And that they felt almost guilty that they couldn't run back to their real estate offices or their banks and announce that they were manic-depressive. I told them it isn't necessary that they do that. What I think *is* necessary is living your life to the best of your *new* ability. It is up to people like me who have access to the media and the support of most of the community I live in to spread the word.

And even for me, I will probably never know what it has cost me to be what I once heard someone refer to as the "mental illness poster child." Personally, it costs me nothing. I only gain from it. It thrills me to talk to someone and see in her eyes that a connection has been made, to see that communion of spirit. It is like an electrical charge when people come up to me in restaurants or public bathrooms and tell me about themselves or some family member. And when I get a letter saying, "I took the bull by the horns and now my husband has been diagnosed," I feel all through me a moment of exhilaration.

I'm grateful that I wasn't so buried from hurt and pain and anger and betrayal that I lost my sensitivity on the way. The way I run my books—my personal journal of credits and debits—losing my sensitivity would be too great a cost. But as for my career, have I made some people uncomfortable enough that they may not want to hire me? I may never know for sure, but I don't think so.

The fact that my colleagues elected me president of the Screen Actors Guild in 1985 gave me publicly the "responsible citizen" title that I had been hoping for for a long time. It made me realize how many people stuck with me, more than I could have imagined. It was not just the numbers of people who voted for me but the people who called other people and asked for the funds to support my campaign. I was mortified that anyone would do that—ask for money for my campaign. But they did, and the people gave. Not only did they give, but they always asked, "How is she? God, we haven't seen her since . . . Send her our loving wishes."

My recovery from manic depression has been an evolution, not a sudden miracle. Four years ago, for instance, we were at our farm in Idaho, and the kids had made a mess and nothing seemed to be going right. It was the kind of scene where, without lithium, furniture would have been thrown, dishes would have been smashed, the kids would have been hit. Instead, it was a lot of yelling, and it had to do with real things that had upset me. And that was okay. But then I found it escalating to a point that *did* worry me. After I was finished screaming at the kids for legitimate reasons, I started railing at Mike unreasonably. And I ran upstairs, slammed the door, and continued yelling. I was raging—white anger—totally disproportionate to anything that had happened—and, finally, I came out of my room and knocked the banister right off the hallway wall.

Then I caught myself before it went any further. I immediately apologized to the kids and to Mike, and we tried to figure out what had happened. We finally deduced that I was exhausted, completely, physically exhausted, and that I was suffering from sleep deprivation. I had been going to bed at two and getting up at five and doing things around the farm and trying to make sure all the kids were happy. It's something that we're very careful about now. For people like me, sleep deprivation is the big enemy.

But that was four years ago. For someone who spent at least 50 percent of her life screaming and yelling about something, I'm now down to, say, 5 percent. Sometimes I even surprise myself. A couple of summers ago, we all went through an incredibly stressful period. We had just moved from Westwood to Encino, and we were painting and rearranging and tearing out walls and adding windows and all that sort of thing. Sean was graduating from high school and we had a huge party, Mack had won a Who's Who writing award from the city, my mother was sick, I was making a speech at a major benefit, my stepdaughters were here for the summer, and Kevin's adoption was being finalized. It's almost a joke when I think about what went on in a two-week span—major life events.

So we decided to get away to our farm in Idaho. I thought, "Just let me get to where I can hear the cows moo or bellow or whatever it is cows do." So a caravan—Mike and I, the girls, a friend, Kevin and the guys, and our three dogs—left for Idaho in two cars.

We got near the farm, pulled up the long two-and-a-half-mile dusty road, and jumped out of the cars. I was dragging behind a little with Kevin when I heard the kids screaming, "Oh, my God, oh, my God." Mike ran in the house and came out looking like a ghost. Nobody knew quite what to say. There was a combination of "Come on in, you've got to see this!" and "Don't come in. Stay where you are."

It turned out that woodpeckers had pecked through several holes right into the house, and they and their little friends from the forest had settled in for the winter. The heat was still on, it was hotter than Hades, and there were billions of flies everywhere, all dead. Everything in that house was dead. Dead birds and bird crap from one end of the house to the other. Downstairs, the pipes had burst and the bottom level of the house, where the kids' bedrooms were, was half deep in water with frogs jumping around in it. Your basic nightmare.

But I didn't freak out. There wasn't even a smattering of a freak-out. I kept waiting for it to happen, but it didn't. We all went in different directions to start cleaning up—and five days and forty thousand dollars later, we had a house again. Had I not been treated, I'm not sure what would have happened. Even had I been able to get through the crisis with clear thinking and organization, I would have no doubt lost it afterward. Over some small item. Over not feeling appreciated. Or whatever.

247

I'm trying to maintain a balance in my life now, and I seem to be succeeding. I want to continue to be an advocate for mental health, and I'm a spokesperson for the National Institute of Mental Health. But I don't want to become so preoccupied with it that it dominates my life. That's another thing I try to impart to people. There comes a point where the mental illness has to stop being the focus of your life. Once you are treated, your world is no longer about depression or mania. It is about living your life— making a nice dinner, reading a book, or writing one, going to a PTA meeting, and feeling comfortable about it. It's no longer thinking of yourself as a "patient."

But you still have to deal with reality. And reality is hard. It is no walk in the park, this thing called Life. It takes practice to do it differently than you used to, and to recognize *your* norm for tolerance of aggravation, or of stress, or of sleep deprivation, or of hunger. And you need to accept that there may be some things about yourself that you don't like. You can work on them, but some of them may always be there. As long as they're not destroying you or those around you, that's okay.

Because of my success with treatment, I don't have to think about manic depression on a daily basis. It has become an adjunct to my life, not central to it. I'm not sure I can ever put things in terms of "normal" even if I hadn't been diagnosed with bipolar disorder. I'm not sure I know what normal is: Healthful and fulfilling is what I want my norm to be.

I've been making a lot of television movies lately, and I feel as though my acting has taken on a new dimension. Earlier this year, two of them were shown—*Prelude to a Kiss*, where I played the mother of the bride, Meg Ryan, in a fairy-tale comedy about a couple's whirlwind love affair that takes a strange and poignant twist, and *Last Wish*, an adaptation of Betty Rollin's beautiful book about helping her cancer-stricken mother commit suicide.

I had suspected that playing Betty Rollin in the television movie was going to be a powerful experience for me, both as an actress and as a person, because of the topic—death—upon which I've been so fixated all my life. But I had no idea that it would allow me, in the safe arena of my workplace, to address how I really felt about death and what it was I wanted to learn. Who would have thought a show would give me that kind of opportunity?

Ironically enough, before I left for Canada to shoot *Last Wish*, I had finally written my own Living Will. I had known, of course, for a long time that Living Wills existed; they just didn't exist for me, not because I didn't believe in them, but because I couldn't face writing one. But in the spring of 1991, after having read Betty Rollin's book and the screen adaptation for it, I felt it was a loving and wise thing to do—loving not just for my husband and my children but for me, too.

With all my fear of death for all those years, it turned out to be a far less monumental experience than I had expected. I thought that the dark clouds would bang together or I would hear the angels singing. But it wasn't. I simply opened the closet door, and it was only a coat hanging there, not a bogeyman. I wrote that I was not to be kept alive on any machinery past the point where there was brain activity, and that I gave the right to my husband and/or my children to authorize removal or ban the use of such equipment. These were my choices, and it relieved the burden for me and for them.

Writing that will helped balance things for me even before I left for Canada. And maybe because I had done it or maybe because of the special people I worked with in this movie—or maybe both—making the movie was an awesome experience. There was an aura that exists when you know that everyone is there, not just for the money, but because they want to be part of this.

To me, this was not a story about a daughter assisting her mother commit suicide when she can no longer stand the agony of cancer. It is a love story, and it begins and is tested long before the cancer is an issue. The day we shot the scene where the mother, played magnificently by Maureen Stapleton, takes the pills that her daughter and son-in-law acquire for her is almost too painful to describe. Putting words to it diminishes it. All of

249

us were so sensitive to the subject, maybe because everyone has or had a mother. It was a unifying experience. We didn't all talk to each other. We'd pass each other and put a hand on someone's arm or just nod. For me, the behavior of Betty Rollins, her husband, and her mother was the ultimate demonstration of love and dignity.

Right after *Last Wish* was finished and I was working in Chicago on *Prelude to a Kiss*, I went through my own personal agony with my mother. I had a call from Mike that she had suffered what seemed to be a heart attack and needed to have a heart catheterization. Otherwise she might be dead in forty-eight hours. I talked to my mom in the intensive care unit, and she told me she was afraid—not afraid to die but afraid of a stroke or being totally incapacitated mentally. Doctors told her that the catheterization could possibly precipitate a stroke, but she said she wanted to try.

Then she said, "Anna, I want to ask you one thing." The question she asked stunned me. "If I die, will your father be there waiting for me?"

I told her that I didn't know about Dad—after all, they had had their differences—but I guessed that her mom and Aunt Lizzie and Uncle Willie would be there. She asked me again, "Will your father be there?"

I paused for a minute, then I told her, "If it's important to you, and you put that in your mind and hold it there and in your heart, you will probably get your wish." I loved the innocence and beauty and pain of that question. It was the only time during that period that I cried. I didn't want to lose my mother, but if I had I would have been at peace because of the communion we had with each other. But in my heart, I wanted to hug her one more time.

Fortunately, I got the chance to do that. She survived the catheterization, and while she gets tired easily, she's the same as she was before. She is a much tinier version of me, no more than four feet five inches tall, because she has osteoporosis. She looks like one of those stuffed Mrs. Santa Claus dolls with her ton of white hair and her red bathrobe. I see her as often as possible.

During the last several months, for the first time in my life, I have not—I'm almost afraid to write this—had those panic attacks about death. Something has happened to me that has enabled me to reach a certain comfort level about death. I've come to believe that whoever I am didn't start on December 14, 1946, and isn't going to end on whatever that mysterious date is in the future. It is a personal sense of enlightenment with no hocus-pocus about it—just, perhaps, a cumulative result of my search ad nauseam of the last forty-something years.

I feel blessed because what I do for a living opens up a whole world for me. And occasionally, as with my panic attacks, it helps me balance my life and come to terms with personal issues.

Sometimes I take the time to look at the awards I've received for my acting and for my work in the mental health field. Some, of course, mean more to me than others. I have three Emmys—eight nominations and three wins. Of course, by society's standards, the Oscar—the one I won for *The Miracle Worker*—is the most prestigious. But the times I didn't win Oscars or Emmys doesn't mean that I didn't do my best work. And the fact is that I have whacked Oscar a couple of times—I mean seriously mangled him.

Until I had children, Oscar had a rough time. Somehow, in many of the outbursts I had where I was in this tirade of throwing things around, sooner or later I'd come across poor Oscar, and I'd hammer him on the floor or send him flying across the room. Usually some monologue went along with it about how stupid and useless all this was. Oscar's been treated now, too, and has a very cushy life.

The Eleanor Roosevelt Award that I received for women's rights activities is one I treasure. But my favorite is the People's Choice Award. That's because it doesn't come from my colleagues or from an expert on acting or filmmaking or from anyone who has anything to do with show business. It comes from the ultimate expert—the audience—and I got it for the series *It Takes Two*.

I'm not certain yet where I want to go with my career. What

251

do I want to do in the next twenty years? Do I expect to be a movie star? No. Would I like to act from time to time? Yes. Sometimes I flirt with the idea of broadening my horizons, either within the world of entertainment—producing, perhaps, or hosting a television show—or doing something else that would be as creatively satisfying to me as performing is . . . but more predictable.

I wouldn't want to do a talk show that just interviews celebrity after celebrity or be on the kind of show where I say, "Now we're going to learn how to cook eggs Benedict." But talk shows are wonderful—people can relate to other people who are candid about what they've been through. It's also a tool through which family members of people with any kind of condition can approach their relatives. They can say, "I saw Patty Duke on *Phil Donahue* or *Oprah* or *Geraldo* or *Sally Jessy*, and she was talking about this illness she has . . . " It gives them an opening.

On the other hand, there is a pull that won't let me get too far away from acting.

About a year ago, it became apparent to me that the things that made me the happiest and most comfortable had very little to do with a big city and glamour. I never did quite fit the glamour mode. It is life with my husband and my family that is my high now. Mike and I have a very unusual relationship: We know each other so well and we are each other's best friend. Mike is straight and steady and honest and kind, and I knew almost as soon as I met him, "This is it. This is the one."

To some people in the outside world our marriage didn't make sense: me, the actress, marrying an army guy who described himself as a "country bmpkin." But for anyone who really knew me, it made perfect sense. What did I want? Some millionaire? What would I do with a millionaire? Someone brilliant to fiddle with my brain? Some slick show-biz nut? None of those. None of those would have allowed me to feel the kind of "ordinary" that I want to feel and the kind of "special" that I need to feel. Mike has a healthy enough ego that he feels safe letting me be in the limelight. And he has freed me to experiment with a different lifestyle. We do not have grand expectations of life. We're really happy with a meat-ball sandwich and a television show or a drive in the country. I feel equal to Mike—but not in the "nice" department because Mike is much nicer than I am. I am awakened every morning with a cup of coffee—and a smile. I had always imagined that marriage had the potential of being this good, but I just couldn't figure out how to do it right . . . until now.

I'm beginning to recognize that no matter what your laundry list of requirements in choosing a mate, there has to be an element of good luck and good fortune and good timing in the right match. I'm very conscious of how Mike and I work on our marriage. We were lucky to coast for a while in a kind of honeymoon phase, and we experienced the exhilaration of financial crisis, awful as it was. In the last few years, we've gotten down to the real married part. It has to do with communication, and how well we're doing forcing ourselves to talk . . . and to listen. I'm more facile with the language than Mike, and that can be intimidating. A naughty habit of mine would be to ask Mike a profound question, then not listen for his answer because he was taking too long to give it. I wanted to jump in and supply the words, the interpretation, and the insight. And then Anna, the judge, noticed I was trying to play both parts. And that if I really cared about what he felt, I had to shut up and let him find a way to express it. So I have been practicing. And it's working.

We're also working on another aspect of our marriage—one that might seem nirvana to others. Mike indulges me, pampers me, and it is wonderful to be so adored and so spoiled. But when Mike was ill in the hospital, in mid-1990, with a staph infection, I found that I was irritated. I didn't know how to put the nozzle in the gas tank because he always filled my car with gas. I didn't know what time the garbage got picked up. I had allowed myself to become so indulged that I was borderline nonfunctional on a practical level. I didn't like that feeling, and I didn't like being perceived that way by friends and neighbors. So one of my tasks now is to choose which indulgences I can handle. The coffee in the morning stays.

We talk freely about things we only hedged about before—the absolute role reversal we have assumed. I earn the money and Mike takes care of the house and the farm and the other stuff. It is blatantly apparent in raising Kevin. I found myself a little put out that Kevin would run to Daddy when he came out of pre-school, and that he would call for Daddy when he woke up at night. It wasn't so much what *I* felt—I worried about other people's perceptions. That old "What will the neighbors think?" is still a very ingrained thing for me. So Mike and I talk about it candidly now. He does the mommy job and I do the daddy job. If we don't like it, we change it. If we do, we're not embarrassed by it. And we practice.

Before we adopted Kevin, we talked a lot about adoption, even to the point where we prepared for what we would do if, at fifteen or eighteen or twenty, he says he wants to look up his biological parents. Sure, it will be like a spear through my heart, but I know that if I'm a good enough person and I really love Kevin, I'll help him do that.

We got that little "angel boy" when he was two days old. His brothers and sisters love him to pieces. And Kevin is no oddball in our family. We have every size, shape, and personality type. So he is part of an eclectic group that I think he'll feel comfortable about as he grows up.

What makes our lives so special is that there is no area we don't discuss and explore, whether it is as important as Kevin or as insignificant as what we want on our pizza. But we don't analyze ourselves into the doldrums either. Our age difference, for instance, loomed larger for me at one point. I'm forty-five, Mike is thirty-seven. I have a picture of myself in my mind as I walk around every day . . . until I look in the mirror, and then I'm stunned. I don't look like the picture of Dorian Gray, but I'm startled to notice that I'm forty-five. Mike insisted that it was my issue, not his. But we talked about it, and I didn't find it necessary to deny that I didn't like my behind three inches lower than it used to be. I joke about why the brain and the ass can't both be where they are supposed to be at the same time. "Cells," I say, "get it together."

In 1990 we bought a tiny Victorian house in Coeur d'Alene, Idaho, not far from the farm. I love the farm, but I don't want to be that isolated in the winter. And I'm living out a childhood fantasy. Our house is in the historic district of a small town with the beauty and purity of the mountains and the lake and neighbors the way I used to read about them in story books. The day we moved in, the neighbors, Skip and Kirstin, came and helped us unload the truck. Others brought fudge and a real welcome mat. There's a woman on one side of us who is in her eighties. She is dear and funny and she has a crush on Mike. There's a man on the other side whose mom died recently. He's a forest ranger, and he gave me all his tomatoes the first summer we moved in. I woke up the first Sunday morning hearing church bells ring. I saw a boy throwing newspapers on the lawns. I felt as though I were living in a Currier and Ives greeting card.

I have been able to get a routine going that I like. I get up every day and think about going to the gym. Someday I may even get there. Mike and Kevin are happy as pigs in slop. They are always going places in what Kevin calls "Daddy's BIG truck." Mike finished the basement and turned it into rooms so we'll have space when the older kids come to visit. For the first time in two years, we took Kevin to day care to give him a little time away from Mommy and Daddy and a chance to play with kids his age. I've also moved my mom out here into a retirement hotel. She says it is the most beautiful place she has ever lived in.

I go to Los Angeles frequently—I played Morgana, the evil sister of King Arthur, in a Prince Valiant animation, new territory for me. I love doing television movies—they are not always made in Los Angeles, so I would have traveled no matter where we lived—and I have a lot of other things to fill the days: producing, acting, directing. Sean and Mack still live in California, so I get a chance to see them when I'm there.

Certainly it isn't "pretty" in Coeur d'Alene all the time. People have their own "chozzerai," but they live at a pace that allows them to say hello and to hear your answer when they ask, "How are you?" In the very beginning, people would ask, "Aren't you Patty Duke?" Now it's "Hi, Anna. How's it going? Does Kevin still have a cold?" The only pressure I feel beside earning enough money to keep the Idaho places and a base in Los Angeles is wondering whether Kevin will outsmart me again today.

Who would have guessed it? I feel very lucky. I have the best of both worlds. And I've done the best I can to ensure enough of a playground here—the farm, riding the weird vehicles, skiing in the winter, lake in the summer—that the kids will want to come often.

Most people are not going to be able to do this kind of thing, mental illness or not. But all of us can examine our priorities and rearrange them if we want to. I saw the possibility that my longtime dream could come true, and I was afraid to take the chance, but I jumped in anyway. I don't have the feeling of waiting for that other shoe to drop, or that I don't deserve being happy. I feel free to enjoy what I have. I believe that in that little package we call hope, there is compensation for all the time that we think may have been wasted or lost. The rate of growth in my mind and my heart in the last seven years is beyond measuring. I see that as God's compensation.

RESOURCES FOR THE MENTALLY ILL AND THEIR FAMILIES

These organizations provide literature and information:

American Psychiatric Association
Division of Public Affairs
Box ABM
1400 K Street NW
Washington, DC 20005
Telephone: 202-682-6220
Medical Director: Melvin Sabshin, M.D.
This organization, the oldest specialty society in the country, was established in 1844. Its 37,000 members are physicians who specialize in the diagnosis and treatment of mental illness. For those interested in the services of a psychiatrist, it offers referrals to one of its seventy-six local psychiatric societies.

DEPRESSION Awareness, Recognition, and Treatment (D/ART)
  Program
National Institute of Mental Health (NIMH)
5600 Fishers Lane, Room 10-85
Rockville, MD 20857
Telephone: For program information: 301-443-4140
For brochures: 1-800-421-4211
Director: Isabel Davidoff
NIMH's D/ART Program (DEPRESSION Awareness, Recognition, and Treatment) was launched in 1988 to bring to the general public

257

and health and mental health care providers science-based knowledge about manic-depressive and other depressive disorders—their symptoms, diagnosis, and treatments. Sponsored by the National Institute of Mental Health, D/ART's national education program is working to reduce the tragic—and frequently unnecessary—suffering of individuals and families by encouraging early recognition of symptoms of mood disorder and use of appropriate treatment. It organizes citizens' advocacy groups and works with major corporations to develop approaches to manage depression in the workplace.

Depression and Related Affective Disorders Association, Inc. (DRADA)
Meyer 3-181
600 North Wolfe Street
Baltimore, MD 21205
Telephone: 301-955-4647
Coordinator: Sally Mink
This organization, established in cooperation with the Johns Hopkins University School of Medicine, is made up of patients, family members, mental health professionals, and others concerned about mood disorders. It was created in 1986 to:

- help patients and families overcome their illnesses and provide a forum through which they can share their experiences with others
- provide information on the psychological and social consequences, and the treatability of these disorders
- educate the public on the biochemical cause of mania or depression
- encourage the development of support services for patients and family and friends of people who suffer from these disorders
- encourage and support research into the cause and treatment of affective illness.

The organization was initiated because several patients of Dr. J. Raymond DePaulo, Jr. at the Johns Hopkins University School of Medicine expressed the wish for a group that would bring together those with mood disorders. Dr. DePaulo kept a list of the requests; when he had a dozen, he contacted Wendy Resnick, a psychiatric nurse, who organized the support group that became DRADA. Ms. Resnick is now director of DRADA's support services. The organization, with more than five hundred members and thrity-two support groups in

258

Pennsylvania, Virginia, Maryland, and Washington, D.C., has produced videos on depression and other mood disorders.

The National Alliance for the Mentally Ill (NAMI)
2101 Wilson Boulevard, Suite 302
Arlington, VA 22201
Telephone: 1-800-950-NAMI
Executive Director: Laurie Flynn
Based in Arlington, Virginia, this is a grass-roots self-help education and advocacy organization that is a referral service for patients and their families. It connects patients to sources of professional help and personal support in their areas and provides free literature about all mental illness, from depression to schizophrenia. In the three weeks following the airing of *Call Me Anna*, Patty Duke's television docudrama based on her first book, twenty-five thousand people called for information about mood disorders.

Laurie Flynn, executive director since 1984, says calls came from patients and their families. So many of them said they called because Patty Duke had "reached" them. "She has this incredible way of connecting with people," says Ms. Flynn, "maybe because they grew up with her or watched her grow up."

NAMI was founded in 1979 by fifty-four people from around the country—members of local support organizations—who came together in Madison, Wisconsin, because they felt the need to form a national organization focusing on people with mental illnesses. Most of them were family members of patients who were feeling burdened by the lack of community facilities, long-term care, and insurance for the mentally ill. During this first meeting, which was sponsored by the Agricultural Extension Service of the University of Wisconsin, a hat was passed and twenty thousand dollars was collected to fund the "front end of a dream." Today that dream has turned into an organization with 140,000 members, who make contributions of a million dollars every year. The board of NAMI is comprised only of patients or their family members.

National Depressive and Manic-Depressive Association (NDMDA)
730 North Franklin Street, Suite 501
Chicago, IL 60610
Telephone: 1-800 82NDMDA
Executive Director: Susan Dime-Meenan
The founding chapter of this organization, an advocacy group, was started in Chicago in 1978 by Marilyn Weiss and Rose Kurland, both

of whom have manic-depressive illness. The first meeting in Ms. Kurland's home brought together seven people who had seen an advertisement the women had placed in a local newspaper. Ms. Weiss remembers the first woman who arrived. She was sixty-four and said it was the first time she had ever talked with anyone who had the same illness she did. On her way out, she remarked, "I just want to tell you that manic-depressives really aren't bad-looking. And we're pretty nice. And really intelligent."

Dr. Jan Fawcett, the Chicago doctor after whom NDMDA's prestigious Jan Fawcett Award has been named (in 1990 it was given to Dr. Frederick K. Goodwin, director of the U.S. Alcohol, Drug Abuse, and Mental Health Administration; in 1992 it will go to Dr. Kay Redfield Jamison, associate professor of psychiatry at Johns Hopkins University School of Medicine), offered his support, urging that a patient group can often provide help beyond the reach of professionals. "I can diagnose someone and I can put them on medication, but to help them stay on the medication and share their thoughts and feelings, support groups can be extremely valuable." Ms. Weiss says that Dr. Fawcett's confidence in her and Ms. Kurland and his conviction that such a group was important gave them credibility. "We weren't just a couple of wackos," she says.

Their next meeting, at a suburban Chicago library, at which Dr. Fawcett spoke, was jammed with people overflowing into the hallway. Those who came included people who were mentally ill, their families, and even doctors who wanted to learn more about manic-depressive illness from those who were experiencing it. The organization grew quickly, published a newsletter, and, in 1981 set up a booth at the American Psychiatric Association's conference in New Orleans. At the time, a biochemical explanation for manic-depressive illness was still a little out of the mainstream. But from that point on, inquiries poured in from all parts of the country, and groups popped up everywhere. Minneapolis. St. Louis. Midland, Michigan. Toronto. New York. In 1986, with 77 chapters in this country and Canada, the National Depressive and Manic-Depressive Association was formed. Marilyn Weiss was the first president.

Today the group has 250 chapters with 35,000 members, and receives approximately four thousand letters a month. Each time the name of the organization appears through the electronic or print media, it results in an average of four hundred telephone calls. It is the only mental health organization that is run by patients; the executive director since 1989, Susan Dime-Meenan, suffers from manic-depressive illness.

National Mental Health Association (NMHA)
1021 Prince Street
Alexandria, VA 22314-2971
Telephone: 703-684-7722
Information Center: 1-800-969-NMHA
President and Chief Executive Officer: John H. Horner
The National Mental Health Association, with a million members, is the nation's only citizens' volunteer advocacy organization concerned with all aspects of mental health and mental illness. It accomplishes its mission as a force for social change through advocacy, education, and alignment with consumer interests and rights. It has chartered organizations in forty-two states, with 550 local affiliates serving their communities through self-help and support groups. Its information center answers hundreds of calls and letters weekly from people requesting information, and it provides brochures and pamphlet series on a variety of mental health topics.

The organization's roots go back to 1909, when Clifford Beers, who had suffered harsh and ineffective treatment as a patient in private and public mental institutions in New Haven, established the Connecticut Society for Mental Hygiene, and, eight months later, the National Committee for Mental Hygiene. That organization, in 1950, merged with the National Mental Health Foundation and the Psychiatric Foundation to form the National Mental Health Association. In 1991 the American Mental Health Fund, started by Jack and Jo Ann Hinckley, parents of the man who tried to assassinate President Ronald Reagan in 1981, also merged into the NMHA.

Since 1973 the organization has awarded the McAlpin Mental Health Research Achievement Award to a researcher whose work contributes to the understanding of mental illness. Mr. McAlpin, who was mentally ill, was devoted to the cause of mental health and the advancement of mental illness research. The 1991 recipient was Dr. Frederick K. Goodwin, director of the U.S. Alcohol, Drug Abuse, and Mental Health Administration. Former recipients include: Dr. David J. Kupfer, professor and chairman of psychiatry at the University of Pittsburgh School of Medicine and director of research training at Western Psychiatric Institute and Clinic; William T. Carpenter, Jr., M.D., Maryland Psychiatric Research Center; Donald F. Klein, M.D., Columbia University, New York State Psychiatric Institute; Paul Greengard, Ph.D., Rockefeller University in New York City; Richard J. Wyatt, M.D., St. Elizabeths Hospital in Washington, D.C.; Jerome D. Frank, M.D., Ph.D., Johns Hopkins University; Douglas W. Heinrich, M.D., Maryland Psychiatric Research Center; Floyd Elliott Bloom, M.D., Salk

Institute Center for Behavioral Neurobiology; Stanley J. Watson, M.D., Ph.D., University of Michigan; Daniel X. Freedman, M.D., University of Chicago; Carol A. Tamaninga, M.D., Maryland Psychiatric Research Center; Neal E. Miller, Ph.D., Rockefeller University in New York City; Lyman C. Wynne, M.D., Ph.D., University of Rochester; Margaret Thaler Singer, Ph.D., University of Rochester; William C. Bunney, Jr., M.D., National Institute of Mental Health; Alexander H. Leighton, M.D., Harvard School of Public Health; Erik H. Erikson, Harvard University; Robert Coles, M.D., Harvard University; Seymour S. Kety, M.D., Massachusetts General Hospital.

REFERENCES
AND
NOTES

Most of the information included in Chapters 2, 4, 6, 8, and 10 came from interviews with the mental health experts listed on pages 274–277, and with patients and their families. In addition, the following references were used.

Introduction: Illness or Eccentricity?

Janice A. Egeland, *Bipolarity: The Iceberg of Affective Disorders?*: research paper presented at Annual Meeting of the American Psychiatric Association, Toronto, Canada, May 1992.

Frederick K. Goodwin and Kay Redfield Jamison, *Manic-Depressive Illness* (New York and Oxford: Oxford University Press, 1990): 3.

Emil Kraepelin, *Manic Depressive Insanity and Paranoia*, trans. R. M. Barclay, ed. G. M. Robertson (Edinburgh: E. & S. Livingstone, 1921, reprinted New York: Arno Press, 1976).

U.S. Department of Health and Human Services, National Institute of Mental Health, D/ART Program, *Bipolar Disorders—Manic Depressive Illness*, DHHS Publication No. (ADM) 90-1609, Alcohol, Drug Abuse, and Mental Health Administration, printed 1989, reprinted 1990.

Chapter Two

Hagop S. Akiskal, "The Bipolar Spectrum: New Concepts in Classification and Diagnosis," *Psychiatric Update: The American*

Psychiatric Association Annual Review, Vol II, American Psychiatric Press, Inc. (1983): 271–92.

Hagop S. Akiskal, et al., "Cyclothymic Temperamental Disorders," *Psychiatric Clinics of North America*, Vol. 2, No. 3 (Dec. 1979): 527–53.

Hagop S. Akiskal and Gopinath Mallya, "Criteria for the 'Soft' Bipolar Spectrum: Treatment Implications," *Psychopharmacology Bulletin*, Vol. 23, No. 1 (1987): 68–73.

Hagop S. Akiskal, "Characterologic Manifestations of Affective Disorders: Toward a New Conceptualization," *Integrative Psychiatry* (May–June 1984): 83–88.

Hagop S. Akiskal, "Validating Affective Personality Types," *The Validity of Psychiatric Diagnosis*, ed. Lee N. Robins, Joseph L. Fleiss, J. E. Barrett (New York: Raven Press, 1989).

Emil Kraepelin, *Lectures on Clinical Psychiatry* (London: Balliere, Tindall & Cox, 1904).

———, *Manic Depressive Insanity and Paranoia*, trans. R. M. Barclay, ed. G. M. Robertson (Edinburgh: E. & S. Livingstone, 1921, reprinted New York: Arno Press, 1976).

Frederick K. Goodwin and Kay Redfield Jamison, *Manic-Depressive Illness* (New York and Oxford: Oxford University Press, 1990).

Harvard Medical School Mental Health Letter, ed. Lester Grinspoon, M.D., Vol. 6, No. 4 (Oct. 1989)

Steven Secunda, et al., "Diagnosis and Treatment of Mixed Mania," *American Journal of Psychiatry* 144 (1987): 96–98.

Ronald R. Fieve, *Moodswing: The Third Revolution in Psychiatry* (New York: Bantam Books, 1975, and reprinted.)

J. Raymond DePaulo, Jr., and Keith Russell Ablow, *How to Cope with Depression* (New York: McGraw-Hill, 1989).

J. Raymond DePaulo, Jr., *How to Cope with Depression: A Guide for Families* (New York: McGraw-Hill, 1989).

Myrna M. Weissman et al., "The Social Role Performance of Depressed Women: Comparison with a Normal Group," *American Journal of Orthopsychiatry* 41 (1971): 390–405.

Myrna M. Weissman and Gerald L. Klerman, "Gender and Depression," *Trends in Neurosciences* 8:9 (Sept. 1985): 416–20.

264

Maggie Scarf, "The More Sorrowful Sex," *Psychology Today* (April 1979): 45–53.

Myrna M. Weissman, "Advances in Psychiatric Epidemiology," *American Journal of Public Health* 77:4 (April 1987): 445–51.

Ellen McGrath et al., *Women and Depression, Risk Factors and Treatment Issues* (Washington, D.C.: American Psychological Association, 1990).

"Schizophrenia and the Brain," Part I, *Harvard Medical School Mental Health Letter*, Vol. 4, No. 12 (June 1988).

E. Walker and M. Green, "Soft Signs of Neurological Dysfunction in Schizophrenia: An Investigation of Lateral Performance," *Biological Psychiatry* 17 (1982): 381–86.

Diagnostic and Statistical Manual, 3d edition revised. American Psychiatric Association.

Andrew A. Nierenberg and Jay D. Amsterdam, "Treatment-Resistant Depression: Definition and Treatment Approaches," *Journal of Clinical Psychiatry* 51:6 (Suppl.) (June 1990): 39–47.

Jay D. Amsterdam et al., "Borna Disease Virus: A Possible Etiologic Factor in Human Affective Disorders?," *Archives of General Psychiatry*, Vol. 42 (Nov. 1985): 1093–1096.

George E. Murphy, "The Physician's Responsibility for Suicide: I: An Error of Commission," *Annals of Internal Medicine* 82 (1975a): 301–5.

——, "The Physician's Responsibility for Suicide: II: Errors of Omission," *Annals of Internal Medicine* 82 (1975b): 305–10.

Peter C. Whybrow et al., *Mood Disorders: Toward a New Psychobiology* (New York: Plenum Press, 1984).

Edward J. Khantzian, "The Self-Medication Hypothesis of Addictive Disorders: Focus on Heroin and Cocaine Dependence," *American Journal of Psychiatry* 142 (1985): 1259–64.

Chapter Four

"When Manic-Depression Is Part of the Family Legacy," *Newsweek* (May 4, 1987): 53.

Richard Burton, *The Anatomy of Melancholy* (London, J. M. Dent & Sons, reprinted New York: Random House, 1977, ed. H. Jackson).

Paul H. Wender, Samuel S. Kety, et al., "Psychiatric Disorders in the Biological and Adoptive Families of Adopted Individuals with Affective Disorders," *Archives of General Psychiatry* 43 (Oct. 1986): 923–29.

A. Bertelsen et al., "A Danish Twin Study of Manic-Depressive Disorders," *British Journal of Psychiatry* 130 (1977): 330–31.

Julien Mendlewicz and John D. Rainer, "Adoption Study Supporting Genetic Transmission in Manic-Depressive Illness," *Nature* 268 (1977): 327–29.

Elliot S. Gershon, "Genetics," Chap. 15 in *Manic-Depressive Illness*, Frederick K. Goodwin and Kay Redfield Jamison (New York and Oxford: Oxford University Press, 1990): 373–99.

Miron Baron et al., "Genetic Linkage Between X-Chromosome Markers and Bipolar Affective Illness," *Nature* (March 19, 1987): 289–92.

Neil Risch et al., "Assessing the Role of X-Linked Inheritance in Bipolar-Related Major Affective Disorders," *Journal of Psychiatric Research* 20 (1986): 275–88.

Elliot S. Gershon et al., "Color Blindness Not Closely Linked to Bipolar Illness: Report of a New Pedigree Series," *Archives of General Psychiatry* 36 (1979): 1422–30.

J. Mendelwicz and J. L. Fleiss, "Linkage Studies with X-Chromosome Markers in Bipolar and Unipolar Illnesses," *Biological Psychiatry* 9 (1974): 275–88.

N. Suzan Nadi, John Nurnberger, Jr., and Elliot S. Gershon, "Muscarinic Cholinergic Receptors on Skin Fibroblasts in Familial Affective Disorder," *New England Journal of Medicine*, Vol. 311, No. 4 (July 26, 1984): 225–30.

Janice A. Egeland et al., "Bipolar Affective Disorder Linked to DNA Markers on Chromosome 11," *Nature* 325:6107 (Feb. 26, 1987): 783–87.

Gina Kolata, "Manic Depression Gene Tied to Chromosome 11," *Science* 235:4793 (March 6, 1987): 1139–40.

John R. Kelsoe et al., "Re-evaluation of the Linkage Relationship Between Chromosome 11 p Loci and the Gene for Bipolar Affective Disorder in the Old Amish Order," *Nature* (Nov. 16, 1989): 238–42.

John R. Kelsoe et al., "Studies Search for a Gene for Bipolar Affective Disorder in the Old Order Amish," *The Psychiatric Times*, Vol. VII, No. 6 (June 1990).

A. McKenzie, "Manic-depression: Suspect gene acquitted," *Science News* (Nov. 10, 1990).

"Depression," Lifestyle-Health Section, *Newsweek* (May 4, 1987).

Solomon H. Snyder, "Cholinergic Mechanisms in Affective Disorder," *New England Journal of Medicine*, Vol. 311, No. 4 (July 26, 1984): 254–55.

Hagop S. Akiskal et al., "The Relationship of Personality to Affective Disorders," *Archives of General Psychiatry* 40 (July 1983): 801–9.

Hagop S. Akiskal, "Interaction of Biologic and Psychologic Factors in the Origin of Depressive Disorders," *Acta Psychiatrica Scandinavica Supplementum*, Vol. 71, No. 317 (1985): 131–37.

Hagop Akiskal, "The Clinical Significance of the 'Soft' Bipolar Spectrum," *Psychiatric Annals* 16:11 (Nov. 1986): 667–71.

———, "Dysthymic Disorder: Psychopathology of Proposed Chronic Depressive Subtypes," *American Journal of Psychiatry* 140:1 (Jan. 1983): 11–20.

Robert M. Post et al., "Conditioning and Sensitization in the Longitudinal Course of Affective Illness," *British Journal of Psychiatry* 149 (1986a): 191–201.

Hagop S. Akiskal et al., "Affective Disorders in Referred Children and Younger Siblings of Manic-Depressives," *Archives of General Psychiatry* 42 (Oct. 1985): 996–1002.

D. H. McKnew et al., "Offspring of Patients with Affective Disorders," *British Journal of Psychiatry* 134 (1979): 148–52.

Jay D. Amsterdam et al., "A Neuroendocrine Test Battery in Bipolar and Healthy Subjects," *Archives of General Psychiatry* 40 (1983b): 515–21.

Elliot S. Gershon et al., "Assortative Mating in the Affective Disorders," *Biological Psychiatry*, Vol. 7, No. 1 (1973): 63–64.

Joseph J. Mendels et al., "Longitudinal Sleep Study in Hypomania," *Archives of General Psychiatry* 25 (171): 274–77.

Cathleen R. Merikangas, "Assortative Mating for Psychiatric Disorders and Psychological Traits," *Archives of General Psychiatry* 39 (Oct. 1982): 1173–80.

J. Raymond DePaulo, Jr., "Assortative Mating in Affective Disorder," Grand Round Minutes, Dept. of Psychiatry and Behavioral Sciences, Johns Hopkins University Hospital, Oct. 14, 1985.

Mark S. Bauer and Peter C. Whybrow, "The Effect of Changing Thyroid Function on Cyclic Affective Illness in a Human Subject," *American Journal of Psychiatry* 143:5 (May 1986): 633–36.

Peter C. Whybrow et al., "Mental Changes Accompanying Thyroid Gland Dysfunction," *Archives of General Psychiatry* 20 (1969): 48–63.

Thomas A. Wehr et al., "Seasonal Affective Disorder with Summer Depression and Winter Hypomania," *American Journal of Psychiatry* 144 (Dec. 1987): 1602–3.

Norman Rosenthal et al., "Seasonal Affective Disorder," *Archives of General Psychiatry* 41 (Jan. 1984): 72–80.

Carla J. Hellekson and Norman Rosenthal, "Phototherapy for Seasonal Affective Disorder in Alaska," *American Journal of Psychiatry* 143 (1986): 1035–37.

Thomas A. Wehr, "Sleep Loss as Possible Mediator of Diverse Causes of Mania," *British Journal of Psychiatry* 159 (1991): 577–78.

———, "Sleep Loss: A Preventable Cause of Manias and Other Excited States," *Journal of Clinical Psychiatry* 50 (12 Suppl.) (1989): 8–16.

J. C. Wu and W. E. Bunney, "Depression: Improvement After Sleep Deprivation," *American Journal of Psychiatry* 147:14 (Jan. 1990): 14.

Yolande B. Davenport et al., "Manic-Depressive Illness: Psycho-dynamic Features of Multigenerational Families," *American Journal of Orthopsychiatry* 49:1 (Jan. 1979): 24–35.

Robert M. A. Hirschfield, "Personality, Life Events, and Other Psychosocial Factors in Adolescent Depression and Suicide," Chap. 9, *Youth in Despair: Preventive Aspects of Suicide and Depression Among Adolescents and Young Adults*, ed. Gerald Klerman (Washington, D.C.: American Psychiatric Press, 1986).

Chapter Six

"Treatment of Mood Disorders—Parts I and II," *Harvard Medical School Mental Health Letters* (Sept., Oct. 1988).

John F. J. Cade, "Lithium Salts in the Treatment of Psychotic Excitement," *Medical Journal of Australia* 36 (1949): 349–52.

Ronald L. Fieve, *Moodswing: The Third Revolution in Psychiatry* (New York: Bantam Books, 1975, and reprinted).

Frederick K. Goodwin and Kay Redfield Jamison, *Manic-Depressive Illness* (New York and Oxford: Oxford University Press, 1990).

Ronald R. Fieve, *Lithium Therapy for Recurring Depression and Manic-Depression*, Pamphlet available at 7 East 67th Street, New York, NY 10021

Lithium and Manic Depression: A Guide, Board of Regents of the University Wisconsin System (Lithium Information Center), 1982, rev., April 1984.

Jan Fawcett, "Studies Show Lithium Helps Alcoholism," *Glenview Announcements*, Living Section (May 2, 1985).

Jay D. Amsterdam et al., "A Possible Antiviral Action of Lithium Carbonate in Herpes Simplex Virus Infections," *Biological Psychiatry* 27 (1990): 447–53.

"Why (Perhaps) Lithium Is Doubly Effective," *Discover* (Feb. 1987).

John Wykert, "Warning: Lithium Pushers Are Dangerous to Your Health," *New York* (Dec. 8, 1975).

"Drugs and Psychiatry: A New Era," *Newsweek* (Nov. 12, 1979): 98–103.

Lewis L. Judd et al., "The Effect of Lithium Carbonate on the Cognitive Functions of Normal Subjects," *Archives of General Psychiatry* 34 (March 1977): 355–57.

Lewis L. Judd et al., "The Effect of Lithium Carbonate on Affect, Mood, and Personality of Normal Subjects," *Archives of General Psychiatry* 34 (March 1977): 346–51.

Kay Redfield Jamison et al., "Patient and Physician Attitudes Toward Lithium," *Archives of General Psychiatry* 36 (July 20, 1979).

Paul B. Lieberman and John S. Strauss, "The Recurrence of Mania: Environmental Factors and Medical Treatment," *American Journal of Psychiatry* 141:1 (Jan. 1984): 77–80.

Felix F. Loeb, Jr., and Loretta R. Loeb, "Psychoanalytic Observations on the Effect of Lithium on Manic Attacks," *Journal of the American Psychoanalytic Association* 35 (1987): 877–902.

Robert M. Post, "Alternatives to Lithium in Bipolar Illness," NDMDA Newsletter (Spring 1989): 5.

Robert M. Post and Thomas W. Uhde, "Carbamazepine in the Treatment of Affective Illness," *The Limbic System: Functional*

Organization and Clinical Disorders, ed. B. K. Doane and K. E. Livingston (New York: Raven Press, 1986).

Abstracts from Consensus Conference on the Role of Anticonvulsants in Bipolar Disorder, Cheyenne Mountain Conference Resort, Colorado Springs (July 1990).

Robert M. Post, Introduction to Portraits of Mania Symposium at which following talks were presented: Susan L. McElroy, "Recent Research on the Use of Anticonvulsants in Bipolar Disorder"; Kay Redfield Jamison, "A Clinical Description of Mania"; Joseph R. Calabrese, "Phenomenology and Treatment of Rapid-Cycling Manic Depression"; Robert H. Gerner, "Treatment of Acute Mania"; William Z. Potter, "Dysphoric Mania and Hypomania." Comments made by Susan Dime-Meenan, executive director, NDMDA. (Washington, D.C., Oct. 3, 1990).

Jay D. Amsterdam and Greg Maislin, "Comparison of Growth Hormone Response after Clonidine and Insulin Hypoglycemia in Affective Illness," *Biological Psychiatry* 28 (1990): 308–14.

Jay D. Amsterdam et al., "Pituitary and Adrenocortical Responses to the Ovine Corticotropin Releasing Hormone in Depressed Patients and Healthy Volunteers," *Archives of General Psychiatry* 44 (1987): 775–81.

Robert M. Post et al., "Dysphoric Mania: Clinical and Biological Correlates," *Archives of General Psychiatry* 46 (April 1989): 353–58.

Hagop S. Akiskal, "Personality as a Mediating Variable in the Pathogenesis of Mood Disorders: Implications for Theory, Research and Prevention," from a presentation at European Medical Research Council Workshop on "Prediction of Course and Outcome in Depressive Illness: Needed Areas for Research." Cork, Ireland, Aug. 1985.

Thomas A. Wehr and Frederick K. Goodwin, "Do Antidepressants Cause Mania?," *Psychopharmacological Bulletin* 23 (1987b): 61–65.

Demitri Papolos, *Primary Affective Disorder*, pamphlet distributed by National Alliance for the Mentally Ill, Arlington, Va.

Harrison J. McCandless, "Management of Depression in the Family Practice Setting: The Continuous Challenge," presented at annual meeting of the American Academy of Family Physicians, Las Vegas (Sept. 1981).

Natalie Angier, "Eli Lilly Facing Million-Dollar Suits on Its Antidepressant Drug Prozac," *The New York Times*, Health Section (Aug. 16, 1990).

Ellen Frank et al., "Three-Year Outcomes for Maintenance Therapies in Recurrent Depression," *Archives of General Psychiatry* 47 (Dec. 1990): 1093–99.

"The Promise of Prozac," *Newsweek* (March 26, 1990): 39–41.

David Gelman, "Drugs vs. the Couch," *Newsweek* (March 26, 1990): 42–43.

Maggie Scarf, "Shocking the Depressed Back to Life," *The New York Times Magazine* (June 17, 1977): 30–40.

Keith Russell Ablow, "Electroshock Reconsidered," *The Washington Post*, Health Section (Sept. 4, 1990): 10.

Joyce G. Small et al., "Electroconvulsive Treatment Compared with Lithium in the Management of Manic States," *Archives of General Psychiatry* 45 (Aug 1988): 727–32.

Frank James, "Sneak Previews of Schizophrenia," *Philadelphia Daily News* (Aug. 15, 1990): 29 (reprinted from *Chicago Tribune*).

DSM-III-R—Diagnostic and Statistical Manual of Mental Disorders, American Psychiatric Association.

Chapter Eight

Two of the major resources referred to for this chapter were

Frederick K. Goodwin and Kay Redfield Jamison, *Manic-Depressive Illness* (New York and Oxford: Oxford University Press, 1990): Chap. 14, and The Program Books from "Moods and Music," a concert featuring the works of Handel, Schumann, Wolf, Berlioz, and Mahler, presented in Los Angeles, California, May 19, 1985, and in Washington, D.C., Nov. 29, 1988.

Emil Kraepelin, *Manic Depressive Insanity and Paranoia*, trans. R. M. Barclay, ed G. M. Robertson (Edinburgh: E. & S. Livingstone, 1921, and reprinted New York: Arno Press, 1976).

Kay Redfield Jamison, *Touched with Fire: Manic-Depressive Illness and the Artistic Temperament* (New York, Free Press/Macmillan, 1992).

William A. Frosch, "Moods, Madness, and Music," *Outlook*, newsletter of the Dept. of Psychiatry, New York Hospital–Cornell Medical Center (Fall 1988): 6.

Norman Kempster, "Begin Reported in Angry Seclusion," *The Philadelphia Inquirer* (June 8, 1983): 21A

Joan Rachel Goldberg, "The Manic-Depressive Entrepreneur," *Success!* (Jan.–Feb. 1987): 54–56.

Connie Bruck, "The World of Business, No One Like Me," *The New Yorker* (March 1991): 40–68.

Kate Ballen, "Campeau Is on a Shopper's High," *Fortune* (Aug. 15, 1988): 70–73.

Jeanie Kasindorf, "The Chutzpah Defense," New York (Nov. 11, 1991): 44.

Phil Patton, "The Man Who Bought Bloomingdale's," *The New York Times Magazine* (July 17, 1988): 16.

C. Lombroso, *The Man of Genius* (London: Walter Scott, 1891).

Laurie Johnston, "AMA Speaker Declares Manic Phase Helps Gifted," *The New York Times* (June 25, 1973).

Nancy C. Andreasen and Ira D. Glick, "Bipolar Affective Disorder and Creativity: Implications and Clinical Management," *Comprehensive Psychiatry*, Vol. 29, No. 3 (May–June 1988): 207–17.

Nancy C. Andreasen, "Creativity and Mental Illness: Prevalence Rates in Writers and Their First-Degree Relatives," *American Journal of Psychiatry* 144:10 (Oct. 1987): 1288–92.

Nancy C. Andreasen and Arthur Canter, "The Creative Writer: Psychiatric Symptoms and Family History," *Comprehensive Psychiatry*, Vol. 15, No. 2 (March–April 1974): 123–31.

Nancy C. Andreasen, "Creativity and Psychiatric Illness," *Psychiatric Annals* 8:3 (March 1978): 23–45.

Kay Redfield Jamison, "Mood Disorders and Patterns of Creativity in British Writers and Artists," *Psychiatry* 52:2 (May, 1989): 125–34.

Donald W. Goodwin, *Alcohol and the Writer* (Kansas City, MO.: Andrews and McMeel: 1988).

Darrell Sifford, "Alcoholism and Writing: A Classic Relationship," *The Philadelphia Inquirer*, Family Section (Dec. 4, 1988): J1.

Hagop S. Akiskal and K. Akiskal, "Reassessing the Prevalence of Bipolar Disorders: Clinical Significance and Artistic Creativity," *Psychiatry and Psychobiology* 3 (1988): 29s–36s.

Joshua Logan, *Movie Stars, Real People and Me* (New York, Delacorte Press, 1978): 342–50.

Nancy J. C. Andreasen and Pauline S. Powers, "Creativity and Psychosis," *Archives of General Psychiatry* 32 (Jan. 1975): 70–73.

B. Bower, "Mood Swings and Creativity: New Clues," *Science News* 132 (Oct. 24, 1987): 262.

Ruth Richards, Dennis K. Kinney, et al., "Creativity in Manic-Depressives, Cyclothymes, Their Normal Relatives and Control Subjects," *Journal of Abnormal Psychology*, Vol. 97, No. 3 (1988): 181–88.

Ruth Richards, "Relationships Between Creativity and Psychopathology: An Evaluation and Interpretation of the Evidence," *Genetic Psychology Monographs* 103 (1981): 261–324.

Ruth Richards, Dennis K. Kinney, et al., "Assessing Everyday Creativity: Characteristics of the Lifetime Creativity Scales and Validation with Three Large Samples," *Journal of Personality and Social Psychology*, Vol. 54, No. 3 (1988): 476–85.

Ruth Richards and Dennis K. Kinney, "Mood Swings and Creativity," *Creativity Research Journal* 3:3 (1990): 202–17.

Daniel Goleman, "A New Index Illuminates the Creative Life," *The New York Times*, Science Times (Sept. 13, 1988): 1.

Eric Shaw et al., "Effects of Lithium Carbonate on Associative Productivity and Idiosyncrasy in Bipolar Outpatients," *American Journal of Psychiatry* 143:9 (Sept. 1986): 1166–69.

Kay Redfield Jamison et al., "Clouds and Silver Linings: Positive Experiences Associated with Primary Affective Disorders," *American Journal of Psychiatry* 137:2 (Feb. 1980): 198–202.

Abraham Meyerson and Rosalie D. Boyle, "The Incidence of Manic-Depressive Psychosis in Certain Socially Important Families," *American Journal of Psychiatry* 98 (1941): 11–21.

Mogens Schou, "Artistic Productivity and Lithium Prophylaxis in Manic-Depressive Illness," *British Journal of Psychiatry* 135 (1979): 97–103.

273

In addition to patients and their families, those interviewed for this book include:

Hagop S. Akiskal, senior science adviser, mood and affective disorders, National Institute of Mental Health

Jay Amsterdam, director of the depression research unit, University of Pensylvania School of Medicine

Nancy J. C. Andreasen, professor of psychiatry and director of the Mental Health Clinical Research Center at the University of Iowa College of Medicine

Harold Arlen, Patty Duke's psychiatrist, practicing in Century City, California

Aaron Beck, pioneer in the study of cognitive therapy and founder of the Center for Cognitive Therapy, Philadelphia

Robert Berchick, clinical director, Center for Cognitive Therapy, Philadelphia

John Blamphin, director of the office of public affairs, American Psychiatric Association, Washington, D. C.

Clarles L. Bowden, professor of psychiatry and pharmacology, University of Texas Health Science Center

David Chowes, president, Manic and Depressive Support Group, Inc., New York

Isabel Davidoff, director of DEPRESSION Awareness, Recognition, and Treatment (D/ART) Program, National Institute of Mental Health

J. Raymond DePaulo, director of the affective disorders clinic, Johns Hopkins University School of Medicine, Baltimore

Susan Dime-Meenan, executive director, National Depressive and Manic-Depressive Association

Donald L. Dyson, associate professor of surgery and psychiatry emeritus, University of Pennsylvania School of Medicine

Janice A. Egeland, professor of the departments of psychiatry and of epidemiology and public health, University of Miami School of Medicine

O. Spurgeon English, psychiatrist practicing in Penn Valley, Pennsylvania, and former chairman of Temple University's department of psychiatry

Jan Fawcett, chairman of the department of psychiatry, Rush Presbyterian St. Luke's Medical Center, Chicago

Ronald R. Fieve, president and clinical director, Foundation for Depression and Manic Depression, New York, professor of clinical psychiatry, Columbia University, and chief of psychiatric research, New York State Psychiatric Institute

Paul Fink, chairman of the department of psychiatry, Albert Einstein Medical Center, Philadelphia, and medical director, Philadelphia Psychiatric Institute

Laurie Flynn, executive director, National Alliance for the Mentally Ill

Ellen Frank, associate professor of psychiatry and psychology, University of Pittsburgh Medical School

Robert H. Gerner, associate research professor, department of psychiatry, University of California, Los Angeles School of Medicine

Elliot S. Gershon, chief of the clinical neurogenetics branch, intramural research program, National Institute of Mental Health

Frederick K. Goodwin, director of the U.S. Alcohol, Drug Abuse, and Mental Health Administration

Alan M. Gruenberg, director of the Dave Garroway Laboratory for the Study of Depression, Pennsylvania Hospital, Philadelphia

Carla Hellekson, Insomnia Treatment and Research Program at Providence Sleep Disorders Center, Seattle

Robert Hirschfeld, professor and chairman of the department of psychiatry and behavioral sciences, University of Texas Medical School at Galveston

Kay Redfield Jamison, associate professor of psychiatry, Johns Hopkins University School of Medicine

Edward J. Khantzian, associate clinical professor of psychiatry, Harvard Medical School at the Cambridge Hospital

David Kupfer, chairman of the department of psychiatry, University of Pittsburgh Medical School

Rose Kurland, co-founder of the National Depressive and Manic-Depressive Association

Ellen McGrath, chairman of the American Psychological Association's National Task Force on Women in Depression

Donald H. McKnew, clinical professor of psychiatry, George Washington University

Joseph Mendels, medical director of the Philadelphia Medical Institute and professor of psychiatry and pharmacology at Thomas Jefferson University College of Medicine

Sally Mink, coordinator, Depression and Related Affective Disorders Association

Steven M. Paul, scientific director, National Institute of Mental Health

Robert M. Post, chief of the biological psychiatry branch, National Institute of Mental Health

William Z. Potter, chief, section of clinical pharmacology, National Institute of Mental Health

R. Arlen Price, associate professor, department of psychiatry and director of the behavioral genetics program, University of Pennsylvania School of Medicine

Robert Prien, chief of the somatic treatments program, affective anxiety disorders research branch of the National Institute of Mental Health

Ruth Richards, associate attending psychiatrist and psychologist at McLean Hospital and assistant clinical professor of psychiatry, Harvard Medical School

Neil Risch, associate professor of public health and genetics, Yale University School of Medicine

Anthony J. Rothschild, assistant professor of psychiatry, Harvard Medical School and clinical director of the affective disorders programs, McLean Hospital

Bette Runck, science writer, U.S. Alcohol, Drug Abuse, and Mental Health Administration

Steven Secunda, consultant to National Institute of Mental Health and private practitioner in Springfield, Pennsylvania

William A. Sonis, director of the mood, sleep, and seasonality program at the Philadelphia Child Guidance Clinic

Marilyn Weiss, co-founder and first president of the National Depressive and Manic-Depressive Association

Myrna M. Weissman, professor of epidemiology in psychiatry, Columbia University College of Physicians and Surgeons and chief, division of clinical-genetic epidemiology, New York State Psychiatric Institute

Thomas A. Wehr, chief of the psychobiology branch, National Institute of Mental Health

Gina White, media affairs director, National Mental Health Association

Peter C. Whybrow, chairman of the department of psychiatry, University of Pennsylvania

INDEX